Hatching Results for Elementary School Counseling

For elementary school counselors and the students they serve.

Hatching Results for Elementary School Counseling

Implementing Core Curriculum and Other Tier 1 Activities

Trish Hatch

Danielle Duarte

Lisa K. De Gregorio

Foreword by Erin Mason

CORWIN

A SAGE Publishing Company

FOR INFORMATION:

Corwin
A SAGE Company
2455 Teller Road
Thousand Oaks, California 91320
(800) 233-9936
www.corwin.com

SAGE Publications Ltd.
1 Oliver's Yard
55 City Road
London EC1Y 1SP
United Kingdom

SAGE Publications India Pvt. Ltd.
B 1/I 1 Mohan Cooperative Industrial Area
Mathura Road, New Delhi 110 044
India

SAGE Publications Asia-Pacific Pte. Ltd.
3 Church Street
#10-04 Samsung Hub
Singapore 049483

Acquisitions Editor: Jessica Allan
Associate Editor: Lucas Schleicher
Editorial Assistant: Mia Rodriguez
Production Editor: Bennie Clark Allen
Copy Editor: Laureen Gleason
Typesetter: C&M Digitals (P) Ltd.
Proofreader: Rae-Ann Goodwin
Indexer: Jean Casalegno
Cover Designer: Celestina Harman
Marketing Manager: Charline Maher

Printed in the United States of America

ISBN: 978-1-5063-8964-6

This book is printed on acid-free paper.

SUSTAINABLE FORESTRY INITIATIVE
Certified Chain of Custody
Promoting Sustainable Forestry
www.sfiprogram.org
SFI-01268
SFI label applies to text stock

18 19 20 21 22 10 9 8 7 6 5 4 3 2

DISCLAIMER: This book may direct you to access third-party content via Web links, QR codes, or other scannable technologies, which are provided for your reference by the author(s). Corwin makes no guarantee that such third-party content will be available for your use and encourages you to review the terms and conditions of such third-party content. Corwin takes no responsibility and assumes no liability for your use of any third-party content, nor does Corwin approve, sponsor, endorse, verify, or certify such third-party content.

Contents

Additional materials and resources related to *Hatching Results for Elementary School Counseling* can be found in the online appendix at **https://www.hatchingresults.com/books/elementary-t1/**.

Foreword

It is my honor to contribute the foreword for *Hatching Results for Elementary School Counseling: Implementing Core Curriculum and Other Tier 1 Activities*. I can personally attest to the passion and dedication that each of the authors has for the school counseling profession. This is a book written with genuine heart, soul, and real-world, been-there-done-that wisdom by three uniquely qualified professionals who truly love school counseling and have dedicated their careers to its growth and advancement. The authors have many years of experience in serving as school counselors, enacting leadership in the profession through a variety of roles and contributions, and training countless school counselors across the country. Readers will be inspired and validated by this practical and approachable text.

Trish Hatch is a longtime colleague, mentor, and friend, whom I met while working as a school counselor a year into my doctoral program. Along with the late, great Judy Bowers, Trish co-authored the original ASCA National Model, a work that profoundly and forever changed the face of the school counseling profession. Having been an early adopter of the ASCA model, I was asked in 2006 to help train other school counselors in the Cobb County School District and had the privilege of meeting Trish when she was brought in by the district coordinator, Gail Smith. As many will attest, Trish's motivational presentation energy is a beloved trademark. Behind this energy, however, is another trademark: an ongoing, committed, fervent thought-storm about the profession that unquestionably excites and challenges you if you have the privilege of getting caught up in it. The kind of deep thought and analysis that Trish engages in about school counseling is contagious, in a very real sense, for those who know and work with her.

I met Danielle, a former student of Trish's, on a visit to San Diego in 2011 and was immediately taken by her confidence and passion. I was convinced that what she had learned from Trish was a launching pad and that she would excel as a school counselor and bring into focus the most important issues of the profession. Danielle has done all that and more, and she is far from done! She has led her state association and participated in White House meetings through the Reach Higher initiative, consistently proving that she is dynamic in many ways. As a trainer and author, Danielle has a unique gift of helping school counselors translate what they know they "should" do into what they "can" do; this is critical to moving the profession forward. Further, her ability to engage actively at the policy level of the education landscape is characteristic of her genuine loyalty to all students. I look forward to watching what she does next.

I met Lisa in 2009 after I began my first academic post at DePaul University, and she was invaluable in helping me understand the unique role of the elementary school counselor in Chicago Public Schools (CPS), a role that was in great contrast to what I had experienced in Georgia. While working in the district office for CPS, she asked me to partner with her in training the first cohort of elementary school counselors to pursue Recognized ASCA Model Program (RAMP), an honor and opportunity for me to leverage relationships with practitioners. Several years later, we were proud to celebrate one of the cohort members as the first elementary school in CPS to achieve RAMP! Perhaps our most challenging work together, an effort for which Lisa was at the forefront, was redefining the role of the elementary school counselor in Chicago to eliminate "case management" (all IEP oversight) from the job description. This was an extremely long and arduous process. Lisa's commitment to this work was steadfast, and in December 2016 it was announced that school counselors now have the contractual right to decline case management duties in CPS.

Like these three esteemed authors, my passion for the profession originates from my time in the field as a school counselor. I worked in several schools and districts in the metro-Atlanta area over a 13-year period and served in several positions in the Georgia School Counselor Association (GSCA). I have also supported the work of school counselors in Illinois and was the state association president from 2012 to 2013. In recent years, I have expanded my connections to school counselors at all levels nationally and internationally through social media, and I am currently training future elementary school counselors at Georgia State University. As a school counselor educator, I often take the practitioner-scholar approach with an emphasis on assisting those in the field in publishing their work from an action research framework. I believe strongly in Tier 1 as the means of reaching all students from a prevention-based perspective, and I have written on topics such as curriculum design, lesson plan development and delivery, and classroom management. All of these experiences reinforce for me that elementary school counselors are and must be extraordinarily versatile in addressing a range of developmental levels and issues, spectacularly creative when it comes to delivering a variety of interventions, and uniquely impactful in setting the stage for what school counseling is for all stakeholders.

Hatching Results for Elementary School Counseling is unlike any other book on the market and is a must-have resource for any practicing or aspiring elementary school counselor. The relevance of this book to the current trends in education, as well as the joys and challenges of school counseling, is undeniable. What readers will enjoy most about this book is its functional application. While theory and research ground the text, its real appeal is found in the strategies that can be implemented immediately. As a thoughtful, real-world look at each of the Tier 1 activities elementary school counselors perform every day, the text demonstrates the authors' credibility and clear grasp of the "art and science" of school counseling.

The book begins with an overview and expansion of how the Multi-Tiered System of Supports (MTSS) framework aligns with the school counseling program and the ASCA National Model. The authors ingeniously introduce a new acronym, "MTMDSS," that keenly incorporates the academic, career/college, and social/emotional domains of a comprehensive school counseling program. School counselors will find the alignment with MTSS intuitive and logical in both theoretical and practical ways and will find the model to be a further means for leveraging support for the roles they have and the services they provide in their building.

The core of the text, a descriptive series of chapters that outlines the entire process, from curriculum decision making, delivery, and assessment to sharing the results of Tier 1 interventions, is where the treasure lies. Each chapter builds seamlessly on the one before it. The chapters on lesson planning, engagement, and classroom management strategies are what every school counselor hungers for *now*, particularly those without a background in teaching. The assessment chapter engages process, perception, and outcome data with a logical model to clear the fog around how to design assessments at the elementary level. Readers learn how to determine lesson effectiveness, whether they are using their own lessons or ones from an existing curriculum. Especially helpful is that throughout these chapters, the authors use a single lesson plan, "Don't Blow Your Top!," with explicit bubble graphics as a tool for articulating and demonstrating the key points within the chapters.

While the focus of the majority of the text is on implementing core curriculum as the primary Tier 1 intervention, a chapter is dedicated to schoolwide activities and programs that reach all students. Readers will find all chapters chock-full of resources, visuals, diagrams, images, templates, stories, and samples that drive every point home. The final "putting it all together" chapter helps school counselors understand the big picture of how to connect Tier 1 interventions to the management system of the ASCA model and how to bring stakeholders on board. While each chapter can be appreciated on its own, readers will find that the intentional sequence and flow of the whole text sets elementary school counselors up for success throughout and smartly brings all the concepts full circle.

If you are seeking a manual for how to implement Tier 1 interventions as an elementary school counselor, this is it! Far from being dry and boring, the authors contextualize every step through their own experiences as school counselors, sometimes with the kind of humor those who work in the profession can truly appreciate. The authors, as voices in the field, bring life to the concepts, sharing numerous resources and graphics in every chapter. If those are not enough, there are even more resources made available online!

Those who enjoy the road-map feel of Trish's *The Use of Data in School Counseling* (Hatch, 2013) will find that this book has a similarly useful style and format. The text and graphics together definitively express the "art and science" of what Tier 1 interventions can look like at the elementary level. Much of what the text offers can be implemented right away, which is what time-strapped school counselors crave. For those who are struggling or stuck as new or seasoned school counselors, the strategies in this text provide that "something else" to try when it seems like all is lost. The tone of the text will make readers feel understood and appreciated in the work that they do, and they will also be challenged to examine how they can make adjustments to their programs to better serve students through Tier 1 interventions.

Too often, school counselors lack preparation in areas such as curriculum and lesson design, classroom management, consultation, workshop delivery, and schoolwide event planning. The authors do a masterful job of filling in gaps that school counselors may have had in their graduate training so that they can be more empowered to implement effective Tier 1 interventions. Today's educator must know recent initiatives, such as the MTSS framework and Positive Behavior Intervention and Supports (PBIS). *Hatching Results for Elementary School Counseling: Implementing Core Curriculum and Other Tier 1 Activities* helps readers connect much of what they do to these initiatives and gives them an expanded MTSS framework that integrates the three domains of a comprehensive school counseling program, based on the ASCA National Model, into a new paradigm. The authors of the book make it clear through this expanded paradigm that elementary school counselors are leaders in the school building who are up-to-date on education reform trends, engaging instructional practices, and the cultural factors that impact the needs of a growing population of diverse learners.

The impact elementary school counselors can have on the students, families, and schools they serve is not to be underestimated. This book is also not to be underestimated; it will incite enthusiasm for those new to the field, recommit those who are seeking fresh ideas, and give the profession a resource that is, to date, unmatched by any other.

Erin Mason, PhD
Assistant Professor
School Counseling and Counselor Education and Practice
Georgia State University
Co-author, *101 Solutions for School Counselors and Leaders in Challenging Times*

Acknowledgments

This work arose from passionate conversations about the need to equip elementary school counselors with greater tools and resources. As former elementary school counselors, we are personally aware of the training, preparation, and knowledge gaps in the profession. Based on our varied experiences, we wrote this book to close these gaps and advance school counselor practices leading to improved student outcomes. We have many colleagues to thank for the time, energy, and resources they have contributed.

Sincerest thanks to Ashley Kruger for multiple best-practice samples and contributions to this text, especially for Chapter 10. Ashley and Nicole Pablo were part of the "think tank" from the start. Both were instrumental in getting this project off the ground by sharing their thoughts on structure and key content. Likewise, Whitney Triplett was key to the initial "brain dump" and organization and has provided helpful feedback as a reviewer. A huge thank-you to the amazing Trisha McHugh for her endless formatting, technical, and administrative assistance. We definitely owe you a huge dish of your favorite lobster mac-n-cheese!

We also appreciate the initial review and feedback given by the school counseling graduate classes of 2018 from San Diego State University and The Ohio State University. Thank you to Dr. Brett Zyromski, who provided feedback on multiple chapters and coordinated the review with his graduate students.

Many thanks to those who provided testimonials, examples, and samples, either in the text or the online appendix of additional resources: Fallbrook Union Elementary School District counselors, Ashley Hansen from Ohio State, Jodi Spoon-Sadlon from the Murrieta Valley Unified School District, Sandra Ruiz from the Alvord Unified School District, Martha Williams and Angela Shanahan from Chicago Public Schools, and Rebecca Lallier from Hartford Schools. Thank you to Inelda Luna, current principal in San Jacinto, for sharing engagement strategies and images to be modified for school counselors in Chapter 5. Special thanks to Dr. M. Rene' Yoesel, Dr. Norm Gysbers, Dr. Carolyn Magnuson, Dr. Bragg Stanley, Carolyn Roof, and Linda Lueckenhoff for the collaborative effort in outlining the development of statewide core curriculum in Missouri and Nancy Sandoval for the investigative work to create the core curriculum and national awareness campaign downloadable resources.

From Trish: I would like to posthumously thank Carol McKinney, for being the most amazing principal an elementary school counselor could ever have had, along with the teachers at Ramona and Butterfield Elementary who so strongly supported my role as school counselor in the late 1980s. Thanks to Lloyd Campbell, Rich Russell, and Louise Bigbie for your mentorship and for believing in me. I'm grateful to my elementary counselor colleagues in Moreno Valley Unified and the grant counselors

I've trained over the years who have committed themselves to creating sustainable programs. *Huge* thanks to Danielle for your positive attitude and for taking the lead on Chapters 4, 5, and 6. Deep appreciation to Lisa for leading the redesign of the Flashlight Presentation and other forms, and for the many nights and weekends dedicated to ensuring the success of this text. Thank you to the graduate students and alumni at SDSU who inspire me to continue to give back to the profession. Thank you to my brother, Paul, for always being there personally and professionally, and to my parents, sons, and family for their never-ending support. To my niece, Allison Hatch, a future school counselor, I hope this text is worthy of your amazing talent. And, finally, to my grandchildren—may they have an awesome elementary school counselor.

From Danielle: I would first like to thank Trish for always inspiring me to do what seems like the impossible—in this case, writing a book—and for continuously supporting me along the way. I would also like to thank all the teachers and administrators I worked with at Alvin Dunn Elementary School in San Marcos, California, including my phenomenal assistant principal, Silvia Ventura-Jacobsen, and teachers Malia Altieri and Jen Vitiello Cohen. Malia's strong expertise in delivering high-quality curriculum provided inspiration content for Chapters 4 through 6. I am also so grateful for the support of former colleagues within the Fallbrook Union Elementary School District, including Megan LaBare, Melissa Lafayette, Zorayda Delgado, Joy Beidel, Leonard Rodriguez, Allen Teng, Candy Singh, and Bill Billingsley. Thanks to my SDSU school counseling cohort members and all of my former graduate students, who have taught me so much. And thank you to Lisa for partnering with us and contributing your diverse experiences to this amazing project. Finally, I would like to thank my parents, Connie and Dave, who are my biggest cheerleaders, and my niece and nephews, who inspire me to dedicate my life to school counseling and education to ensure that they, along with all students, can reach any goal they set their minds to achieve.

From Lisa: I would like to thank my husband, Lorenzo, and my three sweethearts, Quentin, Lillian, and Lucas, for supporting me and granting me time to write. To my kiddos, I love you more than words can express and hope you get the tools you need, not only for school but for life. To my parents, Tony and Wanda, who never got much more than a high school education, thank you for showing me the value of hard work and giving me a childhood that drove me to do more. To my sisters, Eileen, Bernadette, and Emily, thank you for just being you—each one of you is so different, but you all have taught me so much. Deepest respect and gratitude to Trish and Danielle for making this dream come true and for all the laughs—we're a great team! And, last, much appreciation for all my former colleagues at Burnham/Anthony Academy, especially the amazing Sheryl Freeman, Annie May Porthan, Kristen Langdon, Afua Agyeman-Badu, Erving Benson, Megan Fido, Tyrone Lee, Ms. Pondexter, Ms. Kazmi, Ms. Montgomery, and Dr. Linda J. Moore; my former colleagues at the Chicago Public Schools district office; and those many K–8 school counselors in the trenches of Chicago whom I had the pleasure to support in some way. Reflecting back on years of hard work (and all the joys and tears) to write this has been a humbling experience—you are all in my heart, always.

About the Authors

Trish Hatch, PhD, is a Professor at San Diego State University (SDSU), where she was Director of the School Counseling Program from 2004 until 2015. She is the best-selling author of *The Use of Data in School Counseling: Hatching Results for Students, Programs, and the Profession* (2013) and co-author of *Evidence-Based School Counseling: Making a Difference With Data-Driven Practices* (Dimmitt, Carey, & Hatch, 2007) and the *ASCA National Model: A Framework for School Counseling Programs* (ASCA, 2003, 2005).

Trish is the Founder and Executive Director of the Center for Excellence in School Counseling and Leadership (CESCaL) in the College of Education at SDSU and is President and CEO of Hatching Results®, where she has gathered a diverse team of expert school counselors, school counselor educators, and leaders to provide training and consultation across the nation on evidence-based practice and the use of data to improve school counseling programs and increase outcomes for students.

Trish is a legislative advocate and national leader. She has served on multiple state and national school counseling research summit steering committees, including as a national expert consultant on school counseling for the Obama administration at the White House and the U.S. Department of Education. Dr. Hatch is one of five original panel members for the National Panel for Evidence-Based School Counseling Practices and serves on the Advisory Council for the National Evidence-Based School Counseling Conference.

A former elementary school counselor, high school administrator, and central office administrator who oversaw 72 school counselors in 32 high-needs schools, Dr. Hatch has received multiple state and national school counseling awards and was inducted into the H. B. McDaniel Hall of Fame at Stanford University for lifetime achievement in school counseling. She was awarded the American School Counselor Association (ASCA) Administrator of the Year Award, as well as the organization's highest honor, the Mary Gehrke Lifetime Achievement Award. Most recently, she received the National Association of College Admission Counseling's (NACAC's) Excellence in Education Award for "improving the field of education and service to students" and the inaugural California Association of School Counselors' School Counselor Educator of the Year (2016) award.

Danielle Duarte, MS, is a former school counselor with experience at all levels who achieved Recognized ASCA Model Program (RAMP) and Support Personnel Accountability Report Card (SPARC) recognition. She also wrote and served as the Grant Project Director for the federal Elementary and Secondary School Counseling Program Grant in the Fallbrook Union Elementary School District (which awarded $1.1 million and selected only 41 of 566 applicants). Through the grant program implementation, Danielle helped hire, train, and support new school counselors as the district developed comprehensive, data-driven school counseling programs. Currently, Danielle is the Director of Professional Development and an Expert Trainer/Consultant for Hatching Results, LLC. Danielle serves on the Board of Directors for the California Association of School Counselors (CASC), where she was former President (2015–2016); she is an AVID Staff Developer for School Counseling and an adjunct faculty member in San Diego State University's School Counseling Department, and she is heavily involved in Reach Higher initiatives. Danielle is a frequent presenter at state and national school counseling conferences and writes articles featured in school counseling publications, including ASCA's *Professional School Counseling Journal*.

Lisa K. De Gregorio, MS, is currently the Director of Operations and an Expert Trainer/Consultant for Hatching Results®. As a former K–8 school counselor, Lisa earned the Oppenheimer Recognition Award for her social and emotional learning (SEL) and career readiness initiatives, which resulted in a substantial Illinois SEL/Mental Health grant award and her school's selection as one of only six to become a "model elementary school" in Chicago (a system of approximately 450 elementary schools). During more than six years at the Chicago Public Schools' district office as a Lead K–8 Counselor for hundreds of school counselors, Lisa received the inaugural Golden Child award from the Office of College and Career Success, developed K–12 professional learning and resources, managed staff and

special projects, and conducted school visits throughout the city. Lisa is an Education Pioneer Visiting Fellow and was recognized for her systemic change efforts at the district office, at the Chicago Teachers' Union, and as a Board Member of the Illinois School Counselor Association (ISCA) with the Illinois School Counselor Advocate of the Year award in 2015.

Introduction

As a first-year school counselor, I (Trish) recall arriving at my school and being shown to my office. When I opened the desk drawers, I found one file with the names of children identified as "gifted" inside. I had no curriculum, lesson plans, materials, brochures—*nothing*. During graduate school, I performed my school counseling practicum and field site experiences at middle and high schools. I was far less prepared to know where to start at the elementary level, so my work as an elementary school counselor began by supporting the parents of crying kindergarten students and then setting off to develop a plan. Philosophically I believed in proactive, prevention education as opposed to punishment and post-disciplinary intervention. Therefore, I wanted to create a school counseling program that included teaching students the knowledge and skills they needed *before* they encountered problems. I created developmentally appropriate curriculum prior to the creation of the ASCA National Model without use of the Internet, before attending my first school counseling conference, and with no training in how to teach effectively. How wonderful it would have been to have had a book that explained ways to design classroom lessons, teach content to all students, and organize schoolwide events! As I began my work as an elementary school counselor, I was essentially winging it. Working with a caseload of 1,300 students (500 in one school and 800 in the other), I was overwhelmed. Therefore, I set out to design a program that had enough impact to convince the schools and district to utilize funds to purchase additional counseling services, as opposed to more Commodore computers that no one used (I'm dating myself here). As the daughter of a salesman, I also began to "sell" my program.

The purpose of *Hatching Results for Elementary School Counseling: Implementing Core Curriculum and Other Tier 1 Activities* is to provide elementary school counselors, administrators, and graduate students with a hands-on guide to creating and implementing high-quality Tier 1 school counseling systems of support. Building on the content from *The Use of Data in School Counseling: Hatching Results for Students, Programs, and the Profession* (2013), this new text focuses on Tier 1 activities at the elementary level within what we call a Multi-Tiered, Multi-Domain System of Supports (MTMDSS). Tier 1 focuses on schoolwide activities and core curriculum classroom lessons that are provided to *all* students in the academic, social/emotional, and college/career domains and are aligned with the American School Counselor Association (ASCA) National Model. This text provides specific information and examples to directly support elementary school counselors as they design, implement, and evaluate preventative Tier 1 activities to support the development and needs of *all* students schoolwide. As the daughter of a salesman, I also began to "sell" my program (see pages 28–29 for the rest of the story).

Within implementation of the MTMDSS, school counselors, like teachers, provide core subject matter in the three counseling domains for elementary school students. *Hatching Results for Elementary School Counseling: Implementing Core Curriculum and Other Tier 1 Activities* provides clear direction for today's elementary counselor on how to design, teach, assess, and improve core curriculum classroom lessons. The text also provides content on other schoolwide (Tier 1) activities and programs, such as implementing Positive Behavior Intervention and Supports (PBIS), coordinating family education programs, planning schoolwide prevention weeks, organizing peer mediation programs, and more. Included in the text are best practices from school counselors throughout the United States, including some who are now professional trainers and consultants for Hatching Results®. The strategies have been proven to be effective through measuring the impact on students' attitudes, knowledge, skills, and behaviors.

This book is written primarily for practicing elementary school counselors to use as an instruction manual for implementation of schoolwide activities and school counseling core curriculum classroom lessons that are developmental in scope and preventative in nature within Tier 1. Elementary school counselors are expected to create lesson plans, teach classroom curriculum, deliver engaging content, manage classroom behaviors, and provide assessments. Unfortunately, they often receive minimal training in their graduate programs on executing these responsibilities. This text closes the elementary school counselor's knowledge and skill gaps in teaching, learning, and instruction. Through this step-by-step guide on how to measure the impact of school counseling programs, readers will improve their skills and increase buy-in for their own programs.

The content within this book is applicable for use in school counseling graduate courses such as Introduction to School Counseling; Learning, Achievement, and Instruction for School Counselors; Counseling Children and Adolescents; Elementary School Counseling; and any course that teaches prevention and intervention, including Implementation of Multi-Tiered System of Supports for School Counselors. This text will be of benefit to supervisors and students interning or completing field work hours at the elementary school level. Through this resourceful guide for Tier 1 programs and services, school counselors will ensure that all students are benefiting from a comprehensive school counseling program.

Administrators and district and state school counseling coordinators will value this text, as it can assist them in understanding the appropriate role of elementary school counselors within Tier 1 and provides tools, examples, and helpful tips that can be useful for supporting and evaluating school counselors' implementation of the schoolwide program. This text can be further utilized for online learning to support school counselors in their attainment of additional continuing education units (CEUs) for maintenance of state certification or licensure.

Two key areas of focus within the text, in which school counselors often have limited or no training, are *effective teaching strategies* and the *use of measurement tools*. This text provides school counselors with strong skills for teaching core content (a major component of Tier 1), which will lead to better outcomes for both counselors and students. Measuring and quantifying the success of such outcomes is also a critical skill for counselors to have.

When school counselors are competent in using data, they can more accurately measure the impact of their services. There are very few texts written specifically for elementary school counselors and also a lack of evidence-based materials. The need is so great that thousands of elementary counselors have started Facebook groups to share information. Unfortunately, much of the core curriculum and materials shared in these forums are not vetted through any evidence-based approach, and data-driven practices are rarely discussed. As educators, elementary school counselors are held to similar standards and expectations as teachers in terms of setting measurable goals, objectives, and outcomes when providing instruction in the classroom. Within this text, the focus is on using data to measure the impact of education and on evaluating the outcomes of a comprehensive school counseling program.

The federal funding regulations in the Every Student Succeeds Act (ESSA) currently indicate that funds can be spent on hiring and supporting school counselors. As federal accountability measures shift, many states are supporting local control of funding decisions. In California, for instance, there has been a large increase in elementary counselors with the release of local control funding formulas. Now, more than ever, school counselors must be held accountable to show how their programs and services positively impact school climate, academic achievement, attendance, behavior, parent and student engagement, and so on. This text provides examples of how to measure results in all of the areas within Tier 1. Readers can assess their growth and progress relative to these outcomes by utilizing the multiple assessment tools presented throughout the text, including applied activities, check-for-understanding tools, and reader self-assessments. Finally, readers will learn to use data for program improvement as they share results and recommendations with faculty and other stakeholders.

Hatching Results for Elementary School Counseling: Implementing Core Curriculum and Other Tier 1 Activities includes a variety of pedagogical formats, including vignettes from practicing school counselors, featured stories with processing questions, templates for developing lesson plans and action plans, sample classroom lessons (including lesson plans, action plans, PowerPoint slides, pre- and post-assessments, and Flashlight Results presentations), and a variety of graphs and other ways to present school counseling program data. Additional resources are available in the online appendix.

The text will prepare readers to do the following:

- **Attitudes**
  - *Believe* that all students deserve to receive school counseling core curriculum (classroom lessons)
  - *Believe* in the importance of elementary school counselors' taking an active role in core curriculum implementation
  - *Believe* in the importance of developing schoolwide school counseling core curriculum action plans
  - *Believe* that elementary school counselors must assess the impact of their lessons
  - *Believe* that all students deserve to receive schoolwide activities
  - *Believe* in the importance of including parents/families in prevention education to support their children
  - *Believe* that elementary school counselors play a role in schoolwide programs and activities such as coordinating national awareness campaigns and facilitating peer mentoring programs
  - *Feel* confident and competent as they deliver school counseling core curriculum lessons

- **Knowledge**
  - *Explain* the purpose behind standards-based education
  - *Understand* the elementary school counselor's role in a Multi-Tiered, Multi-Domain System of Supports (MTMDSS)
  - *Describe* ways to garner staff input on school counseling core curriculum
  - *Differentiate* between the different types and uses of data as they pertain to core curriculum
  - *Understand* a wide range of classroom management strategies

- **Skills**
  - *Locate*, *compare*, and *select* an appropriate core curriculum for a school or district
  - *Write* high-quality lesson plans with measurable objectives
  - *Create* a school counseling core curriculum action plan for a school or district
  - *Create* pre- and post-tests for assessing students' attitudes, knowledge, and skills
  - *Implement* appropriate classroom management strategies
  - *Teach* core curriculum classroom lessons by incorporating a variety of student engagement strategies to enhance learning
  - *Collect* and *analyze* data to assess students' attitude, knowledge, skill, and behavior changes related to core curriculum and other Tier 1 activities
  - *Share* results from the school counseling core curriculum

1

Multi-Tiered, Multi-Domain System of Supports

A Framework for Tier 1

INTRODUCTION

This text is designed to guide the school counselor in developing, implementing, and evaluating Tier 1 core curriculum and schoolwide activities. As we begin, it will be helpful to provide an overall contextual framework regarding the Multi-Tiered System of Supports (MTSS) and introduce the new Multi-Tiered, *Multi-Domain* System of Supports (MTMDSS) that aligns with the role of the school counselor at any grade level and the American School Counselor Association (ASCA) National Model (ASCA, 2012).

AN INTRODUCTION TO MTSS IN EDUCATION

The Multi-Tiered System of Supports (MTSS) is a comprehensive framework that addresses the *academic and behavioral* needs of all students within the educational system (Cowan, Vaillancourt, Rossen, & Pollitt, 2013; Hawken, Vincent, & Schumann, 2008). Research shows that schools benefit from multiple evidence-based interventions of varying intensity to meet the range of behavioral, social-emotional, and academic needs of all students (Anderson & Borgmeier, 2010; Sugai & Horner, 2009). Combining Response to Intervention (RTI) and Positive Behavior Intervention and Supports (PBIS),

MTSS is a tiered systems approach of increasingly intensive interventions. Like RTI, MTSS facilitates effective universal implementation that focuses on core academic and differentiated interventions to support the academic success of all students. Like PBIS, MTSS is a problem-solving model that employs a continuum of positive, proactive, multi-tiered behavioral interventions (Kennelly & Monrad, 2007; Sugai & Horner, 2009). (See Figures 1.1 and 1.2 for illustrations of the RTI, PBIS, and MTSS models.)

Within the MTSS framework utilized in general education programs, MTSS Tier 1 is the foundation for both academic and behavioral systems of support. Tier 1 contains universal support and core instruction that *all* students receive from their classroom teacher. For example, all students receive multiplication tables in the third grade. Similarly, all students participate in universal instruction on appropriate playground behavior delivered throughout the school. Preventative in nature, Tier 1 programs and activities are implemented with the entire student population. Typically, general education teachers proactively differentiate (modify or adapt) their instructional practices to support students' specialized needs, providing a more challenging or more supportive learning environment as necessary. Within the elementary school, counselors typically participate in presenting a curriculum that aligns with and supports the universal instruction regarding behavior.

Tier 2 within MTSS is comprised of supplemental interventions in addition to Tier 1 core instruction for students identified through the use of data identifiers or indicators as needing additional supports, such as small-group practice and skill building. Teachers and others collaborate to determine the data-driven identifiers that will serve as the mechanism for the students to receive a Tier 2–level intervention (for example, scoring less than proficient on a benchmark assessment). Tier 3 addresses the students with the highest level of need, providing supports of a greater intensity specifically tailored to meet the needs of individual students (Illinois State Board of Education, 2010).

Figure 1.1 Traditional Tiered Educational Models: RTI and PBIS

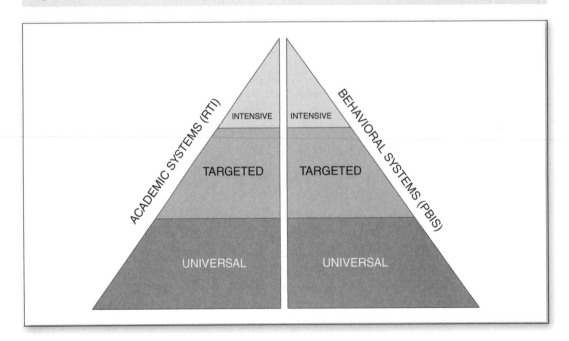

Figure 1.2 Traditional Tiered Educational Models: MTSS

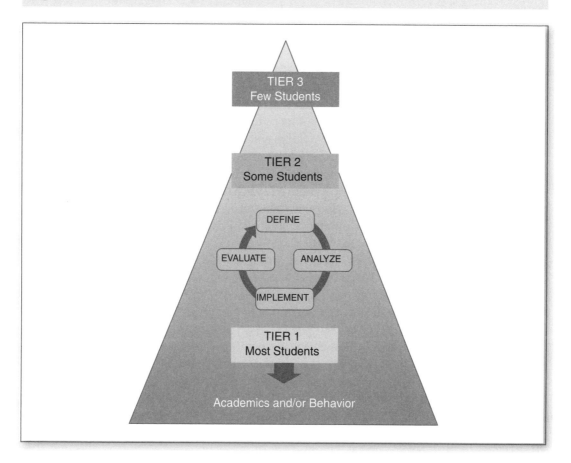

Students who are not responsive to the Tier 1 supports may receive a Tier 2 intervention. These students continue to receive the Tier 1 intervention, but more structure and guidance is provided to assist them in meeting schoolwide expectations. Students receiving Tier 2 supports typically exhibit behavior that is not dangerous to themselves or others, but that is disruptive to their learning or the learning of their peers. Tier 2 interventions are implemented similarly across groups of students who exhibit similar behavior problems and are therefore likely to benefit from the same type of intervention. For example, students who exhibit deficits in social competence (e.g., conflict resolution skills) might participate in a skills group, in which all students in the group receive the same level and intensity of instruction, as well as similar feedback on their behavior. (Anderson & Borgmeier, 2010, pp. 33–34)

CONNECTING MTSS TO SCHOOL COUNSELING: MT<u>MD</u>SS

ASCA calls on school counselors to assist in the academic and behavioral development of students through the implementation of a comprehensive developmental school counseling program based on the ASCA National Model by

- Providing all students with a standards-based school counseling core curriculum to address universal academic, career, and personal/social development
- Analyzing academic and behavioral data to identify struggling students
- Identifying and collaborating on research-based intervention strategies that are implemented by school staff
- Evaluating academic and behavioral progress after interventions
- Revising interventions as appropriate
- Referring students to school and community services as appropriate
- Collaborating with administrators, other school professionals, community agencies, and families in the design and implementation of MTSS
- Advocating for equitable education for all students and working to remove systemic barriers (ASCA, 2008)

While MTSS is focused on two areas (academic and behavioral), school counselors focus on *three* domains: (1) academic, (2) college/career, and (3) social/emotional development. To align with the work of the school counselor, the **Multi-Tiered,** *Multi-Domain* **System of Supports (MTMDSS)** (see Figure 1.3) was designed to align with MTSS as a decision-making framework that utilizes evidence-based practices in core instruction and assessments to address the universal and targeted (data-driven) intervention needs of *all* students in *all* school counseling domains (Hatch, 2017). Note that for purposes of this text, from this point forward, we will simply refer to the three school counseling domains of academic, college/career, and social/emotional development as the three domains.

School counseling programs are an integral part of the total educational program for student success. The entire school community is invested in student academic achievement, college and career readiness, and social/emotional well-being. Schoolwide proactive, preventative, and data-driven intervention services and activities belong to the entire school. Therefore, it is recommended that schools *add the third domain* (college and career readiness) to their MTSS program and create a comprehensive, schoolwide *Multi-Tiered, Multi-Domain System of Supports (MTMDSS)*.

MULTI-TIERED, MULTI-DOMAIN SYSTEM OF SUPPORTS (MTMDSS)

The MTMDSS is a framework (see Figure 1.3) designed specifically for school counseling programs to organize a continuum of core activities, instruction, and interventions to meet students' needs with the goals of (1) ensuring that all students receive developmentally appropriate core instruction in all three domains; (2) increasing the academic, social/emotional, and college/career competencies of all students; (3) ensuring guaranteed interventions for students demonstrating a data-driven need; and (4) maximizing student achievement (Hatch, 2017). The MTMDSS model organizes school intervention services into three levels, or tiers.

Tier 1: Core Program (Universal Supports) (100%)—For All Students

The core program is comprised of the delivery of services that *all students* receive (curriculum, individual student planning, and schoolwide events). A standards- and competency-based school counseling *core curriculum* (formerly called "guidance curriculum") is developmental in nature, preventative and proactive in design, and

Figure 1.3 Multi-Tiered, Multi-Domain System of Supports (MTMDSS)

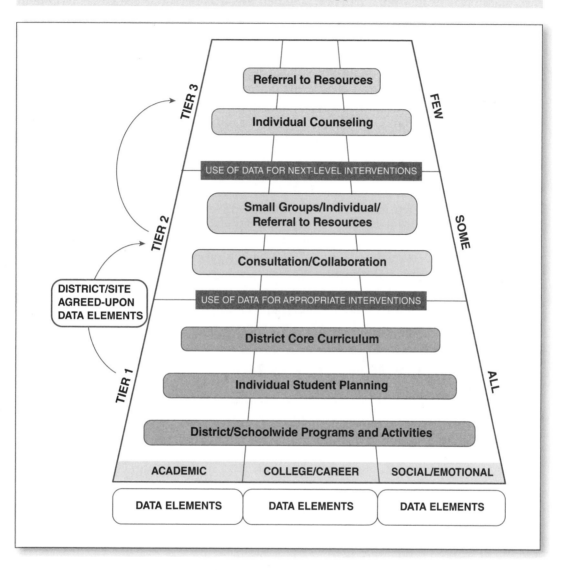

comprehensive in scope. *Individual student planning* includes 4- and 6-year and college/career planning and career readiness (generally for grades 6–12). *Schoolwide activities* for all students, such as national awareness weeks and celebrations (e.g., Red Ribbon Week, Mix It Up, The Great Kindness Challenge), conflict resolution programs, and parent education programs, are provided to all students and/or parents, align with classroom lesson content and standards, and support the core program.

Tier 2: Targeted Interventions (20%)—For Some Students

Similar to what general education teachers do when designing Tier 2 interventions, targeted data-driven interventions (small-group counseling/instruction, referral to interventions on campus, etc.) are designed for students who are identified by prescheduled and predetermined data-screening elements (Hatch, 2017). At the elementary level, these include, for example, attendance rates, behavior infractions, and work skills/study habits (report card marks). In grades 6 through 12, these might also include course failures, credit deficiency, data elements related to college and career readiness, and equity and access issues. Tier 2 interventions include *short-term* progress monitoring and collaboration among teachers, parents/guardians, and the school counselor until improvement and/or referral to appropriate services can be identified and implemented. Tier 2 activities are also designed for students who (1) exhibit barriers to learning; (2) are struggling to achieve academic success; and/or (3) are identified as deserving of instruction and/or supports in addition to Tier 1 curriculum activities (foster youth, dual-language learners, etc.).

Tier 3: Intensive Interventions (5–10%)—For a Few Students

Individualized student interventions (e.g., one-on-one counseling) are designed for students to address emergency and crisis-response events. These include short-term, solution-focused counseling sessions to address life-changing events (divorce, death, imprisonment of a parent, etc.) or unresolved challenges unaffected within Tier 1 and Tier 2. Services are provided on a limited basis and, if issues are unresolved, referrals are made to outside resources (Hatch, 2017). This type of intervention includes *short-term* consultation and collaboration among teachers, parents/guardians, and the school counselor until the crisis is resolved and/or referral to appropriate responsive services can be identified and implemented. Figure 1.4 provides an example of a Multi-Tiered, Multi-Domain System of Supports for the elementary school level.

MTMDSS ALIGNMENT TO TEXT

The purpose of this text is to provide thorough instruction on the activities that school counselors provide within Tier 1. Throughout this text, we will dive deeply into planning, implementing, and evaluating Tier 1 activities, those provided to *all* students "because they breathe." These include school counselor core curriculum classroom lessons at all grade levels, focusing on developmentally appropriate and needs-based topics.

Tier 1 at the elementary level also includes schoolwide activities—those provided and coordinated systemically throughout the entire school. These include, for example, Red Ribbon Week, college and career events, and anti-bullying campaigns, as well as parent education, school transition supports, and conflict resolution programs.

Tier 1 instructional content is developmentally appropriate and standards-based, similar to the curriculum provided by teachers. Rather than conducting "random acts" of Tier 1 lessons and activities, school counselors assess the developmental and data-driven needs of the school and create schoolwide action plans. School counseling activities within the three domains are calendared prior to the start of the year (see Chapter 10). The previous year's data may be used to identify schoolwide and grade-specific needs. The calendar is then shared with faculty, families, and other stakeholders.

ALIGNING MTMDSS WITH THE ASCA NATIONAL MODEL

Activities in the MTMDSS fall within several components of the ASCA National Model (3rd edition), with a recommendation that 80% of time be spent on direct and indirect student services. Previous versions of the ASCA model suggested

Figure 1.4   Multi-Tiered, Multi-Domain System of Supports (MTMDSS) Example

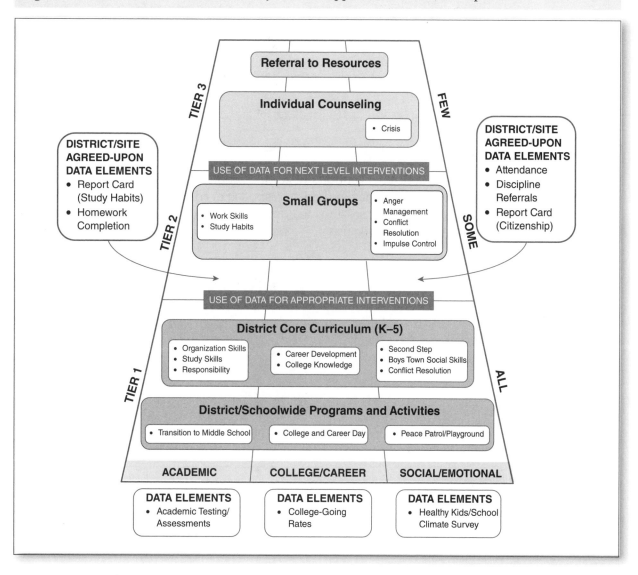

that school counselors spend between 15% and 45% of their time on guidance curriculum (now called core curriculum classroom lessons), depending on their level. Elementary counselors typically teach more lessons (35–45%), while high school counselors teach fewer (15–25%). Although the newest edition of the ASCA model has removed specific recommendations for time within each direct delivery method (see Figure 1.5), the authors still encourage counselors to consider the 35% to 45% timeframe as a guide when first beginning to design and implement their programs (ASCA, 2012, p. 136), but they do not give this as a prescription.

Providing a strong prevention-oriented framework is key to teaching students foundational and developmentally appropriate skills, such as treating others with respect, learning organizational and study strategies, understanding the college readiness and application process, resolving minor conflicts, and beginning the career exploration process. Devoting significant time to teaching classroom lessons and schoolwide activities within the Tier 1 framework provides a strong foundation of evidence-based

ASCA National Model

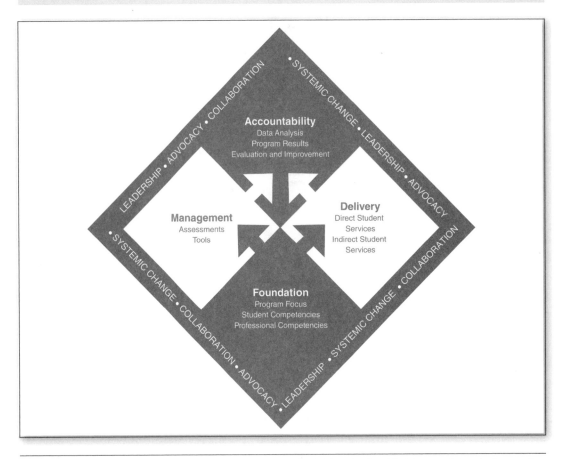

Source: American School Counselor Association (ASCA). (2012). *ASCA national model: A framework for school counseling programs* (3rd ed.). Alexandria, VA: Author.

prevention education programs and services that students need to succeed, which reduces the likelihood of students' qualifying for Tier 2 and 3 interventions.

ALIGNING MTMDSS WITH THE ASCA POSITION STATEMENTS

The *School Counselor and Multitiered System of Supports* position statement was adopted in 2008 and revised in 2014 by the ASCA (see Figure 1.6). It calls on school counselors to be stakeholders in developing and implementing an MTSS that includes but is not limited to RTI and behavioral interventions and supports such as PBIS. According to the position statement, the school counselor's role is to provide *all* students with a standards-based school counseling core curriculum to address universal academic, college/career, and social/emotional development. As school counselors align their work with MTSS and comprehensive school counseling programs designed to improve student achievement and behavior, the MTMDSS model in this text adds the third domain of college and career readiness to MTSS, which typically addresses only academics and behavior. Ensuring an informed, intentional approach to the student core curriculum in all three domains at the Tier 1 level is important, along with helping students with various challenges by providing Tier 2 and 3 interventions.

Figure 1.5 ASCA National Model Suggested Use of Time

ASCA National Model (third edition) Delivery	K-12	ASCA National Model (second edition) Delivery	Elementary	Middle	Secondary
Direct ServicesSchool ◻ Counseling Core Curriculum ◻ Individual Student Planning ◻ Responsive Services **Indirect Services** ◻ Referrals ◻ Consultation ◻ Collaboration	80% or more	Guidance Curriculum	35%-45%	25%-35%	15%-25%
		Individual Student Planning	5%-10%	15%-25%	25%-35%
		Responsive Services	30%-40%	30%-40%	25%-35%
		System Support	10%-15%	10%-15%	15%-20%

Adapted from Gysbers, N.C. & Henderson, P. (2012)
Developing and managing your school counseling program
(5th ed.), Alexandria, VA: American Counseling Association.

Included in Other Components

Program Planning and School Support ▪ Program management and operations (management) ▪ Professional development (foundation and management) ▪ Data analysis (accountability) ▪ Fair-share responsibilities (management)	20% or less

Source: American School Counselor Association (ASCA). (2012). *ASCA national model: A framework for school counseling programs* (3rd ed.). Alexandria, VA: Author.

MTMDSS aligns with the framework of a comprehensive, data-driven school counseling program to meet the needs of all students and to identify students who are at risk. School counselors collaborate with various stakeholders and collect and analyze data to determine the effectiveness of the learning supports.

The MTSS position statement also aligns the ASCA model components with the tiers of supports. For example, for Tier 1: Universal Core Instructional Interventions for All Students, Preventive and Proactive, the following ASCA model activities are suggested:

1. Standards and competencies (foundation)

2. School counseling core curriculum (delivery)

3. Individual student planning direct student services (delivery)

4. Curriculum action plan (management)

5. Curriculum results report (accountability)

6. School data profile (accountability)

This elementary Tier 1 text will include content for five of the six activities. Individual student planning is typically a secondary activity and therefore is not covered in this book. More information on ASCA position statements can be found here: https://www.schoolcounselor.org/school-counselors-members/about-asca-(1)/position-statements.

ALIGNING MTMDSS WITH THE ASCA ETHICAL STANDARDS

The purpose of the *ASCA Ethical Standards for School Counselors* (ASCA, 2016) document is to guide the ethical practices of school counselors. Guidelines that align with Tier 1 in the MTMDSS model include the following:

A.3. Comprehensive Data-Informed Program

School counselors:

b. Provide students with a comprehensive school counseling program that ensures equitable academic, career and social/emotional development opportunities for all students. (ASCA, 2016, p. 3)

Figure 1.6   The School Counselor and Multi-Tiered System of Supports (ASCA)

The School Counselor and Multitiered System of Supports
(Adopted 2008, Revised 2014)

American School Counselor Association (ASCA) Position
School counselors are stakeholders in the development and implementation of a multitiered system of supports (MTSS) including but not limited to response to intervention (RTI) and culturally responsive positive behavioral interventions and supports (CR PBIS). School counselors align their work with MTSS through the implementation of a comprehensive school counseling program designed to improve student achievement and behavior.

The Rationale
An MTSS ensures an informed, intentional approach to help students with various learning challenges. Guided by student-centered data, MTSS teams engaging in data-based problem solving; make decisions about general, compensatory and special education; and assist in the creation of a well-integrated and seamless system of instruction and intervention (Ehren, B, et. al., 2006). Within the framework of a data-driven, comprehensive school counseling program school counselors meet the needs of all students and identify students who are at risk for not meeting academic and behavioral expectations. School counselors collaborate across student service disciplines with teachers, administrators and families to design and implement plans to address struggling students' needs. Data are collected and analyzed to determine the effectiveness of the learning supports for continual improvement efforts over time.

The School Counselor's Role
School counselors assist in the academic and behavioral development of students through the implementation of a comprehensive developmental school counseling program based on the ASCA National Model by:
- Providing all students with a standards-based school counseling core curriculum to address universal academic, career and personal/social development
- Analyzing academic and behavioral data to identify struggling students
- Identifying and collaborating on research-based intervention strategies that are implemented by school staff
- Evaluating academic and behavioral progress after interventions
- Revising interventions as appropriate
- Referring to school and community services as appropriate
- Collaborating with administrators, other school professionals, community agencies and families in the design and implementation of MTSS
- Advocating for equitable education for all students and working to remove systemic barriers

Figure 1.6 (Continued)

The following chart shows how examples of learning supports on a multitiered continuum are applied to a comprehensive school counseling program:

Tiers of Learning Supports	Examples of Learning Supports
Tier 1: Universal Core Instructional Interventions for All Students, Preventive and Proactive	1. Standards and Competencies (Foundation) 2. School Counseling Core Curriculum (Delivery System) 3. Individual Student Planning Direct Student Services (Delivery) 4. Curriculum Action Plan (Management) 5. Curriculum Results Report (Accountability) 6. School Data Profile (Accountability)

Tier 2: Supplemental/Strategic Interventions for Students at Some Risk	1. Standards and Competencies (Foundation)
	2. Individual Student Planning Direct Services (Delivery)
	  a. Small-group action plan
	3. Responsive Services Direct Student Services (Delivery)
	  a. Consultation
	  b. Individual counseling
	  c. Small-group counseling
	4. Closing-the-Gap Action Plan (Management)
	5. Closing-the-Gap Results Report (Accountability)

Tier 3: Intensive, Individual Interventions for Students at High Risk	1. Standards and Competencies (Foundation)
	2. Responsive Services Direct Student Services (Delivery)
	  a. Consultation
	  b. Individual counseling
	  c. Small-group counseling
	  d. Referral to school or community services
	3. Closing-the-Gap Action Plan (Management)
	4. Closing-the-Gap Results Report (Accountability)

Where MTSS interact with school counseling programs, the school counselor can serve in roles of supporter and/or intervener (Ockerman, Mason & Feiker-Hollenbeck, 2012). In the supporting role, the school counselor may provide indirect student service by presenting data or serving as a consultant to a student support team. In intervener role, the school counselor may provide direct student service through the delivery component of the ASCA National Model.

Summary
School counselors implement a comprehensive school counseling program addressing the needs of all students. Through the review of data, school counselors identify struggling students and collaborate with other student services professionals, educators and families to provide appropriate instruction and learning supports within a MTSS. School counselors work collaboratively with other educators to remove systemic barriers for all students and implement specific learning supports that assist in academic and behavioral success.

References
Ehren, B., Montgomery, J., Rudebusch, J., Whitmire, K. (2006). New Roles in Response to Intervention: Creating Success for Schools and Children.

Johnson, E., Mellard, D.F., Fuchs, D., & McKnight, M.A. (2006). Responsiveness to intervention (RTI): How to do it. Lawrence, KS: National Research Center on Learning Disabilities.

Ockerman, M.S., Mason, E.C.M. & Feiker-Hollenbeck, A. (2012) Integrating RTI with school counseling programs: Being a proactive professional school counselor. *Journal of School Counseling* 10(15).

RTI Action Network. Retrieved June 3, 2008 http://rtinetwork.org/?gclid=CNati4-J2ZMCFQEQGgodmTvPaA

Shaprio, E. S. Tiered Instruction and Intervention in a Response-to-Intervention Model. Retrieved June 5, 2008 http://www.rtinetwork.org/Essential/TieredInstruction/ar/ServiceDelivery/1

Source: American School Counselor Association (ASCA). The School Counselor and Multitiered System of Supports: https://www.schoolcounselor.org/asca/media/asca/PositionStatements/PS_MultitieredSupportSystem.pdf.

Activity 1.1

Review the ASCA ethical standards with your administrator. Discuss how a comprehensive school counseling program provides tiered supports to meet the needs of all students.

School counselors:

d. Provide opportunities for all students to develop the necessary mindsets and behaviors to learn work-related skills, resilience, perseverance, an understanding of lifelong learning as a part of long-term career success, a positive attitude toward learning and a strong work ethic. (ASCA, 2016, p. 3)

The ASCA Ethical Standards document can be found in the online appendix and on the ASCA website: https://www.schoolcounselor.org/asca/media/asca/Ethics/EthicalStandards2016.pdf.

The bottom portion of the MTMDSS pyramid (see Figure 1.3) is the largest section and reflects the importance of prevention education. Just as in the Babies in the River story discussed later in this chapter, school counselors can either fill their day with reactive services (i.e., rescuing the babies one after another), or they can get out in front of things and engage in proactive prevention (i.e., teaching the babies how to swim).

Table 1.1 Myths Versus Facts About School Counselors' Role in a Multi-Tiered, Multi-Domain System of Supports

Myth	Fact	Learn More
School counselors only provide Tier 2 and 3 supports	School counselors provide *all* students with a standards-based school counseling **core curriculum** to address universal academic, college/career, and personal/social/emotional development	ASCA position statement about the school counselor in MTSS: http://bit.ly/2n3ouaY
School counselors provide Tier 3 individual counseling to all students	Tier 3 consists of short-term, highly structured interventions and wraparound services defined as "intensive, individual interventions for students at high risk"	ASCA position statement about the school counselor in MTSS: http://bit.ly/2n3ouaY
School counselors provide supports in only one domain (i.e., social/emotional or college/career)	Today's school counselors are vital members of the education team, helping all students in the areas of academic achievement, personal/social development, and college/career development	ASCA executive summary: http://bit.ly/2fZJNqO
Most of the school counselor's time is spent on Tier 2 and 3 supports	The greatest amount of the school counselor's time should be spent on implementing Tier 1 with a high degree of integrity, which is the most efficient means for serving the greatest number of students	"Integrating RTI With School Counseling Programs: Being a Proactive Professional School Counselor," by Ockerman, Mason, and Hollenbeck (2012) Researchers indicate that around 75% to 80% of children should be expected to reach successful levels of competency through Tier 1 delivery (Shapiro, n.d.). "Spending 90% of the school counselor's time with 10% of the students is not the philosophy of intentional guidance." (Hatch, 2013)

Source: Triplett, W. (2017). *Utilizing a multi-tiered system to implement your school counseling program* [PowerPoint slides]. Created for Chicago Public Schools.

Babies in the River

"Babies in the River" is a wonderful parable often told to illustrate the difference between prevention and intervention. Author Trish adapted this version from Pat Martin, a dear friend and colleague.

On a spring afternoon, after the students had left at the end of a minimum day, a group of high school counselors walked to a nearby park area next to a river to eat lunch together for the first time all year. Considering that they rarely even ate lunch at all, this was a treasured event. After a few minutes of talking and eating, Mariana (the school counselor with alphabet A–Hi) noticed a baby floating down the river. Alarmed, she jumped up to assess the situation. As she did, she noticed several babies floating. She screamed for her colleagues to help, and for the next 20 minutes, they retrieved dozens of babies out of the river, until finally the babies stopped floating by. Exhausted, Mariana returned to her picnic and realized that Bob (the school counselor with alphabet Mx–Sm) was missing. Where was Bob? He hadn't been helping rescue the babies? Pretty soon Bob was heard whistling down the walkway. The rest of the group inquired, "Where were you? We were busy retrieving babies, and you were nowhere to be found!"

"Well," he commented, "I decided to go up the river to see how they were getting in! Turns out someone, in their wisdom, decided to build a nursery/preschool next to the river! I noticed that the door had a broken lock, so first I fixed that. Then I realized that the babies didn't know how to swim, so I taught them. Then I learned that the teachers had no floaties, so I bought floaties and put them near the exit, so that if any babies fall in again, the teachers can throw floaties in the water in order for the babies to assist themselves. Finally, I filed a complaint with the city to ensure that no one ever builds a nursery or preschool within a mile of a river again!"

Though the prevention approach is almost always the most appealing, it can be difficult for counselors if they think that shifting to prevention education means turning their back on those students currently in need. It is also not always obvious how to work within the system to redesign how it functions—to build it differently, to partner to train those on the front lines and assist them in understanding how to provide first-level interventions and supports. But this is a requirement if school counselors are going to meet the needs of *all* students, because there is not enough time to rescue every drowning student (hypothetically) and far too many in the caseload.

When counselors spend 80% of their day mired in Tier 2 and 3 reactive services, they may feel like they are in an emergency room rather than a school, and they won't have time for teaching prevention education and for designing systems of support to catch students early. Without a strong prevention system in place, the need for responsive services will continue to grow. By implementing a strong Tier 1 program, complete with classroom lessons and schoolwide activities, students will gain the attitudes, knowledge, and skills necessary to prevent them from needing Tier 2 and 3 services, thereby reducing the time spent in these tiers.

Shifting school counselor program activities from being primarily responsive to being proactive takes commitment, planning, time, and cooperation from administration and faculty alike. As school counselors begin to shift the pyramid to focus more on Tier 1, consideration should be given to addressing the potential challenges of finding balance between the time spent in classrooms and the number of reactive services they previously provided. School counselors will benefit from scaffolding the transitions at their school site to a proactive approach by adding lessons to their Tier 1 action plans each year or by beginning with just one grade level and adding a grade level each year. In addition, when collaborating with teachers and administrators to gain support for Tier 1 in class interventions and participating on leadership teams to create necessary systemic processes, school counselors will improve efficiency and effectiveness as they determine which students are referred for additional Tier 2 and 3 data-driven interventions.

MULTI-TIERED, MULTI-DOMAIN SYSTEM OF SUPPORTS (MTMDSS) ASSESSMENT

Activity 1.2

Please review the Multi-Tiered, Multi-Domain System of Supports (MTMDSS) diagram (Figure 1.3) regarding school counselor activities within an MTMDSS. Next, complete the blank MTMDSS (see Figure 1.7) by listing your current Tier 1, 2, and 3 activities, lessons, and interventions per each domain: academic, college/career, and social/emotional. Look for strengths and potential areas for growth.

Figure 1.7 Blank MTMDSS Diagram

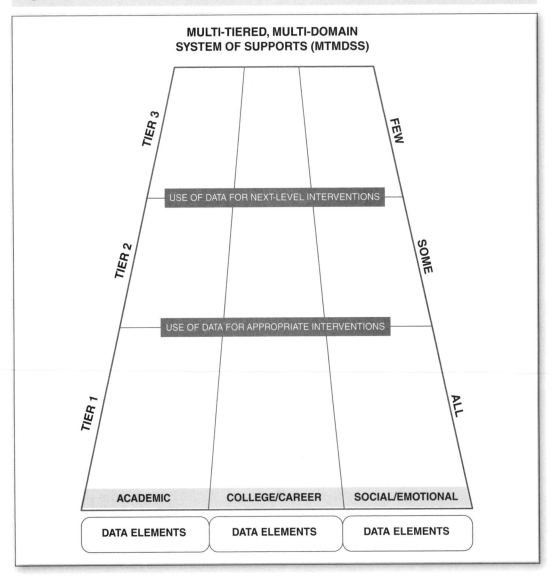

2

Franchising Core Curriculum

TRISH'S STORY

On my trip to Santorini, Greece, last summer, I saw what I thought would be the demise of the island: McDonald's. How could they ruin my favorite island with a franchise? No one would eat there, or so I thought. Soon it was filled with customers from every country purchasing Big Macs, Chicken McNuggets, Filet-o-Fish, fries, chocolate shakes, and, yes, apple pie. Why would people come to Greece and order McDonald's? You guessed it—because they knew what they could count on. No matter where you go in the world, McDonald's has a guaranteed menu—it's part of the franchise requirements. In addition to the "franchise menu," there are culturally appropriate items to satisfy local needs, such as pineapples and Spam on burgers in Hawaii, Ebi filet-o-shrimp burgers in Japan, taro-root pie in China, McCurry in India, and the dreaded McGyro in my beloved Santorini (I have not tried it—yet).

McDonald's is a franchise business. Private entrepreneurs purchase rights to open and run a location of the larger parent company and sign a contractual agreement to follow the company's rules for operation. When a franchisee signs the agreements, he or she agrees to the terms of operating according to the franchisor's requirements, which are dictated by the parent company. The benefits of owning a franchise include the familiarity of the company name and image and training from the parent company on operating the franchise successfully. Failure rates among franchises tend to be lower than among other new businesses, largely because customers generally recognize the company name and know what to expect (Lorette, n.d.).

Figure 2.1 Trish Sees the McDonald's Franchise in Greece

Trish Hatch in 📍 Fira Town, Santorini.
June 12, 2016 · ✆ ▾

Oh no.... There goes the island. This is a disaster.

WHAT IS FRANCHISING?

In school counseling, there is no national "franchisable" core curriculum ready to purchase and implement. There's nothing that parents can "count on" when they come into an elementary school. School counseling standards and curricula often vary from state to state, district to district, site to site, and counselor to counselor. Some states have set up common expectations and provide sample curriculum recommendations, but most leave decisions about expectations for consistent delivery up to individual districts, schools, and counselors. Imagine if this happened at McDonald's. It would cease to be a franchise and would be more like a mom-and-pop hamburger shop, where prices and expectations of food quality and preparation vary from place to place. While local control gives power to schools and districts to select the curriculum best suited for their students' needs, the fact that school counselors provide inconsistent curriculum in schools affects what the "customer"—in this case, parents and students—can count on.

WHAT CAN STUDENTS, PARENTS, AND TEACHERS EXPECT (COUNT ON) FROM SCHOOL COUNSELING PROGRAMS?

The purpose of a Schoolwide Core Curriculum Action Plan is to ensure that "every student gets every*thing*!" By virtue of breathing, *all* students are guaranteed to receive instruction from the school counseling program, and all students get everything (i.e., the entire curriculum designed for their grade level). The Schoolwide Core Curriculum Action Plan, which is used when creating and presenting the school counseling core curriculum, is similar to a teacher's scope and sequence. Just as teachers collaborate to determine grade-level expectations, scope and sequence, and pacing charts for timely delivery of subject content, school counselors are called on to collaborate and create similar documents to ensure that all students are on target to receive common instruction from school counseling programs.

Just as a standardized curriculum exists for math, science, and language arts, a "franchisable" core curriculum is intended to provide a message of consistency regarding expectations for student learning among schools and across districts and states. In the same way that parents come to know that their fifth graders will be taught state capitals in social studies starting in January, so too will they understand that the school counseling lesson for January is about resolving conflicts with friends, which supports a school counseling competency. Teachers will meet to agree on "essential standards" or "power standards" for each grade level; similarly, school counselors will collaborate with other elementary counselors in the district and site administrators to determine which content is most appropriate for students at each grade level. During planning, school counselors will take students' developmental levels into consideration, along with site-specific and data-driven needs.

THE 80/20 APPROACH

Ideally, approximately 80% of the curriculum should be created as franchisable, school to school, within a district. When selecting the 80% franchisable curriculum that will be consistent school to school within a district, school counselors are encouraged to follow the same process of standards-based educational expectations as teachers do. Therefore, school counselors are recommended to include a thorough review of the American School Counselor Association's (ASCA's) domains (academic, career, and social/emotional) and *Mindsets & Behaviors for Student Success* standards in creating developmentally appropriate scaffolding of attitudes, knowledge, and skills in the areas of academic, college/career, and social/emotional learning. When developing the school counseling franchisable curriculum districtwide, attention to site-specific needs can be built into lesson planning. For example, while respect and anti-bullying will be taught to all fourth- and fifth-grade students districtwide, a school counselor with high numbers of rumors reported at his school will incorporate this content within the lesson.

The subsequent 20% is reserved for a specific schoolwide curriculum based on local and/or school site needs. In reviewing schoolwide data, a youth behavior risk survey may indicate a high percentage of students who report that they are experimenting with alcohol. In this scenario, the school counselor may want to add lessons to address this data-driven need. Similarly, if students report high levels of cyberbullying or sexual harassment (discipline data), it would be more efficient and effective to conduct the curriculum in classes or grade levels with high numbers of offenders than it would be to remove students from class to conduct multiple group or individual interventions. Sometimes an overabundance of Tier 2 referrals suggests that a more efficient and effective way of managing student behavior would be to add an additional classroom lesson to the action plan. This may be temporary and should be based on school site data. There is no magic number or percentage that determines when a counselor should stop seeing students in small groups and instead conduct additional classroom curriculum; this is a conversation best discussed with school administration. Systemic thinking could also be applied to student report card data (Duarte & Hatch, 2014). Imagine, for example, that report cards indicate a high percentage of students in the fourth grade with *needs improvement* or *unsatisfactory* marks on the study habits portion of the report card. A school counselor might be tempted to facilitate multiple time-consuming small counseling groups or individual sessions for these students. When Tier 2 or 3 interventions become all-encompassing, it may be time to consider a Tier 1 curricular or more schoolwide programmatic approach to address this systemic need for study habits.

SCHOOLWIDE CORE CURRICULUM ACTION PLANS

The ASCA National Model: A Framework for School Counseling Programs (ASCA, 2012) presents the use of three types of action plans, one of which is the School Counseling Core Curriculum Action Plan. Schoolwide Core Curriculum Action

Plans are standards driven and ensure that every student gets every*thing* (again, the whole curriculum designed for each student's grade level). What content will every student receive because he or she came through the schoolroom door? What can we tell each parent and teacher that each student will receive from the school counseling program as a first, third, or fifth grader?

Developmental in design, preventative in nature, and comprehensive in scope, the Schoolwide Core Curriculum Action Plan guarantees that families, students, teachers, and other stakeholders know exactly what curriculum their student will receive and at what time throughout the year. The curriculum, much like math or science, is competency driven, created by school counselors and student service professionals to address the standards and competencies (ASCA, 2014). The school counselors, in collaboration with site administrators (or, in some cases, district coordinators), determine what content will be covered in each lesson and align it with the standards. School counselors create an action plan, calendar these lessons, and collect process, perception, and outcome data. Lessons are either selected or designed by school counselors to become consistent (or franchisable) from school to school to ensure that when students transfer within a district, they will receive the same curriculum from the school counseling program. For example, just as all third graders are taught multiplication, so too are all students taught the lesson on problem-solving steps.

Although different districts approach the development of core curriculum differently, collaboration is key. Within one school district, the counselors may choose to use the pre-developed *Second Step* Violence Prevention Program (Committee for Children, 2014) and design additional lessons that align with the academic and college/career domains. In another district, the entire curriculum may be self-generated by the school counselors. In either case, school counselors within a district work collaboratively to ensure consistency in the lesson content that they develop and deliver.

Figure 2.2 is an example of a Schoolwide Core Curriculum Action Plan shared by co-author Danielle, indicating the specific curriculum that every student in the district will receive from the school counseling program in elementary school. Care is also taken to ensure that all three school counseling domains are addressed, with attention to a minimum number of agreed-upon lessons for each grade level. Being at an elementary school, the school counselor added the lesson times rather than the subject area.

GUIDELINES FOR CREATING SCHOOLWIDE CORE CURRICULUM ACTION PLANS

Schoolwide Core Curriculum Action Plans contain

- Grade(s)
- Lesson topic(s)
- The ASCA domain and *Mindsets & Behaviors* standards to be addressed
- A description of the curriculum that the school counselor or counseling team will provide
- A timeline for the start and completion of each activity
- Process data (i.e., the number of students impacted)
- When class lessons will be taught (by class/subject)
- Perception data (attitudes, skills, and knowledge)

Figure 2.2 Example Core Curriculum Action Plan

Example K–5 School Counseling Core Curriculum Action Plan

Adapted from Alvin Dunn Elementary Action Plan

Grade Level	Core Curriculum Lesson Topic	American School Counselor Association (ASCA) Domain + Mindsets & Behaviors	Curriculum and Materials	Projected Start/ Projected End	Projected Number of Students Impacted	Time of Lesson	Evaluation Methods: How Will the Results Be Measured?
K	Second Step Unit 1 Skills for Learning (5 lessons)	Social/Emotional M 2, M 3, B-LS 4, B-SMS 6, B-SS 3	Second Step Violence Prevention Program	September – January	100	Every other week @ 12:15	Teacher Feedback Survey Results
	Second Step Unit 2 Empathy (6 lessons)	Social/Emotional M 6, B-LS 1, B-SMS 1, B-SS 2, B-SS 4	Second Step Violence Prevention Program	February – June		Burkey - Mon Hernandez - Tues Wurster - Thurs	
1	Second Step Unit 1 Skills for Learning (5 lessons)	Social/Emotional M 2, M 3, B-LS 4, B-SMS 6, B-SS 3	Second Step Violence Prevention Program	September – January	110	Weekly: Ray/Colburn: Mon @ 2:45 Kincaid: Thurs @ 2:20 Cruz: Tues @ 2:40 Cerda: Thurs @ 2:40 Reynolds: Thurs @ 11:35	Monitoring citizenship marks on report cards & Teacher Feedback Survey Results
	Second Step Unit 2 Empathy (6 lessons)	Social/Emotional M 6, B-LS 1, B-SMS 1, B-SS 2, B-SS 4	Second Step Violence Prevention Program	February – April			
	Second Step Unit 3 Emotion Management (5 lessons)	Social/Emotional B-SMS 1, B-SMS 2, B-SMS 5	Second Step Violence Prevention Program	May – June			
	School Counselor Welcome & Appreciating Differences	Social/Emotional M 3, B-SS 4, B-SS 7	Book: *It's Okay to Be Different*	September			
	College & Career Awareness	Career M 4, B-LS 7	Books: *L M N O Peas & Lookout College, Here I Come!*	January			
	Anti-Bullying	Social/Emotional M 3, B-SS 4, B-SS 9	Book: *Stop Picking on Me*	March			
2	Second Step Unit 2 Empathy (6 lessons)	Social/Emotional M 2, B-LS 1, B-SMS 1, B-SS 2, B-SS 4	Second Step Violence Prevention Program	September – January	100	Every other week @ 11:05 DeMarco – Mon Nicolai – Tues Hernandez – Wed Navarro – Thurs	Monitoring citizenship marks on report cards & Teacher Feedback Survey Results
	Second Step Unit 3 Emotion Management (6 lessons)	Social/Emotional B-SMS 1, B-SMS 2, B-SMS 5	Second Step Violence Prevention Program	February – April			
	School Counselor Welcome & Respect Lesson	Social/Emotional M 3, B-SS 4, B-SS 7	School Counselor – Generated Lesson	September			
	College & Career Awareness	Career M 4, B-LS 7	Books: *L M N O Peas & Lookout College, Here I Come!*	January			n/a
	Anti-Bullying	Social/Emotional M 3, B-SS 4, B-SS 9	Book: *Stop Picking on Me*	March			Behavior referral rates

Example K–5 School Counseling Core Curriculum Action Plan

Adapted from Alvin Dunn Elementary Action Plan

Grade Level	Core Curriculum Lesson Topic	ASCA Domain + Mindsets & Behaviors	Curriculum and Materials	Projected Start/End	Projected Number	Time of Lesson	Evaluation Methods
3	Second Step Unit 2 Empathy (4 lessons)	Social/Emotional M 2, B-LS 4, B-SMS 6, B-SS 4, B-SS 5	Second Step Violence Prevention Program	September – December	90	Every Other Week: Vitiello/Martinson Mon @ 2:00 Sanchez Tues @ 2:00	Monitoring citizenship marks on report cards & behavior referral rates
	Second Step Unit 3 Emotion Management (6 lessons)	Social/Emotional B-SMS 1, B-SMS 3, B-SMS 7	Second Step Violence Prevention Program	January – March			
	Second Step Unit 4 Problem Solving (3 lessons)	Social/Emotional B-LS 1, B-SMS 7, B-SS 2, B-SS 6	Second Step Violence Prevention Program	April – June			
	School Counselor Welcome & Respect Lesson	Social/Emotional M 3, B-SS 4, B-SS 7	School Counselor – Generated Lesson	September			n/a
	Red Ribbon Week	Social/Emotional M 1, B-LS 1, B-SMS9, B-SS 9	Counselor-generated anti-drug/alcohol lesson	October			n/a
	College & Career Readiness	Career M 4, B-LS 7, B-SMS 5	Counselor-generated college lesson; College & Career Day	January			Pre/Post Survey
	Stand UP to Bullying Month	Social/Emotional M 3, B-SS 4, B-SS 9	Book: *My Secret Bully*; 4 Corners Lesson; Stand UP to Bullying Calendar	March			Behavior Referral Rates
4	Second Step Unit 1 Empathy & Skills for Learning (4 lessons)	Social/Emotional M 2, M 3, B-SMS 6, B-SS 4, B-SS 5	Second Step Violence Prevention Program	September – December	100	Weekly: Salmon: Mon @ 1:30 Walker: Tues @ 1:30 Miring off: Wed @ 9:00 Vandervort: Tues @ 11:30	Monitoring citizenship marks on report cards
	Second Step Unit 2 Emotion Management (6 lessons)	Social/Emotional B-SMS 1, B-SMS 3, B-SMS 7	Second Step Violence Prevention Program	January – March			
	Second Step Unit 3 Problem Solving (7 lessons)	Social/Emotional B-LS 1, B-SMS 7, B-SS 2, B-SS 6	Second Step Violence Prevention Program	April – June			
	School Counselor Welcome & Respect Lesson	Social/Emotional M 3, B-SS 4, B-SS 7	School Counselor Generated Lesson	September			n/a
	Red Ribbon Week	Social/Emotional M 1, B-LS 1, B-SMS9, B-SS 9	Counselor-generated anti-drug/alcohol lesson	October			n/a
	College & Career Readiness	Career M 4, B-LS 7, B-SMS 5	Counselor-generated college lesson; College & Career Presenters Day	January			Pre/Post Survey
	Stand UP to Bullying Month	Social/Emotional M 3, B-SS 4, B-SS 9	Book: *My Secret Bully*; 4 Corners Lesson; Stand UP to Bullying Calendar	March			Behavior Referral Rates

(Continued)

Figure 2.2 (Continued)

Example K–5 School Counseling Core Curriculum Action Plan

Adapted from Alvin Dunn Elementary Action Plan

5	Second Step Unit 1 Empathy & Skills for Learning (4 lessons)	Social/Emotional M 3, B-LS 4, B-SMS 10, B-SS 1, B-SS 5	Second Step Violence Prevention Program	September – December			Monitoring citizenship marks on report cards CA Healthy Kids Survey
	Second Step Unit 2 Emotion Management (7 lessons)	Social/Emotional B-SMS 1, B-SMS 2, B-SMS 6	Second Step Violence Prevention Program	January – March			
	Second Step Unit 3 Problem Solving (7 lessons)	Social/Emotional B-LS 9, B-SMS 7, B-SS 2, B-SS 5	Second Step Violence Prevention Program	April – June			
	School Counselor Welcome & Respect Lesson	Social/Emotional M 3, B-SS 4, B-SS 7	School Counselor Generated Lesson	September		Weekly: Hayashi: Mon @ 8:50 Falk: Thurs @ 1:30 Watters: Fri @ 12:20	n/a
	Red Ribbon Week	Social/Emotional M 1, B-LS 1, B-SMS9, B-SS 9	Counselor-generated anti-drug/alcohol lesson	October	90		CA Healthy Kids Survey
	College & Career Readiness	Career M 4, B-LS 7, B-SMS 5	Counselor-generated college lesson; College & Career Presenters Day	January			Pre/Post Survey
	Stand UP to Bullying Month	Social/Emotional M 3, B-SS 4, B-SS 9	Book: *My Secret Bully*; 4 Corners Lesson; Daily Calendar	March			CA Healthy Kids Survey Pre/Post Survey
	Transition to Middle School	Academic & Social/Emotional M 2, B-LS 8, B-SMS 10, B-SS 9	Counselor Generated; Trip to Feeder MS	April & May			Monitoring Ds/Fs in students' 6th grade year

Principal's signature _____ Date _____ Date of staff presentation _____ Prepared by _____

- Outcome data (achievement-related and achievement results)
- The name of the individual responsible for delivery
- An indication that the plan has been reviewed and signed by the administrator

The number of lessons delivered may vary depending on the student-to-counselor ratio or the extent to which the school counselors deliver all lessons or assist others in the delivery of the curriculum (such as when school counselors supervise interns or paraprofessionals, or when elementary teachers deliver social/emotional learning programs like Student Success Skills). Because the school counseling curriculum is delivered to all students, the numbers per grade level appear under "Projected Number of Students Impacted." Some curricula are generated by the school counselor, and other curricula may come from prepackaged programs, but all include a method for evaluation that will be discussed later in this text.

While some lessons include immediate and/or long-term evaluation tools, this is not to imply that the school counselor would measure every lesson in every way annually. Rather, the Schoolwide Core Curriculum Action Plan may provide a list of which perception and outcome data might be reviewed or examined as significant data points that align with each curriculum lesson. The school counseling team selects a few lessons each year to evaluate and improve, based on their alignment with schoolwide and/or program goals (discussed further in Chapter 3).

INSTRUCTIONS FOR COMPLETING AN ACTION PLAN

When completing an action plan, refer to these guidelines:

Grade(s)

It is important to ensure that every student receives access to the achievement of competencies; therefore, school counselors teach core curriculum classroom lessons to all students within each grade level.

Lesson Topic

When deciding which content you'll provide to every student, it will be helpful to review your developmental crosswalk of the ASCA *Mindsets & Behaviors for Student Success* standards (discussed further in Chapter 4) and the three domains of academic, college/career, and social/emotional development. Which standards do you want to be certain to address? Which of the three domains are taught within each grade level throughout the year? Ideally, and with a low ratio, school counselors want to address each domain, but this may not be possible. Consider your priorities and begin in that domain. Priorities might include areas that the data indicate need the most attention. Perhaps your Youth Risk Behavior Survey or school climate survey results indicate that you have a high number of students who are feeling unsafe at school, who have been victims of bullying, and so on. Based on these data, you might prioritize this lesson and therefore address the social/emotional domain. School counselors can then add on a few core curriculum lessons each year until all domains are addressed.

ASCA Domain and Mindsets & Behaviors Standards

In this section school counselors will list the appropriate counseling domain(s) covered by the lesson. Then the school counselor will look at the ASCA *Mindsets & Behaviors* standards. In this section write in the abbreviations of the most important standards to be covered by the lesson.

Curriculum and Materials

This column asks you to identify the specific content to be taught in the classroom lesson. For example, the competency might be study skills, but the content will vary by grade level and student population. Fourth-grade students may receive the study and test-taking skills curriculum using the Sunburst *Super Study Skills* video (AIM Education, 2010), or first graders may participate in career exploration through reading the book *LMNO Peas* (Baker, 2010) and completing a "When I Grow Up" worksheet. By tracking the different curricula being used, and measuring and comparing the results of lessons, school counseling teams can determine which curriculum and materials are most effective. These formal and informal assessments allow for program improvement and prevent costs associated with purchasing ineffective curriculum. In addition, if the curriculum to be used is documented, it can be easily referenced each academic year.

Projected Start/End

Knowing when an activity will occur and when it will be completed is essential to team planning. This facilitates intelligent planning of when events will occur in the school system. For example, teaching test-taking strategies is most effective when done just prior to statewide standardized test administration. Doing it months before or after students have been tested would miss the critical teaching moment. Similarly, teaching conflict resolution skills would be more appropriate in the beginning of the school year than at the end, as the skills might be forgotten over the summer.

Lesson Presented During Time/Subject

When school counselors are deciding the subject area in which to deliver their core curriculum lessons, it is important to recognize and appreciate the standards and competencies that the classroom teachers are required to address. Effort should be made to infuse lesson activities across the curriculum, as opposed to impacting only one academic area, if applicable at elementary school. This section can also be used to include the time of recurring lessons. Through collaboration and alignment of lessons, school counselors gain staff buy-in and mutual support for lessons.

Process Data

The number of students impacted by each classroom lesson is indicated in this section. School counselors will document the approximate number of students in each grade level and add it to this section, and school counselors are advised to schedule their lessons when all students are present (i.e., when students are not out of class for speech or adaptive physical education).

Perception Data

Before the delivery of classroom lessons, it is important for the school counselor to consider the criteria by which success will be measured. What are the attitudes, knowledge, and skills to be taught? Will the perception data be measured by a pre- and post-test? In this section, counselors will fill out what they hope students will believe, know, and be able to do after the lesson is taught.

Outcome Data

Achievement-related and achievement data are the ultimate outcomes aligned with school counseling core curriculum lessons. Student achievement data consist of outcome data focusing on academic achievement; at the elementary level, these measures include benchmark scores, standardized test results, and academic proficiency levels. Achievement-related data are the data elements, determined by research, that support student achievement. In elementary school, student achievement data include attendance rates, behavior, parent engagement, and so forth (Hatch, 2013). What outcome data can be assessed by the lesson: attendance, behavior, and/or achievement? Consider how these types of data can be collected. For more on how these types of data can be collected, see Chapter 8.

School Counselor(s)

At the bottom of the action plan, list the name(s) of the school counselor(s). For teams with multiple school counselors, you can also add a column to the action plan specifying the individual who will be responsible for each lesson. In some situations, school counselors implement some core curriculum lessons, while others teach lessons in collaboration with teachers (often the case for the Committee for Children's *Second Step*).

The Administrator's Signature

The signature of the administrator ensures collaboration and agreement with the proposed activities of the comprehensive school counseling program. Although this section is not included in the original ASCA template, it is added in the plan provided here to encourage support and awareness from school leadership. Additionally, a date scheduled for a faculty presentation to share this information is also included on the action plan, so that counselors can discuss their program and provide a calendar indicating when the lessons will be delivered, allowing time for teachers to prepare in advance. Additional discussion about the importance of utilizing planning calendars is presented in Chapter 10. The action plan can also be shared with families and included on the school counseling program website.

Figure 2.3 is an ASCA Action Plan Template adapted to add the time or subject during which the lesson will be presented and signature items at the bottom of the action plan. Additional templates are available online. School counselors are encouraged to use and adapt these templates to meet the needs of their school counseling program.

Figure 2.4 is the beginning of an action plan created by a new school counselor who was assigned to multiple elementary schools. To ensure consistency, the counselor

Figure 2.3 Core Curriculum Action Plan Template

SCHOOL COUNSELING CORE CURRICULUM ACTION PLAN

Templated Adapted from

AMERICAN SCHOOL COUNSELOR ASSOCIATION

School Counseling Program Goals:

Core Curriculum Lessons and Related to Goals:

Grade Level	Lesson Topic	ASCA Domain and Mindsets & Behaviors Standard(s)	Curriculum and Materials	Projected Start/End	Lesson Presented During Time/Subject	Process Data (Projected number of students affected)	Perception Data (Type of surveys/ assessments to be used)	Outcome Data (Achievement, attendance and/or behavior data to be collected)

Principal's Signature	Date	Date of staff presentation	Prepared by

Source: American School Counselor Association. School Counseling Core Curriculum Action Plan: https://www.schoolcounselor.org/school-counselors/asca-national-model/asca-national-model-templates.

Figure 2.4 Core Curriculum Action Plan From the First Year of School Counseling

Fallbrook Union Elementary School District
Core School Counseling Curriculum Action Plan
Fallbrook Street Elementary ~ La Paloma Elementary ~ Live Oak Elementary ~ Mary Fay Pendleton ~ William H. Frazier Elementary

Grade Level	Core Curriculum Lesson Content	American School Counselor Association (ASCA) Domain + Mindset & Behavior Standards	Curriculum and Materials	Projected Timeframe
K-3	Healthy Decision Making & Good Choices (Red Ribbon Week)	Social/Emotional M 1 B-SMS 9 B-SS 2	Book: *No!...And I Mean No, Let's Say NO to Drugs!* Red Ribbon Week Pledge	October
	College & Career Awareness	Career M 4 & 6 B-LS 7 B-SMS 5	Books: *L M N O Peas & Mahalia Mouse Goes to College*	January
	Respect & Anti-Bullying	Social/Emotional M 3 B-LS 5 B-SS 5 & 8	Book: *It's Okay to be Different* & Activity	March
4-6	Healthy Decision Making & Good Choices (Red Ribbon Week)	Social/Emotional M 1 B-SMS 9 B-SS 2	School Counselor–generated Anti-Drug/Alcohol Lesson + STAR Decision-Making	October
	College & Career Exploration	Academic & Career M 4 & 6 B-LS 7 B-SMS 5	School Counselor–generated College & Career Lesson	January
	Respect & Anti-Bullying	Social/Emotional M 3 B-LS 5 B-SS 5 & 8	Book: *Bully Beans* & Role-Play Scenarios	March
	Transition to Middle School (6th)	Academic & Social/Emotional M 2 & 3 B-LS 10 B-SMS 10	Potter Jr. High (led by Potter Administrators & School Counselors) Where Everybody Belongs (WEB) Day at Potter	May

District Director of Student Services _____   Date _____

School counselor: How many lessons should counselors teach per grade level?

Trish's answer: It depends. Imagine that your school counseling program is like a house. All houses have kitchens, bathrooms, and bedrooms. Some houses have only two bedrooms, while other larger homes have four or five bedrooms. But they all have bedrooms. Similarly, all school counseling programs have similar components—core lessons, small-group interventions, parent education, and so forth. If a school counselor has a larger caseload, it doesn't mean that he or she gives up on one of the components of the program. Rather, the counselor provides fewer small-group interventions or lessons if he or she has a larger caseload. Depending also on the curriculum taught and available resources, some school counselors may collaborate to co-teach curriculum with teachers, while others will decide to teach the curriculum themselves.

In 1987, I was a new school counselor with 800 students at one school and 500 at another (for a total of 1,300). Due to the large caseload, I focused on providing only a few lessons for all levels. In conversation with my administrators at each school, we decided to focus most of the prevention lessons on the grade levels that needed the most assistance (third and fourth). By focusing on these grade levels that had the greatest needs (indicated by the most referrals to the office), I was able to measure impact and share results.

I organized my week to teach lessons two days per week (one day at each school) and small groups two afternoons per week, with two mornings for individual counseling and one day for planning, participating at meetings, and so on. By planning four to five lessons per day, I was able to calculate the number of lessons I could reasonably teach each year. Then, looking at the calendar and the number of classes at each grade level, I scheduled about 80% of the weeks (working around the beginning and end of school, testing, etc.). Once my impact was seen at those levels, the administrators advocated for hiring a full-time counselor at each school. When I was finally able to be full-time at just one school, I was able to provide monthly lessons at each grade level. I share this story to remind school counselors that even with a huge caseload, through strategic problem solving, advocacy, and measuring results, school counselors can make a difference and improve programs and services for all students.

"franchised" her curriculum across all schools by teaching the same topics, and she will make minor modifications to her lessons to meet site-specific needs. One strength of this plan is that students will receive instruction in all three domains over the course of their K–6 experience. In her first year, she doesn't have any curriculum and begins by creating one lesson for primary grades and one lesson for upper grades for each topic. In year two, she will build on the lessons by expanding, diversifying, and differentiating instruction for different grade levels and creating new lessons to add to her action plan (so as to not repeat the same lessons). The school counselor will need to add methods of evaluation to her action plan and begin measuring results to show the impact of teaching the core curriculum. What else do you notice in this action plan? What do you like about the plan? What is missing? How might you improve it?

WAYS TO DELIVER CORE CURRICULUM

As part of the planning process, school counselors will collaborate with teachers to determine the best times to present classroom lessons. Note that in Figure 2.2 the core curriculum action plan includes specific times for scheduled lessons. Ideally, school counselors will select times when teachers can be present and involved in the lessons so that they can enhance and reinforce the content after school counselors leave. However, school counselors may have to be flexible to ensure that content is taught in a way that best serves everyone. In some situations, the school calendar will require counselors to be flexible in their scheduling of lessons. Below are some suggestions for school counselors as they are planning to teach core curriculum:

- Intentionally tune into what teachers are covering in their various classes so that you can look for connections between the academic standards and Mindsets & Behavior Standards to push into core subjects to deliver counselor-led lessons or co-teach lessons. By sharing your lesson plan ideas that align with teachers' content (e.g., a lesson on calculating GPA during math; a lesson on cultural diversity during social studies; a lesson on stress relief including art/music during electives), you can leverage your time in the classroom and increase opportunities for collaboration (Mason, 2010).
- Consider delivering lessons during teachers' prep periods if no other time is available. Every effort should be made to encourage the teacher to remain during the school counselor's lesson, as students will benefit from the

teacher's reinforcing concepts after the counselor leaves and until the next lesson, for example, by adding feelings vocabulary that the counselor discussed to a classroom word wall. In addition, many school counselors are not credentialed as teachers, which may raise union or legal issues in some districts. While teaching a lesson during a prep period without the teacher is preferable over not teaching the curriculum at all, the best scenario is when teachers and counselors are present in the classroom together.

- Flip the delivery of large-group or classroom lessons! Prerecord a video to be shown by classroom teachers and provide a lesson plan and/or activity for students to complete during or after the video. This option works well to enhance schoolwide activities such as Red Ribbon or Kindness Week, when the school counselor may not have time to present in all classrooms. It can help alleviate some of the day-to-day challenges of school counselors, who often feel pulled in many different directions, especially when a counselor has a large caseload or limited access to students. In a flipped classroom, students watch online presentations, collaborate in online discussions, or complete tasks outside the classroom, which may lead to more consistent content delivery and provide more effective and efficient classroom interactions between school counselors and students (Mason, Gupta, Sowers, & Sabens, 2014).

- Advisory or homeroom teachers can participate in the delivery of the school counseling curriculum in upper grades. Counselors can collaborate with advisory teachers to provide instruction; however, care must be taken to ensure the quality of content and instruction through the assessment process. Advising and homeroom can support the school counseling program as one delivery model within the core curriculum, but this method is not intended to be the sole means of delivery. School counselors are advised to create detailed lesson plans and provide them to teachers prior to the lesson, along with methods for evaluation.

- Depending on class size and space, combining two classes of students together can be another means to teach core curriculum. Grouping students can double the school counselor's time, but a note of caution: Assess student outcomes to ensure that the same level of learning is taking place compared to teaching each class individually. More students means that fewer individuals are able to share answers with the group, and students may be more likely to get distracted. Strong classroom management skills on the part of the school counselor are also important to prevent off-task behaviors.

- In schools where upper-grade students have electives, such as technology, AVID (Advancement Via Individual Determination), or health, school counselors are encouraged to work with the elective teacher and/or to co-instruct. Rather than duplicate content on topics such as cyber-safety, anti-drugs/alcohol, or college exploration, the school counselor can collaborate to ensure that counseling lessons are not repetitive for students.

School counselor: Sometimes teachers leave the classroom when I am teaching to make copies or go to the bathroom . . . is that okay?

Authors' answer: We recommend that teachers be both present and engaged during the school counseling lesson so that they will understand and reinforce concepts taught after the counselor leaves. Teacher involvement in classroom lessons assists students in their learning, such when the teacher shares a personal example related to the topic or helps students complete an activity. Additionally, because elementary school counselors teach in each classroom only once per week to once per month, reinforcement can be supported by teachers. While teachers may have to leave for an emergency or the school schedule can be such that teachers have prep time, ideally teachers are in the class and participating when the counselor is teaching. School counselors can include teachers in the lessons by letting them know in advance that they will ask them a question about the topic, require assistance for students with an activity, or issue a homework assignment. This strategy can be particularly effective for a teacher who hasn't previously been engaged when the counselor is leading instruction.

CORE CURRICULUM: ENSURING VALUE ADDED

How school counselors approach entering the teacher's classroom matters. It is appropriate to be aware and respectful that any interruption of instructional learning time is indeed just that—an interruption of the student's instruction. During an age of increased accountability for student outcomes, teachers are equally concerned about student achievement and success. Thus, it would not be surprising to find that, from time to time, school counselors encounter faculty or administration who appear initially resistant to the implementation of core curriculum. In addition, in districts where elementary school counseling is a new role, counselors may initially encounter confusion or pushback as to when, where, why, and how they will garner time for instruction from administrators and/or teachers. As the school counselor is beginning the work of franchising the curriculum, it is recommended that he or she meet with administrators and faculty to discuss the core curriculum as part of the comprehensive school counseling program. This should include discussion of ways in which the school counselor's curriculum will add value and contribute in a meaningful way to the instructional learning environment and student development in the three domains (academic, college/career, and social/emotional). It may help to compare the counselor's core curriculum action plan to the teacher's use of scope and sequence and to share lesson plans and assessment tools. Finally, teachers will be less concerned about an interruption of instructional time if they can clearly see the value to their students. In the authors' experience, teachers most often complain about core curriculum lessons when they experience the lesson as a "random act of guidance" by a school counselor who has poorly prepared curriculum, appears unable to control the classroom, and does not assess student learning. School counselors do not have to be credentialed teachers, but they must know how to teach. Therefore, school counselors are encouraged to use a variety of student engagement strategies and to use strong classroom management (see Chapters 5 and 6). Confident school counselors seek feedback from the teachers at their school and engage them in the improvement process, for example, by using the Core Curriculum Lesson Feedback Tool provided in Chapter 6.

Figure 2.5 shows a flyer for the core curriculum based on monthly themes in an easy-to-read format for parents, created by counselors in the Romoland School District in California. The counselors added graphics and included the mindsets and behavior standards students would be learning in the descriptions for the monthly topics. What are other ways to advertise the core curriculum to families?

Figure 2.5 Monthly Core Curriculum Topics Flyer for Families

School Counseling Core Curriculum Monthly Themes & Standards
Boulder Ridge Elementary
By School Counselor, Mrs. Toledano, M.A.Ed., PPS

AUGUST	SEPTEMBER 
Role of the School Counselor & Positive Affirmations Self-confidence in ability to succeed. Sense of belonging in the school environment. Create relationships with adults that support success.	*Behavioral Expectations & Attendance* Self-confidence in ability to succeed. Apply self-motivation and self-direction to learning. Demonstrate ability to assume responsibility. Demonstrate self-discipline and self-control.
OCTOBER	NOVEMBER
Kindness & Anti-Bully Awareness Demonstrate personal safety skills Demonstrate advocacy skills and the ability to assert when necessary	*Personal Safety & Respect* Demonstrate personal safety skills. Demonstrate effective coping skills when faced with a problem.
DECEMBER	JANUARY
Feelings, Communication, & Self-esteem Belief in development of whole self, including a healthy balance of mental, social/emotional and physical well-being. Gather evidence and consider multiple perspective to make informed decisions. Demonstrate social maturity and behaviors appropriate to the situation and environment. Demonstrate empathy.	*Setting Goals &* *Growth Mindset* Demonstrate perseverance to achieve long and short term goals. Self-confidence in ability to succeed. Belief in using abilities to their fullest to achieve high-quality results and outcomes.
FEBRUARY	MARCH
How to Be a Friend, Get Along with Others, & Solve Conflicts Gather evidence and consider multiple perspective to make informed decisions. Create positive and supportive relationships with other students. Demonstrate social maturity and behaviors appropriate to the situation and environment.	*Test Taking Skills & Mindfulness* Belief in development of whole self, including a healthy balance of mental, social/emotional and physical well-being. Positive attitude toward work and learning. Use time-management, organizational and study skills
APRIL	MAY
Learning About Jobs & Career Paths Self-confidence in ability to succeed. Belief in using abilities to their fullest to achieve high-quality results and outcomes. Understanding that postsecondary education and lifelong learning are necessary for long-term career success.	*Summer Safety & Character Traits* Belief in development of whole self, including a healthy balance of mental, social/emotional and physical well-being. Self-confidence in ability to succeed.

Franchising Parent Education

Just as school counselors determine franchisable curriculum for students, so too should they provide parent education that is pre-planned, consistent, aligned with student developmental needs, and calendared, assessed, and improved each year. Some beginning school counselors prefer to loosely design their parent education program by utilizing a drop-in approach, which may consist of a monthly coffee with the counselor or an occasional parent education workshop. However, elementary counselors are encouraged to design an intentional curriculum that all parents will receive each year from the comprehensive counseling program.

To determine the content of the parent lessons, elementary counselors may want to conduct a needs assessment like the one in *The Use of Data in School Counseling* (Hatch, 2013) or review parent/family feedback on the school or district's climate survey to design the curriculum to address top priorities. Another option is to align the parent education to core curriculum topics being taught to students so that parents/guardians receive similar instruction and ideas to reinforce the concepts at home. For instance, during Red Ribbon Week, the lesson would cover drug and alcohol prevention tips for parents and would review key concepts taught to students. Like students and teachers, families should be able to know what they can count on from the school counseling program each year. Ideally and when at all possible, seek ways to collaborate with other counselors to franchise parent education from school to school within your district. To the extent that counselors design a consistent instructional curriculum and calendar it each year, parents will come to know and trust what they can expect from the school counseling program as foundational. Then, as needs arise or a crisis occurs, school counselors can add or build upon the parent education as necessary.

Figure 2.6 shares a sample from co-author Danielle, who held preplanned family workshops for the year to align with the core curriculum for students. Note the alignment with topics to be addressed for families and the curriculum action plan from Figure 2.2. For example, parents receive instruction about *Second Step* during September when school begins, and later in April the topic of fifth graders' transition to middle school is covered, which aligns with the students' lesson and field trip to the middle school.

Figure 2.6 Parent Academy Flier

Figure 2.6 (Continued)

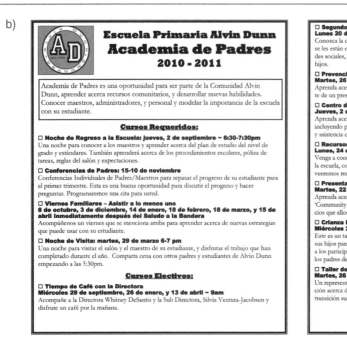

Whether you are a new or veteran school counselor, creating a parental core curriculum is an essential component of a comprehensive school counseling program and contributes to the foundation of Tier 1 core curriculum and school activities within the framework of a Multi-Tiered, Multi-Domain System of Supports (MTMDSS).

BEST PRACTICES FOR SUCCESSFUL PARENT EDUCATION PROGRAMS

The involvement of parents and families in their children's education is critical to students' academic success. To ensure parent and family engagement and a successful program, follow these suggestions:

- Create a welcoming school climate for parents. Depending on the time of day, offer snacks and beverages if possible or some time for social networking. Be positive and let parents/guardians know that they are valued. Consider providing transportation funding assistance and translators if needed.
- Offer attendance incentives if possible. Don't underestimate the draw of free school store supplies or spirit wear, a special parking space, or some door prizes! Seek donations from local businesses.
- Establish timely and effective school-to-home and home-to-school communication that suits the community. Whenever possible, schedule all workshops for the school year in advance and distribute flyers at Back to School events at the start of the school year.
- Make sure topics are relevant to parents and are based in strengthening knowledge and skills to support and extend their children's learning at home.

- Connect students and families to community resources as much as possible. Consider providing a personal greeting and welcome packet for all parents visiting the school that includes a community services directory/list, important school contact information, the annual school counseling calendar and brochure, and coupons to local businesses.
- Create a "suggestion or comment" box (both electronic and onsite) for families to anonymously provide their questions, concerns, and recommendations for the school counseling program.

Templates of essential documents you need to offer a Family Connection Workshop Series at your school, including a reproducible Record of Attendance Punch Card to track points earned for each workshop attended toward a celebratory closing party and incentives, are featured in Figures 2.7, 2.8, and 2.9, and the online appendix.

Figure 2.7 Family Connection Workshop Series Announcement Flyer

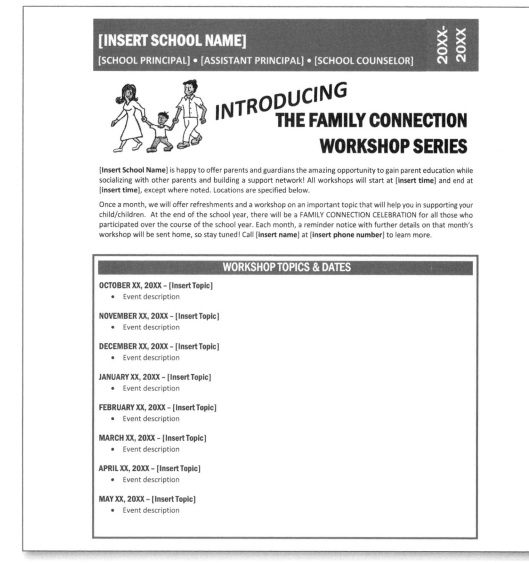

Source: Illustration by Gogis Design, http://www.gogisdesign.com.

Figure 2.8 Family Connection Workshop Series Reminder and RSVP Flyer

[INSERT SCHOOL NAME]
[SCHOOL PRINCIPAL] • [ASSISTANT PRINCIPAL] • [SCHOOL COUNSELOR]

20XX-20XX

REMINDER!!
THE FAMILY CONNECTION
WORKSHOP SERIES

ATTENTION PARENTS & GUARDIANS:

You are invited to participate in the FAMILY CONNECTION SERIES brought to you by **[insert school name]**! Remember, you will earn 100 points each time you attend a workshop in the series. At the end of the school year, there will be a CELEBRATION where you will have the opportunity to "shop" for great prizes based on the number of total points you have earned according to your Family Connection Attendance Punch Card. The more workshops you attend, the more points you will have to "spend"!

Also, to kick things off, the CLASSROOM WITH THE GREATEST PERCENTAGE OF PARENTS attending our very FIRST workshop on **[Insert Date]** at **[insert building/location]** from **[insert time]** to **[insert time]** will win a CLASSROOM PIZZA PARTY, sponsored by **[insert organization]**! This month's workshop is entitled **[Insert Workshop Title]**. This workshop will cover **[Insert workshop description]**.

If you will attend in October, please return the RSVP Form below or respond online at **[Insert Link]** no later than **[insert date]** so that we can be sure to have adequate refreshments and materials. Simply complete the portion below and submit to your child's teacher ONLY IF YOU WILL BE ATTENDING. See you on **[insert weekday, insert date]**!

**********************************Tear/Cut Here**********************************

FAMILY CONNECTION WORKSHOP SERIES: [INSERT MONTH] 20XX
Return to Classroom Teacher or RSVP online by **[insert date]**! If you have more than one student, please list each.

_____ YES! I will be in attendance on **[insert date]**. Number attending: _____

Student Name: _____ Room #: _____

Student Name: _____ Room #: _____

Parent/Guardian Signature: _____ Phone #: _____

RSVP Online at: [Insert link]

Source: Illustration by Gogis Design, http://www.gogisdesign.com.

Figure 2.9 Family Connection Workshop Series Record of Attendance Punch Card

online resources

[INSERT SCHOOL NAME]

For each workshop you attend, have this Record of Attendance Card punched/signed by a staff member. Each punch is worth 100 points.

Parent/Guardian Name: ____________________

Phone: ____________ E-Mail: ____________

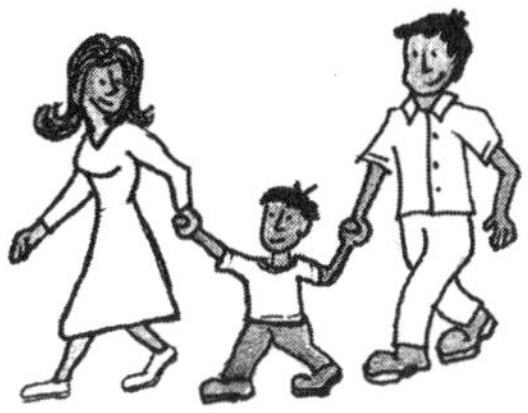

OCTOBER	NOVEMBER	DECEMBER	JANUARY
◎	◎	◎	◎
FEBRUARY	MARCH	APRIL	MAY
◎	◎	◎	◎

THE FAMILY CONNECTION WORKSHOP SERIES

RECORD OF ATTENDANCE CARD

20XX-20XX

[INSERT SCHOOL NAME]

For each workshop you attend, have this Record of Attendance Card punched/signed by a staff member. Each punch is worth 100 points.

Parent/Guardian Name: ____________________

Phone: ____________ E-Mail: ____________

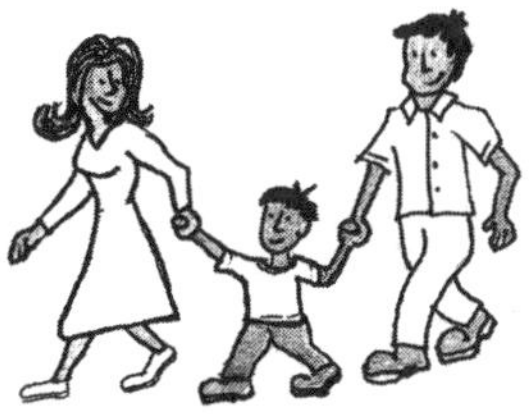

OCTOBER	NOVEMBER	DECEMBER	JANUARY
◎	◎	◎	◎
FEBRUARY	MARCH	APRIL	MAY
◎	◎	◎	◎

THE FAMILY CONNECTION WORKSHOP SERIES

RECORD OF ATTENDANCE CARD

20XX-20XX

Source: Illustration by Gogis Design, http://www.gogisdesign.com.

Determining Core Curriculum

When I started as an elementary counselor at Burnham/Anthony Mathematics and Science Academy in Chicago (K–8), I arrived to find that the previous counselor, who had been simultaneously working on getting a principal's license, had so many roles and duties in the school that the school counseling program had been seriously neglected. I first set out to clean and organize the entire office, which had records from the 1960s, stacks of paper, and clutter everywhere, even purchasing paint on my own and enlisting my parents to help me paint the walls and dust away cobwebs! With order in my surroundings, I could focus on developing what I saw as an immediate need—a curriculum for students. The self-generated "Live Every Day With Character" program was composed of weekly classroom guidance lessons that I created or gathered from books or free online resources; these lessons were all connected to a monthly character value and life skill and included relevant morning announcements and an in-service workshop for teachers with grade-level specific resources. I developed a college and career awareness afterschool program, "Capture Your Dreams: The Choice Is Yours," with curriculum for the middle grades, and I turned a media cabinet into a resource center for academic, social/ emotional, and college/career development materials, complete with decorated library card pockets for each staff member. Both programs got the attention of the district office, and soon thereafter we were selected to become one of 10 "model" schools (out of more than 650 schools at the time!) with the award of an Illinois Mental Health/Social-Emotional Learning grant, which we received mainly because the district was aware of our strong school counseling program and commitment to a holistic approach to student learning. With the grant, we had the financial means and freedom to select a prepackaged schoolwide curriculum—anything we could possibly want! Although the staff were still trying to figure out what to make of me and my exuberant enthusiasm, now finding myself as the grant coordinator, I engaged staff in a planning process that spanned an entire school year prior to even implementing the curriculum in classrooms.

Figure 3.1 The Art and Science of School Counseling

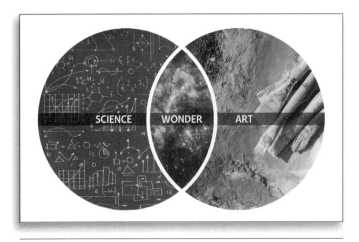

Source: Illustration by Gogis Design, http://www.gogisdesign.com.

INTRODUCING THE ART AND SCIENCE OF SCHOOL COUNSELING

Counseling is an art. For decades, school counselors have been providing counseling to students, staff, and parents utilizing active listening skills, reflective listening, conflict resolution skills, mediation, and so forth. The counseling skills taught to future school counselors are truly the "art" of the profession. The "science" of school counseling, although some might think of it as new, has been present since the profession began. However, in the last two decades, school counselors have been called on to use data, report results, and implement evidence-based practices (ASCA, 2012; Dimmitt, Carey, & Hatch, 2007; Hatch, 2013).

School counseling is increasingly becoming a beautiful combination of art *and* science in practice. The *science* of employing data to drive school counseling programs means identifying specific needs of students and providing evidence-based interventions to impact student achievement, and the *art* is found in employing various counseling theories and strategies to meet the unique situation. Within this framework, the *science* of a more clinical or mental health scientific perspective is combined with the *art* of a person-centered, rapport-building practice of a practitioner. This is reflected even in today's school counselor preparation programs. Just think—do you possess a Master of Science (MS) or a Master of Arts (MA) degree? Both are graduate programs offered by colleges and universities across the country; the main difference between an MA and MS degree is that an MA applies to arts and humanities degrees, while an MS applies to scientific and technical degrees. The difference can be seen through the types of courses required, the sequence of study, and possibly the culminating thesis, capstone project, and/or fieldwork requirements. The art and science of school counseling have implications when counselors plan for core curriculum in the classroom—the best lessons have a balance of both.

EVIDENCE-BASED PRACTICE AND CORE CURRICULUM

Recently there has been a strong movement toward evidence-based practice (EBP) and implementation of an "evidence-based school counseling program" built from research and data, but what does this really mean? The EBP movement originated in the medical field and is defined as "the integration of [the] best research evidence with clinical expertise and patient values" (Sackett, Straus, Richardson, Rosenberg, & Haynes, 2000, p. 1). The approach combines the best available research with the medical practitioner's integration of knowledge and clinical skills. Evidence-based practice has been applied to nursing, counseling in psychology, and, most recently, to school counseling (Dimmitt et al., 2007). Dimmit et al. (2007) propose a model of evidence-based school counseling practice that encourages school counselors' use of

Figure 3.2   A Model of Evidence-Based School Counseling Practice

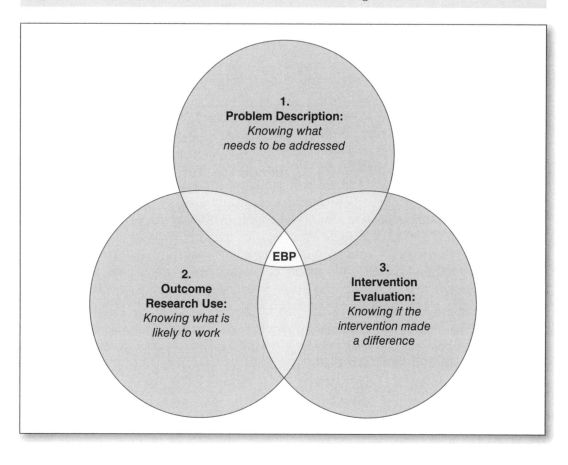

data to determine (1) the needs that will be addressed (the problem description), (2) which practices or interventions should be implemented (using outcome research), and (3) whether the interventions or practices utilized were effective (the evaluation of the curriculum or intervention; see Figure 3.2).

EBP and a Research-Based Curriculum

Applying EBP to school counseling curriculum delivery commonly refers to selecting a curriculum that was previously found to be effective, delivering this curriculum, and measuring its impact with the school population. A prepackaged research-based curriculum, such as the Committee for Children's *Second Step* program, has been found to enhance student outcomes, including improvements in social skills, increased empathy, and less adult intervention in minor student conflicts (Frey, Nolen, Edstrom, Hirschstein, 2005; Low, Cook, Smolkowski, & Buntain-Ricklefs, 2015). Utilizing an EBP approach, school counselors implement a research-based curriculum while evaluating the lesson with perception data and monitoring results to ensure positive outcomes for their particular student demographic. Prepackaged research-based curriculum programs can be quite costly and, in many cases, can have multiple lessons (typically far more than the school counselor has time to deliver alone). These program choices are often schoolwide decisions, as school counselors must partner with teachers to ensure that comprehensive delivery systems are in place.

EBP and a School Counselor–Generated Curriculum

In some cases, school counselors may lack access to funding or support to implement a schoolwide research-based curriculum. In other cases, no research-based product might exist in the topic area (e.g., a lesson on the transition to middle school). In these situations, school counselors are encouraged to use their professional wisdom (knowledge and experience) as a guide to designing their own lessons that align to research-based best practices. Within this approach, school counselors use their knowledge of and experience with the students they serve to generate a curriculum that meets the developmental needs of their students. They (a) research content and resources; (b) create lesson plans and actively teach the lessons using a variety of engagement strategies; (c) measure students' gains in attitudes, knowledge, and skills; (d) assess achievement-related and achievement data aligning with the lesson content; and (e) diligently evaluate their materials and lessons to make modifications as needed. Within this approach, school counselors evaluate perception data (attitude, knowledge, and skills) to determine that the learning objectives for the lessons have been met, and they use the results to make decisions regarding any changes to core curriculum they deliver and/or the school counseling program overall. School counselors who generate core curriculum employ a systematic procedure for gathering good-quality data from routine practice and align the work of the school counselor within the evidence-based model approach.

EBP and a Statewide Curriculum

Some states have created a statewide curriculum for school counselors to utilize when teaching classroom lessons. A list of some statewide curricula is provided later within this chapter in Figure 3.7. A statewide curriculum can be very helpful for school counselors as they're beginning to implement their program, because it provides them with immediate resources that they can add to their curriculum action plan. The challenges may be similar to those outlined in Table 3.1 for counselor-generated curriculum. The process of creating a statewide curriculum can be comprehensive and lengthy. The following box presents comments submitted by Dr. M. René Yoesel regarding Missouri's process and experience. More information on the history of this process can be found in the online appendix.

Missouri's Comprehensive School Counseling Program

The State of Missouri has developed a Comprehensive School Counseling Program, which includes K–12 lesson plans arranged by standard. This process has required field tests, curriculum updates, and lots of collaboration between school counselors, counselor educators, the Missouri Department of Elementary and Secondary Education, and the Missouri School Counselor Association. The authors of this book learned more about the process of creating the statewide program from Dr. Norm Gysbers, Dr. Carolyn Magnuson, Dr. Bragg Stanley, Carolyn Roof, and Linda Lueckenhoff, as submitted by Dr. M. René Yoesel.

Q: Describe the rationale/need for developing a curriculum framework for your state.

A: The rationale began with an awareness that local, state, and national educational reform efforts did not address the development of the nonacademic skills required of all students' success—the skills that school counselors emphasized in their work. To address this need, we started with a vision of what graduating students needed to know, understand, and be able to do (in addition to academic skills) in order to be successful. We applied basic, universal domains of human development and the factors that facilitate and block that development. From there, the curriculum framework was developed.

Q: Explain the process for developing the curriculum—who was involved, what resources did you utilize, how did you develop/crosswalk lessons, and how long did it take?

A: The development of the actual curriculum (sample classroom lessons for each aspect of the curriculum framework) began in 2004, and the first phase was completed in 2009. However, this was preceded by many years of creating materials that led to the need to develop a resource of sample strategies for full implementation of the Missouri Comprehensive School Counseling Program components.

Prior to the creation of the writing team, a meeting was held with the Missouri Department of Elementary and Secondary Education's (DESE's) assistant commissioner for curriculum and instruction and the coordinator of the K–12 academic curriculum areas. The idea was introduced that the comprehensive "guidance" school counseling program *should* be a part of the department's academic curriculum efforts/materials. This was a risk, as the individuals making the pitch for the integral role of the statewide plan were not DESE employees, but the meeting was successful!

The Comprehensive Guidance (School Counseling) Program writing team members utilized the ASCA standards and the Missouri Show-Me Standards (and subsequent iterations) to crosswalk units and lessons. This process resulted in developing awareness among users that there is an interrelationship of the ASCA model and the Show-Me Standards and the Missouri Comprehensive Guidance (School Counseling) Program Curriculum Framework. In turn, it gave users "talking points" for conversations with classroom teachers, school administrators, and school boards.

Q: How long did it take?

A: Depending on your perspective, 40+ years (or 5 years, or forever), because development is ongoing.

Q: What has been the response/utilization of the curriculum?

A: Both have been excellent! One example is the fact that on the first day the classroom curriculum was active online, the Missouri Center for Career Education server was overloaded. The national response is reflected in one beginning school counselor's unsolicited response at a national meeting—she used one of the lessons during a supervisory visit, and her supervisor said it was the best lesson she had seen. Many states have implemented the Missouri "model," and the curriculum has been used internationally as well. Most important are the data gathered in a statewide study demonstrating the effectiveness of full implementation.

Q: If you could do it over again, what might you do differently, and what are the next steps?

A: We trusted the process, took risks, believed in the program, and built on available resources at each step of the way. Next steps include continuing to review, revise, and renew existing materials to ensure that they are relevant to the needs of today's school counselors. DESE continues to fund and facilitate a state writing team that ensures that materials are rigorous and relevant.

Source: R. Yoesel, personal communication, April 27, 2017.

The art and science in school counseling might also be referred to as practice informing research, and research informing practice. These may be inseparable concepts. Neither element is complete on its own; they are complementary. Research-based prepackaged curricula are typically easy to use, graphically organized, clearly written, and aligned with standards. They often include extension activities, assessments, and parent/family engagement components. Well-researched and well-designed school counselor–generated lessons meet the specific needs of the school population to produce successful student outcomes. Most often, counselors will design school counseling programs with both a research-based curriculum and school counselor–generated lessons within Tier 1. The combination allows for school counselors to utilize best practices while slightly modifying prepackaged lessons and/or adding additional topics as needed. With experience and time, school counselors will determine core curriculum lessons that best fit the needs of their students. Regardless of whether the school counselor utilizes research-based curriculum or school counselor–generated curriculum, collecting perception and outcome data is most important. See Chapter 8 for more on assessment.

Table 3.1 Research-Based Curriculum Versus School Counselor–Generated Curriculum

Research-Based Curriculum		School Counselor–Generated Curriculum (self-generated or located online—may also apply to some state curricula)	
Benefits	Challenges	Benefits	Challenges
Evidence supporting effectiveness	EBP still requires school counselors to create local measures to assess impact	Allows counselors to be creative and add the "art" of school counseling	School counselors must create their own lessons through trial and error, and must evaluate and improve lessons regularly
Prepackaged	Costly and may become outdated, requiring expensive fees for replacement	Free	It takes time to make/ revise/locate lessons—so it is not "free" if you add up the costs of the extra duties of creating/ modifying the curriculum
Readymade— typically easy to pick up and teach with little prep	May not culturally align with the needs of local students and may be outdated	Can create/revise curriculum to meet cultural or other needs of the student population	Requires prep time to create lessons
Proven impact through research	Many lessons are needed to implement/ teach with fidelity	Counselors can collaborate to divide up lessons to create/revise	Lessons may be haphazard and not scaffolded as in prepackaged programs
Many lessons	Too many lessons for the school counselor to teach alone (requires consolidation or selecting a few)	Online lessons are easy to locate and are often well vetted by many counselors	May lend itself to personal preferences and overly heavy in one domain, versus balancing the three domains

Research-Based Curriculum		School Counselor–Generated Curriculum (self-generated or located online—may also apply to some state curricula)	
Benefits	Challenges	Benefits	Challenges
Packaged in sequential/ scaffolded lessons	Not as impactful if randomly taught	Can take local developmental needs into account	Often is created in a vacuum
When teachers buy in, the whole school supports delivery	Requires teacher buy in	Can be very tech-savvy, cutting-edge, and engaging for students with a skilled school counselor	May be less sophisticated if a school counselor lacks tech training/tools
May have some assessment tools (typically self-reported behaviors)	May not include perception assessments (counselors may have to create their own)	Self-generated content allows pre-/ post-tests to align better with attitudes, knowledge, and skills	May require assessment tools and rubrics to be created
May be scripted— easy to pick up and go	Scripted—may not be in line with the counselor's voice or may hinder creativity	May be helpful for first-year counselors who are just starting to learn by creating their own material	Risk of random acts of curriculum

School Counseling Program SMART Goals

Prior to determining what core curriculum to teach, school counselors are advised to create overarching program SMART goals that the curriculum will support. SMART goals are **S**pecific, **M**easurable, **A**ttainable, **R**esults-Oriented, and **T**ime-Bound. They align with a Multi-Tiered, Multi-Domain System of Supports (MTMDSS), as each goal targets one area of focus within the academic, college/career, or social/emotional development domains, with tiered levels of prevention and intervention. When designing school counseling program SMART goals, school counselors can best prepare by collecting reference documents, such as state performance indicators, district strategic plans, and school improvement goals. Through strategically connecting the goals of school counseling programs to established state and local targets, school counselors show how they align their work to support these initiatives. In this way, the services and activities that school counselors provide are integrated into the comprehensive school system. See Table 3.2 for tips on writing a SMART goal, and see Figure 3.3 for an example goal, with school counseling program activities supporting that goal.

RESOURCES

Resources for a Research-Based Curriculum

How can school counselors identify evidence-based programs and products that have been proven to be effective? Since 2002, the What Works Clearinghouse

Table 3.2   Tips for Writing SMART Goals

Specific What is the specific issue based on our school's data?	In order to be **SPECIFIC (S)**, look up data that align to the areas of focus. For instance, if a school goal is to reduce the number of suspensions and behavior referrals, the school counselor can find out the number and percentage of each from the previous school year (see Figure 3.3). School counselors want to choose an area of need, and the data help determine what is and isn't an area on which to focus.
Measurable How will we measure the effectiveness of our interventions?	Once baseline (previous year) data are determined, consider how to continually collect the **MEASURABLE (M)** data needed to assess progress toward the selected goal. In Figure 3.3, the school counselor uses a query from the student information system, Infinite Campus.
Attainable What outcome will stretch us but is still attainable?	Determining the rate at which a success will be **ATTAINABLE (A)** is slightly more subjective. While you want to choose a goal that will stretch you, you don't want to be stretched to an unrealistic level. Think about students who are getting mostly Ds and Fs—instead of pushing them to get straight As, you would encourage them to focus simply on getting all passing grades, to create a more attainable goal that would not leave them discouraged—in this same way, school counselors also want to choose an objective that will push them in a realistic way. In Figure 3.3, the school counselor chose a 15% decrease—a goal of reducing the number of referrals from 82 in the previous year to 70 that year.
Results-Oriented Is the goal reported with results-oriented data (process, perception, and outcome)?	In order to ensure that a goal is **RESULTS-ORIENTED (R)**, school counselors consider process, perception, and outcome data. See Chapter 8 for more information about different types of data.
Time-Bound When will our goal be accomplished?	Considering when the goal will be accomplished makes it **TIME-BOUND (T)**. Generally, school counseling program goals are created for the year, and periodic checks (monthly, quarterly, etc.) are important, as is tracking progress toward the goal. In Figure 3.3, the school counselor tracked the number of behavior referrals each month to assess whether she was on track. By checking regularly, the school counselor is able to provide additional prevention or intervention activities as needed to help reach the goal.

(WWC), part of the U.S. Department of Education's Institute of Education Sciences, has been a central and trusted source of scientific evidence on education programs, products, practices, and policies by focusing on high-quality research to answer the question "What works in education?" (see Figure 3.4). The WWC reviews the research to determine which studies meet rigorous standards and summarizes the findings so that educators and schools can make informed decisions to improve student outcomes. For examples, refer to the WWC's website at http://ies.ed.gov/ncee/wwc.

In their mission to help make evidence-based social and emotional learning (SEL) an integral part of education from preschool through high school, the Collaborative for Academic, Social, and Emotional Learning (CASEL) synthesizes the research of others and conducts its own original research on curriculum and

Figure 3.3 Example School Counseling Program SMART Goal

XYZ K-6 School
Area of Focus: Reducing Behavior Referrals (Social/Emotional)

Specific Issue What is the specific issue based on our school's data?	In the 2015-16 school year, there were 127 referrals. In the 2016-2017 school year, there were 82 referrals.
Measurable How will we measure the effectiveness of our interventions?	Referral data will be collected from Infinite Campus.
Attainable What outcome would stretch us but is still attainable?	2017-2018 goal - 15% decrease (70 referrals)
Results-Oriented Is the goal reported in results-oriented data (process, perception and outcome)?	Outcome - referrals on Infinite Campus.
Time Bound When will our goal be accomplished?	Monitor the progress monthly/each trimester to assess progress. Final goal accomplished end of the 2017-2018 school year (70 or fewer referrals)

By the end of 2016-2017 there will be a 15% decrease in school-wide referrals (70 or fewer referrals).

Aligns with School District LCAP Goal 3: Create and maintain optimum learning and working environment for students and staff.

Aligns with State/Local Performance Standards
- Suspension Rate
- School Climate

Activities to Address the Goal
• All student in grades kindergarten through 6 will receive a minimum of 10 Second Step classroom lessons teaching emotional regulation & problem solving (see yearly calendar) • School counselor will be an active member of the PBIS Team • School counselor will assist in developing and presenting staff in-service presentations on topics including proactive classroom management, reasons for referrals, restorative practices • School counselor will support the implementation of school-wide positive leadership incentives • School counselor will support the creation and presentation of school-wide expectations • School counselor will provide intentional interventions for students with 2+ significant referrals (small group and/or individual counseling) • Monitor the data monthly/each trimester to determine areas of focus as well celebrate successes

Figure 3.4 What Works Clearinghouse Website

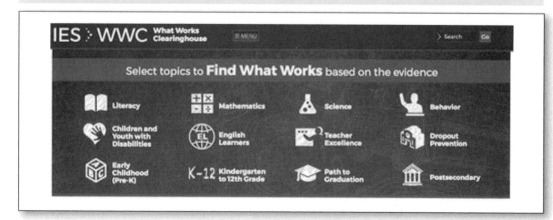

Figure 3.5 2013 CASEL *Program Guide*

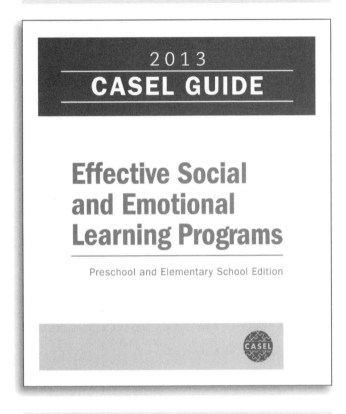

Figure 3.6 Navigating Social and Emotional Learning From the Inside Out

programs. To address educators who want to know which programs will promote social and emotional competence in their students, CASEL develops and publishes reviews of evidence-based SEL programs, including the CASEL *Guide to Effective Social and Emotional Learning Programs— Preschool and Elementary School Edition* (CASEL, 2013; see Figure 3.5). This free, consumer-friendly guide (1) identifies and rates well-designed school-based programs that incorporate SEL practices and classroom instruction, (2) shares best-practice guidelines for district and school teams on how to select and implement SEL programs, and (3) offers recommendations for future priorities to advance SEL research and practice. You can access the CASEL *Program Guide* at http://www.casel.org/guide.

A new guide published in May 2017 by researchers at the Harvard Graduate School of Education and commissioned by the Wallace Foundation, *Navigating SEL from the Inside Out* (Jones et al., 2017; see Figure 3.6), aims to steer school districts through the thicket of SEL, out-of-school time, and classroom management curriculum and approaches by offering profiles of 25 evidence-based programs, most of which are designed for children in pre-K through fifth grade.

Options include the *Mutt-i-grees* program, where students imagine how dogs might feel in a situation; the *I Can Problem Solve* curriculum, where students look at a picture of a boy pushing another boy out of line and engage in hypothetical discussion; and the *4Rs* (Reading, Writing, Respect, and Resolution) program, which utilizes children's literature to spark conversations about bullying and respecting differences, for example. Because options are so plentiful, the publication includes worksheets and summary tables to guide staff as they consider their priorities and goals in choosing a program. Access the document at http://www.wallacefoundation.org/knowledge-center/Documents/Navigating-Social-and-Emotional-Learning-from-the-Inside-Out.pdf.

Figure 3.7   Statewide Core Curriculum Web Resources

STATE-WIDE CORE CURRICULUM RESOURCES		
WEBSITE	URL	DESCRIPTION
Connecticut's Comprehensive School Counseling Curriculum	http://www.sde.ct.gov/sde/lib/sde/PDF/DEPS/Special/counseling.pdf	Guide to comprehensive school counseling program development.
Hinsdale (NH) School District's Curriculum	http://www.hnhsd.org/curriculum/all/guidance.pdf	School counseling curriculum including response to intervention resources, ASCA competencies, student services organizational chart, referral forms, and career development framework.
Iowa Department of Education: School Counseling	https://www.educateiowa.gov/school-counseling	Resources relating to SMART goals, managing and delivering a school counseling program, action plans, and the use of data.
Missouri Department of Elementary and Secondary Education: Guidance and Counseling Support Materials	https://dese.mo.gov/guidance-counseling-support-materials	Sample guidance units and lessons represent a complete set of units for each element of the Guidance and Counseling K-12 grade-level expectations.
Public Schools of North Carolina: Guidance Curriculum for the Comprehensive School Counseling Program	http://www.dpi.state.nc.us/docs/curriculum/guidance/resources/programs-study.pdf	Guide to comprehensive school counseling program development K-12.
State of Washington: K-12 Education	http://k12.wa.us/SecondaryEducation/CareerCollegeReadiness/default.aspx	Secondary education and K-12 supports including resources, templates and curriculum development for school-wide program.
Tucson Unified School District: Guidance and Counseling	http://tusd1.org/Departments/Counseling/CounselorResources/ElementaryGuidanceCurriculum/tabid/79283/Default.aspx	Curriculum geared toward the elementary setting.
West Virginia Department of Education	http://wvde.state.wv.us/counselors/links/advisors/lesson-plans.html	Lesson plans and handouts on a variety of topics.

Resources for a School Counselor–Generated Curriculum

Unlike many classroom teachers, who may teach one or two subjects or grade levels, elementary counselors may create developmentally appropriate and engaging lessons for up to nine grade levels, if they are in a K–8 school. Therefore, quickly identifying low and no-cost resources to help school counselors get started is essential. Refer to Figure 3.7 for a list of online web links to statewide core curriculum resources. This is an excerpt of a full table of No Cost Web Resources for Self-Generated Elementary School Counseling Curriculum found in the online appendix, which can be used in creating lessons and student activities.

FACTORS TO CONSIDER IN SELECTING AND DEVELOPING CORE CURRICULUM

Fidelity of Evidence-Based Programs

The fidelity of evidence-based program implementation and the proposed effects are diminished when programs are not delivered as prescribed. Some school counselors or schools may choose to develop core curriculum by combining lessons from different evidence-based curricula because they like the topics or find them particularly useful. In addition, evidence-based programs may include so many classroom lessons that school counselors reduce the numbers of lessons within their scope and sequence. School counselors are reminded that changes in adherence to the curriculum, exposure (the number of classroom lessons taught), quality of delivery, or program differentiation (using other programs) can result in modified results. This is not to discourage the use of an evidence-based program because adjustments need to be made; rather, it is to ensure full awareness of the potential impact on outcomes.

Legal Issues and Lesson Plans

As school counselors use online classroom lessons and piece together their curriculum, they may encounter blogs and online resources such as *TeachersPayTeachers* and *We Are Teachers*, which provide an online marketplace for teachers and counselors to sell original classroom lesson plans. However, those who sell their lesson plans online might be acting outside of copyright laws. Critics cite ethical pitfalls (plagiarism and a lack of quality) in this intellectual property and caution that there may be a chance that these "authors" don't actually own the copyright to the classroom materials they produce, because this content may have been developed for their current position. District employment contracts may assign copyright ownership of materials produced for the classroom to the teacher (or school counselor), which means that educators have rights to "sell" their self-generated curriculum. However, the Copyright Act of 1976 stipulates that, without any written agreement stating otherwise, materials created by teachers in the scope of their employment are deemed "works for hire"; therefore, the school owns them (Walker, n.d.). In sum, prior to purchasing any self-generated curriculum online, school counselors should do their best to ensure that the lessons are of high quality; also, prior to posting or selling materials themselves, school counselors are advised to read their employment contracts to prevent legal issues.

Collaboration in Lesson Plan Development

Today's online learning communities and technology applications make it possible to connect the individual and collective talents of beginning and experienced school counselors worldwide in collaborating to develop and share effective lessons—there is no need to start from scratch with this approach! By using Dropbox or creating a Google Drive shared folder, it is possible to divide tasks between counselors in a school, within a district, or even within a state through a state association.

Additional Ways to Select a Curriculum

When school counselors have more curriculum to deliver than time allows (given counselor-to-student ratios or other responsibilities), it's helpful to provide teachers with a survey of the predetermined lessons and ask them to prioritize which lessons they prefer. Perhaps the teachers are already teaching students how to use their agenda planners. In this case, that lesson is not one the elementary counselor needs to deliver. A sample of a counselor survey is provided in the online appendix and in *The Use of Data in School Counseling: Hatching Results for Students, Programs, and the Profession* (Hatch, 2013) on pages 114 and 115. School counselors may want to survey their teachers regarding the extent to which they perceive their students to be exhibiting the attitudes and behaviors aligned with noncognitive factors. Based on *Teaching Adolescents to Become Learners: The Role of Noncognitive Factors in Shaping School Performance* (Farrington et al., 2012), published by the University of Chicago, the Noncognitive Needs Survey is a tool for prioritizing school counseling core curriculum. It is pictured in Figure 3.8 and is available in the online appendix.

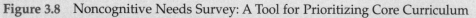

Figure 3.8 Noncognitive Needs Survey: A Tool for Prioritizing Core Curriculum

online resources

Hatching Results, LLC
NONCOGNITIVE NEEDS SURVEY
A Tool for Prioritizing School Counseling Core Curriculum

TEACHER NAME: _____ CLASSROOM #: _____ DATE: _____

SUBJECT/GRADE: _____ TIME: _____

INSTRUCTIONS: To the best of your knowledge and based on your *own* observations during the current school year only, please rate your classroom's demonstration and proficiency of certain noncognitive factors and skills.

ACADEMIC BEHAVIORS

1. The majority of students in my class effectively demonstrate:	5 Always	4 Usually	3 Sometimes	2 Rarely	1 Never
a. Work completion (homework, projects, class work, etc.)	☐	☐	☐	☐	☐
b. Organizational skills (materials/desk/backpack)	☐	☐	☐	☐	☐
c. Participation skills (active listening/engaged/contribute)	☐	☐	☐	☐	☐
d. Study skills (exhibited in school and/or at home)	☐	☐	☐	☐	☐

COMMENTS:

ACADEMIC PERSEVERANCE

2. The majority of students in my class effectively demonstrate:	5 Always	4 Usually	3 Sometimes	2 Rarely	1 Never
a. Grit (staying focused on task despite obstacles)	☐	☐	☐	☐	☐
b. Tenacity (determination and resolve)	☐	☐	☐	☐	☐
c. Delayed gratification	☐	☐	☐	☐	☐
d. Self-discipline	☐	☐	☐	☐	☐
e. Self-control (forgo short-term needs for long-term goals)	☐	☐	☐	☐	☐

COMMENTS:

Hatching Results®, LLC
Based on the *Teaching Adolescents to Become Learners: The Role of Noncognitive Factors in Shaping School Performance (2012)* by the University of Chicago

---

(Continued)

Figure 3.8   (Continued)

ACADEMIC MINDSETS

3. In my assessment, the majority of students in my class believe:	5 Always	4 Usually	3 Sometimes	2 Rarely	1 Never
a. They belong to the academic community	☐	☐	☐	☐	☐
b. Their ability and competence grow with effort	☐	☐	☐	☐	☐
c. They can succeed in their school work	☐	☐	☐	☐	☐
d. They see value in their work	☐	☐	☐	☐	☐

COMMENTS:

LEARNING STRATEGIES

4. The majority of my students in my class are proficient in the following areas:	5 Always	4 Usually	3 Sometimes	2 Rarely	1 Never
a. Study Skills (can identify/use)	☐	☐	☐	☐	☐
b. Metacognitive Strategies (thinking about thinking)	☐	☐	☐	☐	☐
c. Self-regulated Learning (ability to pause self)	☐	☐	☐	☐	☐
d. Goal-Setting (ability to set goals)	☐	☐	☐	☐	☐

COMMENTS:

SOCIAL SKILLS

5. The majority of students in my class demonstrate proficiency in:	5 Always	4 Usually	3 Sometimes	2 Rarely	1 Never
a. Interpersonal Skills	☐	☐	☐	☐	☐
b. Empathy	☐	☐	☐	☐	☐
c. Cooperation	☐	☐	☐	☐	☐
d Assertion	☐	☐	☐	☐	☐
e. Responsibility	☐	☐	☐	☐	☐

COMMENTS:

Hatching Results®, LLC
Based on the *Teaching Adolescents to Become Learners: The Role of Noncognitive Factors in Shaping School Performance (2012)* by the University of Chicago

College and Career Readiness in Elementary School

While much of the curriculum at the elementary level focuses on the social/emotional and academic domains, a Multi-Tiered, Multi-Domain comprehensive school counseling program includes college and career development. Elementary school counselors are encouraged to provide schoolwide lessons and activities, such as career fairs, college visits, and job exploration activities. Following the

Figure 3.9   NOSCA's Eight Components of College and Career Readiness Counseling

(Continued)

Figure 3.9 (Continued)

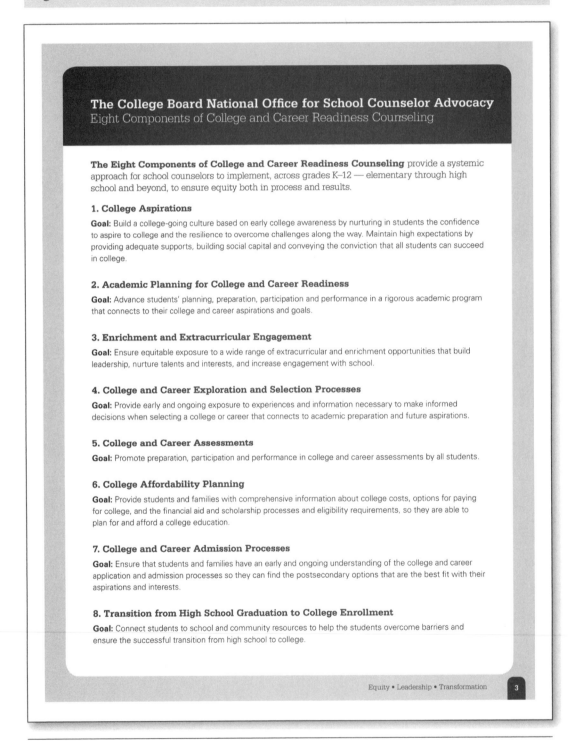

The College Board National Office for School Counselor Advocacy
Eight Components of College and Career Readiness Counseling

The Eight Components of College and Career Readiness Counseling provide a systemic approach for school counselors to implement, across grades K–12 — elementary through high school and beyond, to ensure equity both in process and results.

1. College Aspirations

Goal: Build a college-going culture based on early college awareness by nurturing in students the confidence to aspire to college and the resilience to overcome challenges along the way. Maintain high expectations by providing adequate supports, building social capital and conveying the conviction that all students can succeed in college.

2. Academic Planning for College and Career Readiness

Goal: Advance students' planning, preparation, participation and performance in a rigorous academic program that connects to their college and career aspirations and goals.

3. Enrichment and Extracurricular Engagement

Goal: Ensure equitable exposure to a wide range of extracurricular and enrichment opportunities that build leadership, nurture talents and interests, and increase engagement with school.

4. College and Career Exploration and Selection Processes

Goal: Provide early and ongoing exposure to experiences and information necessary to make informed decisions when selecting a college or career that connects to academic preparation and future aspirations.

5. College and Career Assessments

Goal: Promote preparation, participation and performance in college and career assessments by all students.

6. College Affordability Planning

Goal: Provide students and families with comprehensive information about college costs, options for paying for college, and the financial aid and scholarship processes and eligibility requirements, so they are able to plan for and afford a college education.

7. College and Career Admission Processes

Goal: Ensure that students and families have an early and ongoing understanding of the college and career application and admission processes so they can find the postsecondary options that are the best fit with their aspirations and interests.

8. Transition from High School Graduation to College Enrollment

Goal: Connect students to school and community resources to help the students overcome barriers and ensure the successful transition from high school to college.

Equity • Leadership • Transformation　3

Source: National Office of School Counselor Advocacy. Retrived from https://secure-media.collegeboard.org/digitalServices/pdf/advocacy/nosca/11b-4383_ES_Counselor_Guide_WEB_120213.pdf.

recommendations of the National Office of School Counselor Advocacy (NOSCA), the Eight Components of College and Career Readiness serve as foundational considerations for curriculum, schoolwide activities, and parent education within a comprehensive school counseling program. The College Board (2012) has a free *Elementary School Counselor's Guide: NOSCA's Eight Components of College and Career Readiness Counseling* (College Board, 2012; see Figure 3.9), which is available in the online appendix. Additionally, Kids2College is a free college exploration program that promotes college and career readiness and an increase in elementary students' knowledge about college. For more information, go to http://www.kids-2-college.org.

SELECTING AN EVIDENCE-BASED CURRICULUM

Selecting a schoolwide or districtwide curriculum is a serious investment of time and resources. The process may involve professional development training and the support of the entire school. Therefore, careful planning and execution cannot be overstressed when making strategic decisions leading to the successful selection and implementation of an evidence-based curriculum; selection and planning may take an entire school year prior to full implementation. Below are steps to consider when selecting a large-scale, schoolwide evidence-based curriculum:

1. **Form a team/committee.** The involvement of the principal and other leadership team members is essential. Identify other participants on a voluntary basis and from a range of grade levels and disciplines. Consider adding parents and/or community members to the team. The elementary school counselor on the team is vital in this process.

2. **Identify needs and set priorities.** Gather useful data, such as the school improvement plan, needs assessments, school climate data, and student self-report surveys, to identify areas of concern and to inform decisions. Review the vision and mission of the school/district to help set priorities and align with SMART goals.

3. **Get educated.** As a team and using the CASEL *Program Guide*, for example, review the overview descriptions and program ratings to identify three to four curricula that stand out as options to best meet your needs and budget. Visit the programs' websites to learn more, watch videos of the curricula in action, search the web for feedback and reviews, talk to other colleagues, and contact the sales representatives at the selected curriculum companies to request that sample curricula be sent for in-person review. Consider visiting schools that have implemented the curricula to discuss benefits and pitfalls. If there is agreement, narrow the curricula choices further to two or three, if possible.

4. **Involve stakeholders.** Elementary school counselors are encouraged to conduct an in-service for *all* faculty and staff about the rationale for an evidence-based curriculum, the goals and intended impact, the plan for roll-out, and so on to start to build internal capacity. You should present an overview of each evidence-based program, playing any videos of the various curricula being delivered if available, and allowing time for everyone to browse through the actual sample curricula for themselves.

Enlisting the support of elementary faculty is essential to successful implementation later, as faculty at this level are typically far more cohesive and decision making tends to be more collaborative. (Refer to the sample professional development day agenda pictured in Figure 3.10 for more ideas.)

5. **Select the curriculum.** Conduct a democratic vote to determine which curriculum is most desired by the staff. Once you've decided, you can negotiate the purchase of the curriculum and arrange any necessary training dates or determine the details for parent/family engagement and partnerships. Elementary school counselors are perfectly suited to perform this leadership role.

6. **Promote program adoption.** Now that you've selected a program and invested in it, you can build excitement by communicating to students and families. Your team may offer family workshops featuring the new curriculum as a topic, include information on the school website or in the school newsletter, coordinate a student talent show using a theme related to the new curriculum or a celebratory student body assembly where some classes act out a skit, and so forth. Create special T-shirts or lanyards for the core team members to wear during parent-teacher conferences, report card pickup, or other family events that state "Ask me about [insert name of curriculum here]." Consider displaying flyers of the curriculum in the hallways or the cafeteria, where families may be gathered and waiting. See the example in Figure 3.11 of weeklong activities planned for students and families at the end of a planning year to build excitement and promote the new things to come in the fall.

7. **Communicate clearly.** For a successful kickoff in implementing the curriculum, make sure that there is clear and timely communication to staff and faculty so that they are aware of expectations, key dates and scheduling, available resources, and so on. See Figure 3.12 for a flyer for students and parents that was issued at the start of the school year.

8. **Establish a review process.** Establish a review process to continuously improve students' learning and experience through regular inquiry and data collection. If you haven't done so already, this may be an excellent time to create an Advisory Council for your school counseling program.

LISA'S STORY CONTINUES . . .

Luckily for me, knowing that I couldn't do it alone, I had already spoken to my principal about forming a voluntary Social and Emotional Learning (SEL) Committee to work with me on various initiatives related to school climate, so my principal was able to select members from that group to participate on the Grant Committee as well. We reviewed data in our school improvement plan and school climate survey results to guide discussions about our priorities and the changes we wanted to see. Symbolically, we adopted the slogan "Plant the Seeds of Hope" for the year. As part of the grant, we underwent an intensive series of professional development led by CASEL, attended presentations by groups such as the Committee for Children and Lions Club International about their curriculum, and were assigned a coach to work with us.

Ultimately, we utilized the ratings and descriptions in the CASEL Program Guide to get educated, contacted various sales reps for sample curricula to preview, and narrowed it down to four curricula to present to the entire staff for selection. Our principal gave the SEL and Grant Committees permission to conduct a full day of in-service for the entire staff, wherein we covered topics such as the importance of SEL, the grant plan, and curriculum options, with time allowed to peruse the samples. Trust me—Edutopia's videos about the value of SEL go far in winning staff over, making the connection, and tugging at the heartstrings! We put it to a vote that day and ended up with a tie, so we shared additional information on things to consider and voted again.

Now that we had a clear winner, we began to promote the program to students and families. For example, during parent/teacher report card pickup, members of the committee wore wooden hearts that I had painted, attached to ribbons, which read "Ask Me About SEL," and we played Edutopia videos on SMART boards in the hallways as parents waited for their turn to visit with the teachers. I created communication materials for families, such as an SEL brochure and a newsletter that were distributed; we also conducted a full week of celebratory activities, including an assembly where students presented class skits and rap songs about life skills and the new curriculum coming the following year.

With the new academic year, we introduced Second Step and PBIS while I launched a Student of the Month incentive program and some new school spirit initiatives. Confident in the change to come and the steps we had taken, we fulfilled our goals and modified our slogan to "Planting the Seeds of Change." Within a couple years' time, we saw unbelievable gains in our outcome data that got recognized by the mayor and state on multiple occasions! Our school, with 95% of our student population receiving free and reduced lunch, made it on the popular annual list of top schools issued by Chicago magazine and was often showcased by Jean-Claude Brizard, former Chief Executive Officer of Chicago Public Schools from 2011 to 2012. Beyond great leadership and quality instruction, the contributions of the SEL and Grant committees and the resulting impact on the climate and students cannot be denied in fostering our school's success.

As noted previously, Figures 3.10 through 3.12 present some of the documents that align with the selection of a schoolwide curriculum and the implementation of an SEL program at Burnham/Anthony Math and Science Academy.

Figure 3.10   Lisa's full Professional Development Day agenda conducted by the SEL Committee. Though the program was led by the school counselor, note the team effort—various members conducted different sessions.

BURNHAM/ANTHONY MATH & SCIENCE ACADEMY
Dr. Linda J. Moore, Principal   •   Ms. Sheryl Freeman, Assistant Principal   •   Social & Emotional Learning Committee

'PLANT THE SEEDS OF HOPE'
PROFESSIONAL DEVELOPMENT DAY AGENDA
FEBRUARY 11ᵀᴴ

8:30- 9:00   Staff Breakfast Social in Cafeteria   *(Provided by: Social and Emotional Learning Committee Members)*

9:00- 9:15   Children and Family Benefits Unit Resources   *(Presented by: Ms. Carolina Casillas)*

9:15- 10:00 Team Building in Room # 107   *(Presented by: Ms. Agyeman & Mr. Benson)*
- Ice Breaker Activity

10:00- 11:00 SEL Presentation in Room # 106   *(Presented by: Ms. May)*
- Activity: Self Assessment checklist (Tool 33)
- Power Point Presentation & Movie Clip
  - SEL Defined
  - Importance of SEL
  - Burnham/Anthony SEL Vision Statement
- Activity: SEL 'elevator speech'

11:00- 11:10 BREAK

11:10- 12:10 SEL Motivational Speaker in Room # 107   *(Presented by: Mr. Jeremiah Henderson)*

12:10- 12:45 LUNCH in Cafeteria   *(Provided by Administration)*

12:45- 1:30 IL SEL/Mental Health Grants Presentation in Room # 107   *(Presented by: Ms. Krotiak)*
- Overview of SEL/ Mental Health Grants
  - Introduction of Steering Committee
- Year One Activities and Goals
  - Integrating SEL with Core Academic Content (Tool 32 or 36) and Outside the Classroom (Tool 34)
  - Curriculum Options
- Activity: 'Plant the Seeds of Change' with students
- Year Two Activities and Goals

1:30- 2:00   Mini-Focus Groups in Room # 107   *(Presented by: Ms. May)*
- Identify school's positive qualities and strengths that supports achieving our SEL vision
- Identify barriers in achieving our SEL vision

2:00- 2:15   SEL Reflection Activity   *(Presented by: Ms. Krotiak)*

2:15- 2:30   Closing Activity   *(Presented by: Ms. May)*

2:30- 2:45   Concluding Remarks   *(Presented by: Dr. Moore and Ms. Freeman)*

Figure 3.11 Lisa's detailed notice to staff about planned SEL Week celebration activities to promote and share the good news with students and parents about new Tier 1 programming beginning the next school year.

BURNHAM/ANTHONY MATH & SCIENCE ACADEMY

Dr. Linda J. Moore, Principal ● *Ms. Sheryl Freeman, Assistant Principal* ● *Social & Emotional Learning Committee*

Introducing our special Introduction to SEL Week!

"SEL–Teaching Lessons for School and Life"

MAY 12th through MAY 16th

Dear Teachers and Staff,
As you know, as part of our social and emotional learning initiative, we are celebrating and sharing the good news with students next week! Please review this sheet for details about what is planned . . .

WEEK LONG POSITIVE INCENTIVE ACTIVITY: Each teacher will be given <u>classroom specific</u> colored-flowers (enclosed). All week long, give a student a flower if you observe them being respectful, being safe, being responsible, or being their best. Instruct students to write their name in the middle of the flower and write one-three sentences describing what they did. Track flowers distributed on sheet provided. Burnham Staff and Student Council (Anthony Bldg.) will collect on daily basis and place for display on '**Blooming With SEL**' bulletin board. The classroom with greatest percentage of flowers awarded at each building will win a class pizza party <u>and</u> free Dress Down Day!! Winners will be determined by Incentive Committee.

MONDAY, May 12th: *Kick-Off Assembly.* Buses will arrive at 9:15am to begin boarding students for arrival at Trumball Park by 10am for an assembly. Kindergarten will sit on the floor in the gymnasium, with 1st grade, 2nd grade, and so on seated behind them to ensure visibility. There will be various skits and speeches made. Return to school is scheduled for 12:00pm. Students will eat lunch in their classrooms upon their return to the building. They are asked to bring a bagged lunch; Cafeteria Manager will prepare a bagged lunch if necessary.

TUESDAY, May 13th: *School Beautification Day.* A schedule will be provided to teachers with notice of allotted time to spend outdoors landscaping and cleaning. Upon completion of outdoor activity time, each class is to engage in indoor cleaning time spent beautifying the classroom. This is a Dress Down Day for students— they should be wearing clothes that they can get dirty. Please be mindful of students with allergies.

WEDNESDAY, May 14th: Alternate 'School Beautification Day' if poor weather the day prior.

THURSDAY, May 15th: *SEL Classroom Lesson & Time Capsule Reflection.* Every teacher is asked on this date to set aside time for students to reflect on the week and set goals for the following school year, just as the school has been doing. Enclosed you will find a grade appropriate classroom lesson to conduct on SEL that focuses on conflict resolution and how to treat others with respect. Afterwards, please discuss with students and have them complete the grade-appropriate FALCON PRIDE goal sheet enclosed. READ each question carefully to the students; encourage them to reflect on this school year and what they hope to achieve next year. Once students have completed the forms, please collect and file in their cumulative folder 'time capsule' so that next Fall we can return it to each student as a beginning reminder.

FRIDAY, May 16th: *SEL Celebration.* Students will have a FREE Dress Down Day if they wear their grade level colors. At students' normal lunchtimes, students will have a picnic outside (**Note: All lunch periods are extended 20 minutes**). Students can bring their own lunch to school; Cafeteria Manager will make bagged lunches as necessary. Anthony students will eat lunches outside on lunch tables. Upon return from lunch, K & 1st grade will watch a movie in Room 101; 2nd & 3rd grade will watch a movie in Room 107; 4th & 5th grade in Room 116; 6th, 7th, & 8th grade in their own classrooms separately. Teachers must select their own age-appropriate movie with a positive, SEL message and seek approval from Administration. Ms. Krotiak has primary-aged cartoons available or "Emmanuel's Gift". Other possible titles include: "Miracle", "Pay It Forward", "Dream Writers", "Music of the Heart", "The 11th Hour", etc. After showing the movie, please discuss with thought-provoking questions. Popcorn will be made in both buildings and given to students.

Figure 3.12 Lisa's flyer for students and parents detailing the new Tier 1 initiatives in place and "The Way to Be" program at Burnham/Anthony Academy.

Burnham/Anthony Math & Science Academy—Teaching Lessons for School and for Life!!

SEL IN ACTION AT BURNHAM/ANTHONY!

CELEBRATE SEL WITH US ON OCTOBER 3rd!!

WHAT IS SEL?

Social and Emotional Learning (SEL) involves processes through which people develop fundamental emotional/ social abilities to recognize and manage emotions, develop caring and concern for others, establish positive relationships, make responsible decisions, resolve conflicts respectfully, and make ethical and safe choices.

We are proud to announce that we are **committed** to focusing on academic skills as well as teaching social and emotional learning skills to create and maintain safe, caring learning environments. We are **excited** to introduce **FIVE great SEL initiatives this school year**—Second Step curriculum, the Falcon Four Student Code of Conduct, the SEL agenda planner, the school-wide positive rewards system, and the Student of the Month program!!!

SECOND STEP: Students from K through 8th will be taught this curriculum on a weekly basis. It provides instruction in SEL skills and structures opportunities for children to practice, apply, and be recognized for using these skills throughout the day. It is an award-winning violence prevention program. Students will learn and practice vital social skills, such as empathy, emotion management, problem solving, and cooperation. This program is research-based; it has been shown to reduce discipline referrals, improve school climate by building feelings of inclusiveness and respect, and increase the sense of confidence and responsibility in students. We are fortunate to offer this to our students!

'THE FALCON FOUR—THE WAY TO BE' AT OUR SCHOOL: *This year, we have **FOUR** school-wide expectations for all students:* **Be Safe, Be Respectful, Be Responsible, and Be Your Best!!** *This applies no matter where the student may be. These expectations comprise our **Student Code of Conduct**. In order to recognize students who follow these rules and expectations, Staff can award a child with an entry form for prize drawings in each building!!! All Staff wear a lanyard with a vinyl pocket that contains entry forms. This way, we can instantaneously provide one to a student who demonstrates the proper WAY TO BE at our school!*

SEL AGENDA PLANNER SALE GOING ON NOW!!

Only $3

A GREAT tool to help students keep track of their assignments and monthly calendar while learning about character values & positive role models! **Get yours today!!!**

STUDENTS OF THE MONTH!!

Each month, a boy and girl in each building will be awarded as Student of the Month for excellence in Second Step, academics, conduct, and character. They will be featured on a bulletin board display and earn a coupon for a Dress Down Day of their choice!

SPECIAL ACTIVITY

Friday, October 3rd

Come celebrate these great new initiatives and learn more about them at our SEL KICK-OFF ASSEMBLY AT ANTHONY BLDG. starting at 10:00am

4

Lesson Plans

DANIELLE'S STORY

"I haven't been a teacher before."

"My school counseling program didn't train me in how to teach a classroom lesson."

"I don't feel comfortable being in front of a class of students."

"The curriculum I have is very prescriptive, and I don't know how to make lessons interesting and fun."

These are all comments I've heard from many school counselors regarding core curriculum classroom lessons, and I, too, have felt similarly. Although my graduate program had a course titled "Learning, Achievement, Instruction," I still felt somewhat unprepared to fully design curriculum and teach students using engagement strategies and strong classroom management skills. I actually cringe when thinking back to some of the first lessons I taught as an elementary school counselor, remembering how nervous I was and how much I talked at the students rather than engaged them in the content of the lesson. Thankfully, I was supported by patient and helpful mentor teachers and had the good fortune to work in districts implementing strong teacher training using models such as Direct Interactive Instruction (Action Learning Systems, 2012).

Over the years, I enhanced my teaching skills and have learned how to (1) write measurable objectives aligned with standards, (2) incorporate a variety of engagement strategies within my lessons, (3) improve my classroom management skills, and (4) easily assess what students have learned at the end of my lesson through multiple measures. Although some school counselors may not see the value in attending teacher trainings, these professional development opportunities have drastically improved my teaching skills and abilities. One of my favorite compliments is when teachers are surprised that I haven't been a classroom teacher, or when they tell me that I use all the same strategies as they do.

School counselors sometimes worry about "taking" teachers' time away from instruction in their content area and may even face resistance in getting into classrooms, which is why it is even more important for school counselors to demonstrate strong instructional practices. When

(Continued)

(Continued)

teachers see school counselors teaching to standards (yes, school counselors have standards, too!), facilitating active participation throughout core curriculum classroom lessons, and assessing student learning, professional respect improves. Strong teaching and learning leads to teachers' welcoming school counselors into classrooms as they see the value of what students are learning.

Chapters 4 through 6 are designed to provide the reader with the attitude, knowledge, and skills needed to effectively teach and engage students through core curriculum classroom lessons.

LESSON PLAN DEVELOPMENT COMPONENTS

Just as teachers design lesson plans, school counselors preparing to teach content in the classroom setting do so as well (Lopez & Mason, n.d.). In Chapter 2, counselors determined content for franchisable curriculum. This chapter expands on the development of curriculum for agreed-upon topics to support school counselors' development of lesson plans. Descriptions of each lesson plan component and ways to incorporate best practices of teaching and learning within a well-developed lesson plan are included. Some sections of the lesson plan are more straightforward and shorter, while other sections are longer, are not typically taught in school counseling graduate programs, and include more detailed descriptions and instruction. Throughout this chapter, readers are encouraged to reference our full lesson plan example (shown in Figure 4.25, beginning on page 84).

Lesson plan development includes these components, which are expanded upon in the following text:

1. Lesson subject and title

2. Grade level of students

3. Learning objectives

4. Standards

5. Materials

6. Procedure

7. Plan for evaluation

8. Follow-up

Lesson Subject and Title

When designing a lesson, first consider the subject area. Is the lesson focused on learning how to solve problems, career exploration, or test taking strategies, for example? A general topic such as one of these would be the lesson subject. School counselors create a title that aligns with agreed-upon franchised curriculum topics (see Chapter 2) and, if possible, is also interesting. For instance, a problem-solving lesson can be named "We Can Do It! Solving Problems With One Another." Learning about test-taking strategies can be titled "Let's Ace That Test!" Although this is written first on the lesson plan, school counselors will likely fill in this section after the lesson objectives and procedure have been completed, to ensure that the title aligns with the content.

Grade Level of Students

Within the lesson plan, school counselors will indicate the age or grade level of students for which the lesson is designed. Considering the developmental level of students is important, especially in elementary school, to ensure that the content is age-appropriate. Generally, the following grades can be grouped together: kindergarten and first grade; first and second; second and third; third and fourth; fourth and fifth; and fifth and sixth. Some lesson modification may be needed, such as differentiating instruction to support students who are more advanced or those who need additional help to access the content.

Learning Objectives

Creating measurable learning objectives is one of the most important components of lesson design, and therefore this will be discussed in depth. Learning objectives are brief statements describing what students will learn during the course of a classroom lesson. Objectives are the most important learning takeaways, so they are to be determined *prior* to planning the rest of the lesson. While some might think of classroom activities first, and frame objectives to align with what they want to teach, objectives are meant to drive the lesson content, rather than the other way around. By beginning with the end in mind, school counselors plan objectives by thinking about the attitudes, knowledge, and skills they want their students to obtain by the end of the lesson.

How to Counsel (Teach) Like a Champion: The Four Ms

Doug Lemov's *Teach Like a Champion 2.0* (2015) discusses the "Four Ms" for writing an effective classroom lesson objective: (1) **m**anageable, (2) **m**easurable, (3) **m**ade first, and (4) **m**ost important. These four criteria are designed to make the lesson useful and effective (see Table 4.1).

Figure 4.1 Lesson Plan: Lesson Subject and Title

Lesson Plan Template

1. Lesson Subject and Title:
2. Grade(s):
3. Learning Objective(s):
4. Standards:
5. Materials:
6. Procedure:
7. Plan for Evaluation: How will each of the following be collected?
   - Process Data:
   - Perception Data:
   - Outcome Data:
8. Follow-Up:

Lesson plan adapted from ASCA

Figure 4.2 Lesson Plan: Grade Level of Students and Learning Objectives

Lesson Plan Template

1. Lesson Subject and Title:
2. Grade(s):
3. Learning Objective(s):
4. Standards:
5. Materials:
6. Procedure:
7. Plan for Evaluation: How will each of the following be collected?
   - Process Data:
   - Perception Data:
   - Outcome Data:
8. Follow-Up:

Lesson plan adapted from ASCA

Figure 4.3 Doug Lemov's *Teach Like a Champion 2.0: 62 Techniques That Put Students on the Path to College*

Table 4.1 Teach Like a Champion: The Four Ms

Teach Like A Champion: 4 Ms	
Manageable	An objective should be of a size and scope that can be taught in a single lesson.
Measurable	An objective should be written so that your success in achieving it can be measured, ideally by the end of the class period.
Made first	An objective should be designed to guide the activity, not to justify how a chosen activity meets one of several viable purposes.
Most important	An objective should focus on what's most important on the path to college, and nothing else.

Source: Lemov, D. (2014). Teach Like a Champion 2.0: 62 techniques that put students on the path to college, 2nd edition. San Francisco, CA: Josey-Bass.

Using the school counseling lens, the following questions and descriptions are framed for counselors to consider as they are planning their lesson objectives:

Manageable: Can this objective effectively be taught within the course of one school counseling lesson? School counselors' classroom time is limited. It's tempting to squeeze too much into one lesson by over-planning. However, quality is much better than quantity. When too much content is squeezed into one lesson (usually only 35 minutes to an hour), content focus is affected—and therefore so are the student outcomes. School counselors are encouraged to consider the most important learning takeaway for the lesson and to focus on teaching the targeted objectives extremely well.

Measurable: How can I assess student learning of this objective? First, when writing an objective, school counselors want to consider how to measure what students have learned. Using pre- and post-tests to measure student learning is one form of assessment, yet there are other ways to do this as well. Accurately completing an activity, filling out a "ticket out the door," or even orally completing sentence frames are all ways to measure student learning. When writing an objective, school counselors can incorporate the measures within their objective with one simple word: *by*. For example: "Students will explain ways to be respectful to their classmates *by* completing a ticket out the door listing one or more examples of showing respect." While not every lesson objective must be written to be specifically measurable, best practice states that at least one objective is directly measurable.

Made first: Why is it important to create my objective prior to the rest of my lesson plan design? As discussed previously, designing the objective to guide

Table 4.2   Activity 4.1

Look at the examples below demonstrating how an unmeasurable learning objective was transformed into a measurable objective. Consider how you can make the additional "Not Yet Measurable" objectives measurable.

Not Yet Measurable	Measurable
Students can describe two or more careers they are interested in for the future.	Students can describe two or more careers they are interested in for the future by completing a career exploration activity.
Third-grade students can explain problem-solving steps.	Third-grade students can explain problem-solving steps by participating in role-play scenarios of conflicts.
Fifth graders demonstrate their knowledge of the elective classes offered at the feeder middle school.	Fifth graders demonstrate their knowledge of the elective classes offered at the feeder middle school by accurately filling out an elective sheet.
Kindergarten students can understand how other people feel.	
Students demonstrate their knowledge of test-taking strategies.	
Third and fourth graders can show respect to one another.	

the activity, rather than to justify how the activity meets one of multiple outcomes, is recommended. While it is important to review and fine-tune the objective after the lesson is created, writing the objective prior to lesson design helps better ensure that the intended goal of the lesson will be met through the delivery of content.

Most important: What is most important for students on their path to mastery of content? In *Teach Like a Champion 2.0*, Lemov (2015) discusses the importance of all curricula being focused on helping students achieve the goal of postsecondary readiness. While he is specifically addressing teachers, the message is similar for school counselors. Although the three domains of focus for school counselors are academic, career, and social/emotional development, ultimately teaching students skills in each area helps ready them to become active members of society after graduating from high school. Therefore, when considering objectives, it is important for school counselors to plan their class time wisely, ensuring that each school counseling core curriculum lesson supports student learning and students' growth on their path to becoming productive members of society.

Bloom's Taxonomy

In addition to Lemov's Four Ms, school counselors can also utilize Bloom's Taxonomy when creating lesson objectives. The taxonomy pyramid (see Figure 4.4) shows how remembering and understanding make up the foundation of learning, with subsequent levels promoting deeper thinking and creativity. Rather than focusing on students' solely knowing or understanding concepts, creating lessons that will move

> ### Bloom's Taxonomy
>
> Developed under the leadership of Dr. Benjamin Bloom, Bloom's Taxonomy was created to promote higher levels of thinking within education. This framework categorizes educational goals and has been applied within the K–12 and college setting since the 1950s, and it is still relevant today. Within the framework, there are six categories: (1) remember, (2) understand, (3) apply, (4) analyze, (5) evaluate, and (6) create (Armstrong, n.d.).

students to higher levels of thinking ensures that they can apply, analyze, evaluate, and create using their base knowledge.

The first category, *remembering* knowledge, is the foundation on which the other categories are built, as depicted in the pyramid shown in Figure 4.4. Students need to first remember and recall content, and then utilize this information to build their skills and abilities to the most complex level of creating. As students put information into practice, deeper levels of learning occur, and they progress from basic *understanding* to *applying* and *analyzing*, up through *evaluation* and *creation*. For example, after students can explain problem-solving steps (within the category of understanding), their ability to *apply* the steps to a role-play scenario and compare/contrast when to use different solutions exhibits higher levels of thinking using their base knowledge. As school counselors create objectives and lessons, considering Bloom's Taxonomy and its accompanying verbs (see Figure 4.26 at the end of the chapter) encourages critical thinking as students apply, analyze, evaluate, and create with the information they learn. While not every lesson objective must be at the level of *apply* or above, best practice is to write at least one objective per lesson at the Bloom's Taxonomy level of *apply* or higher.

Figure 4.4 Bloom's Taxonomy

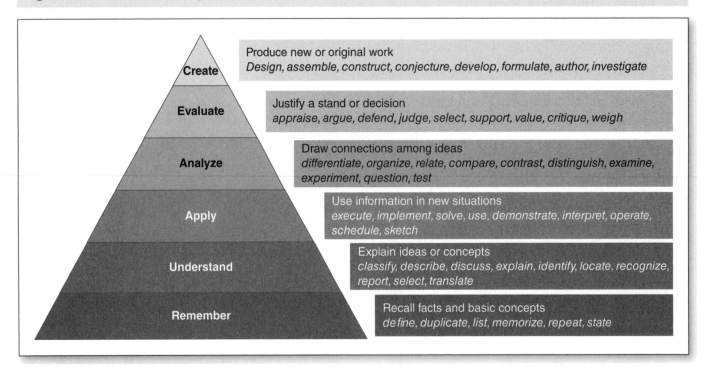

Table 4.3 Activity 4.2

Below are the objectives that were previously made to be measurable (from Activity 4.1). Now look at how these objectives have been transformed to further include the Bloom's Taxonomy levels of apply, analyze, evaluate, or create. Consider how to make the additional objectives fit into the level of apply or above.

Bloom's Taxonomy Level: Remember or Understand	Bloom's Taxonomy Level: Apply, Analyze, Evaluate, or Create
Students can *describe* two or more careers they are interested in for the future by completing a career exploration activity.	Students can *compare and contrast* two or more careers they are interested in for the future by completing a career exploration activity.
Third-grade students can *explain* problem-solving steps by participating in role-play scenarios of conflicts.	Third-grade students can *model* problem-solving steps by participating in role-play scenarios of conflicts.
Fifth graders *demonstrate* their knowledge of the elective classes offered at the feeder middle school by accurately filling out an elective sheet.	Fifth graders *apply* their knowledge of the elective classes offered at the feeder middle school by accurately filling out an elective sheet.
Kindergarten students can *understand* how other people feel by correctly identifying feelings on picture cards.	
Students demonstrate their *knowledge* of test-taking strategies by completing a test-taking strategy worksheet.	
Third and fourth graders can *show* respect to one another by filling out a "ticket out the door" listing one or more ways of being respectful.	

Standards

In 1996, the American School Counselor Association (ASCA) created the *ASCA National Standards for Students* (revised in 2004), with specific competencies and indicators in the academic, career, and personal/social domains (Campbell & Dahir, 1997). Each indicator was clearly defined, for example:

A:A3.1 *Take responsibility for their actions*

C:B1.1 *Apply decision-making skills to career planning, course selection and career transition*

PS:B1.2 *Understand consequences of decisions and choices*

In 2014, ASCA shifted to the *Mindsets and Behaviors for Student Success: K–12 College- and Career-Readiness Standards for Every Student*, which still incorporate the three domains of academic, career, and social/emotional development (previously personal/social), but within the broader context of two categories: mindsets and behaviors. The Mindset Standards include six items "related to the psycho-social attitudes or beliefs one has about oneself in relation to academic work" (Sparks & ASCA, n.d., slide 1) that school counselors will encourage students to develop. The Behavior Standards fall into three categories of Learning Strategies, Self-Management Skills, and Social Skills, with nine to

Figure 4.5   Lesson Plan: Standards

Lesson Plan Template

1. Lesson Subject and Title:

2. Grade(s):

3. Learning Objective(s):

4. Standards:

5. Materials:

6. Procedure:

7. Plan for Evaluation: How will each of the following be collected?

   - Process Data:
   - Perception Data:
   - Outcome Data:

8. Follow-Up:

Lesson plan adapted from ASCA   AMERICAN SCHOOL COUNSELOR ASSOCIATION

ten standards under each area. These behavior standards are "commonly associated with being a successful student" (Sparks & ASCA, n.d., slide 29).

Many school counselors trained in the *ASCA National Standards for Students* found them to be very straightforward and easy to align with each grade level. Standards were used to develop a comprehensive school counseling program, building on student learning each year. Curriculum crosswalk tools were used by school counselors to check off which standards were taught in which grades, with the goal of students' mastering all the *ASCA National Standards for Students* within their K–12 education.

The ASCA *Mindsets and Behaviors for Student Success* are much broader, which can be helpful as well as challenging. Oftentimes school counselors teach skills that don't fit into only one domain of academic, career, or social/emotional. For instance, Behavior Learning Strategies Standard 1 is "demonstrate critical-thinking skills to make informed decisions." School counselors can easily explain ways in which this standard can be applied to academic, career, and social/emotional domains. The ASCA *Mindsets and Behaviors for Student Success* were created based on best practices and a survey of research, including the noncognitive factors in the University of Chicago's literature review *Teaching Adolescents to Become Learners* (Farrington et al., 2012). Similar to the Common Core State Standards, the ASCA mindset and behavior standards are focused on college and career readiness within all aspects of learning. Therefore, the ASCA *Mindsets and Behaviors for Student Success* are up-to-date with current research and can be applied broadly within the school counselor role to best support student development.

A challenge with the mindset and behavior standards' broad and vague nature, especially for those who are familiar with the specificity of the previous standards, is that implementation and application are left up to the interpretation of school counselors. Using Behavior Learning Strategies Standard 1 again ("Demonstrate critical-thinking skills to make informed decisions"), school counselors can teach multiple concepts to address this standard—conflict resolution, saying no to drugs and alcohol, tattling versus reporting, and more. The *ASCA Mindsets and Behaviors for Student Success* allow for flexibility in teaching content, but they are less directive for school counselors unsure of what to teach.

The *ASCA Mindsets and Behaviors for Student Success* can be applied to all grade levels in a developmentally appropriate manner. While adapting the standards to meet the diverse needs of K–12 students, the variance also causes a challenge if trying to crosswalk and teach the standards across all grade levels. While teachers use their standards as a framework from which to create lesson objectives, the *ASCA* mindset and behavior standards can make this more challenging because they are so

Figure 4.6 ASCA *Mindsets and Behaviors for Student Success: K–12 College- and Career-Readiness Standards for Every Student*

The ASCA Mindsets & Behaviors for Student Success: K-12 College- and Career-Readiness Standards for Every Student

Each of the following standards can be applied to the academic, career and social/emotional domains.

Category 1: Mindset Standards
School counselors encourage the following mindsets for all students.

M 1. Belief in development of whole self, including a healthy balance of mental, social/emotional and physical well-being
M 2. Self-confidence in ability to succeed
M 3. Sense of belonging in the school environment
M 4. Understanding that postsecondary education and life-long learning are necessary for long-term career success
M 5. Belief in using abilities to their fullest to achieve high-quality results and outcomes
M 6. Positive attitude toward work and learning

Category 2: Behavior Standards
Students will demonstrate the following standards through classroom lessons, activities and/or individual/small-group counseling.

Learning Strategies		Self-Management Skills		Social Skills	
B-LS 1.	Demonstrate critical-thinking skills to make informed decisions	B-SMS 1.	Demonstrate ability to assume responsibility	B-SS 1.	Use effective oral and written communication skills and listening skills
B-LS 2.	Demonstrate creativity	B-SMS 2.	Demonstrate self-discipline and self-control	B-SS 2.	Create positive and supportive relationships with other students
B-LS 3.	Use time-management, organizational and study skills	B-SMS 3.	Demonstrate ability to work independently	B-SS 3.	Create relationships with adults that support success
B-LS 4.	Apply self-motivation and self-direction to learning	B-SMS 4.	Demonstrate ability to delay immediate gratification for long-term rewards	B-SS 4.	Demonstrate empathy
B-LS 5.	Apply media and technology skills	B-SMS 5.	Demonstrate perseverance to achieve long- and short-term goals	B-SS 5.	Demonstrate ethical decision-making and social responsibility
B-LS 6.	Set high standards of quality	B-SMS 6.	Demonstrate ability to overcome barriers to learning	B-SS 6.	Use effective collaboration and cooperation skills
B-LS 7.	Identify long- and short-term academic, career and social/emotional goals	B-SMS 7.	Demonstrate effective coping skills when faced with a problem	B-SS 7.	Use leadership and teamwork skills to work effectively in diverse teams
B-LS 8.	Actively engage in challenging coursework	B-SMS 8.	Demonstrate the ability to balance school, home and community activities	B-SS 8.	Demonstrate advocacy skills and ability to assert self, when necessary
B-LS 9.	Gather evidence and consider multiple perspectives to make informed decisions	B-SMS 9.	Demonstrate personal safety skills	B-SS 9.	Demonstrate social maturity and behaviors appropriate to the situation and environment
B-LS 10.	Participate in enrichment and extracurricular activities	B-SMS 10.	Demonstrate ability to manage transitions and ability to adapt to changing situations and responsibilities		

Source: American School Counselor Association (2014). Mindsets and Behaviors for Student Success: K-12 College- and Career-Readiness Standards for Every Student. Alexandria, VA: Author.

broad. Therefore, school counselors may find it easier to create a strong measurable learning objective first, and then align the *ASCA Mindsets and Behaviors for Student Success* to the created objective, rather than the other way around. Whether designing objectives based on standards or connecting standards to objectives, core curriculum classroom lessons must be standards-based, but the process to get there is up to the individual school counselor.

Figure 4.7   ASCA Mindsets and Behaviors Program Planning Tool

ASCA MINDSETS & BEHAVIORS: PROGRAM PLANNING TOOL

AMERICAN SCHOOL COUNSELOR ASSOCIATION

This form is a tool you can use in planning your overall school counseling curriculum. Indicate the grade level in which you plan to address any standard in the cells below as well as how the standard is addressed (core curriculum-CC, small group-SG, closing-the-gap-CTG). It isn't necessary to address each standard each year.

	Grade Level/Delivery		
	Academic	Career	Social/ Emotional
Mindsets	*Indicate grade level and how addressed (core curriculum-CC, small group-SG, closing the gap-CTG)*		
M 1: Belief in development of whole self, including a healthy balance of mental, social/ emotional and physical well-being			
M 2: Self-confidence in ability to succeed			
M 3: Sense of belonging in the school environment			
M 4: Understanding that postsecondary education and lifelong learning are necessary for long-term career success			
M 5: Belief in using abilities to their fullest to achieve high-quality results and outcomes			
M 6: Positive attitude toward work and learning			
Behavior: Learning Strategies			
B-LS 1: Demonstrate critical-thinking skills to make informed decisions			
B-LS 2: Demonstrate creativity			
B-LS 3: Use time-management, organizational and study skills			
B-LS 4: Apply self-motivation and self-direction to learning			
B-LS 5: Apply media and technology skills			
B-LS 6: Set high standards of quality			
B-LS 7: Identify long- and short-term academic, career and social/emotional goals			
B-LS 8: Actively engage in challenging coursework			
B-LS 9: Gather evidence and consider multiple perspectives to make informed decisions			
B-LS 10: Participate in enrichment and extracurricular activities			
Behavior: Self-Management Skills			
B-SMS 1: Demonstrate ability to assume responsibility			
B-SMS 2: Demonstrate self-discipline and self-control			
B-SMS 3: Demonstrate ability to work independently			
B-SMS 4: Demonstrate ability to delay immediate gratification for long-term rewards			
B-SMS 5: Demonstrate perseverance to achieve long- and short-term goals			
B-SMS 6: Demonstrate ability to overcome barriers to learning			
B-SMS 7: Demonstrate effective coping skills when faced with a problem			
B-SMS 8: Demonstrate the ability to balance school, home and community activities			
B-SMS 9: Demonstrate personal safety skills			
B-SMS 10: Demonstrate ability to manage transitions and ability to adapt to changing situations and responsibilities			
Behavior: Social Skills			
B-SS 1: Use effective oral and written communication skills and listening skills			
B-SS 2: Create positive and supportive relationships with other students			
B-SS 3: Create relationships with adults that support success			
B-SS 4: Demonstrate empathy			
B-SS 5: Demonstrate ethical decision-making and social responsibility			
B-SS 6: Use effective collaboration and cooperation skills			
B-SS 7: Use leadership and teamwork skills to work effectively in diverse teams			
B-SS 8: Demonstrate advocacy skills and ability to assert self, when necessary			
B-SS 9: Demonstrate social maturity and behaviors appropriate to the situation and environment			

© 2003, ASCA National Model: A Framework for School Counseling Programs. American School Counselor Association

Source: American School Counselor Association. ASCA Mindsets & Behaviors: Program Planning Tool. Retrieved from https://www .schoolcounselor.org/school-counselors/asca-national-model/asca-national-model-templates.

This ASCA Mindsets and Behaviors Program Planning Tool (see Figure 4.7) helps school counselors plan their schoolwide counseling curriculum. School counselors identify the grade level and domain (academic, career, social/emotional) in which they plan to address the standards. In some districts, such as Wisconsin's Green Bay Area Public School District, this tool has been used during discussions with teachers as school counselors plan their schoolwide curriculum in collaboration with faculty. Keep in mind that it is not necessary to address each standard each year.

Table 4.4 Activity 4.3

Below are the objectives that were created in Activities 4.1 and 4.2. Notice how one or two ASCA *Mindsets and Behaviors for Student Success* standards were applied to several of the objectives. Consider how to add mindset and behavior standards to the additional objectives.

Learning Objective	ASCA Mindset and Behavior Standards That Apply to the Objective
Students can compare and contrast two or more careers they are interested in for the future by completing a career exploration activity.	M 4. Understanding that postsecondary education and life-long learning are necessary for long-term career success B-LS 7. Identify long- and short-term academic, career and social/emotional goals
Third-grade students can model problem-solving steps by participating in role-play scenarios of conflicts.	B-LS 1. Demonstrate critical-thinking skills to make informed decisions B-SS 5. Demonstrate ethical decision-making and social responsibility
Fifth graders apply their knowledge of the elective classes offered at the feeder middle school by accurately filling out an elective sheet.	B-LS 8. Actively engage in challenging coursework
Kindergarten students apply their understanding of how other people feel by correctly identifying feelings on picture cards.	
Students analyze and apply their knowledge of different types of test-taking strategies by accurately completing a test-taking strategy worksheet.	
Third and fourth graders can show respect to one another by developing and completing a "ticket out the door" listing one or more ways of being respectful.	

Materials

In this section, list all the materials needed for the school counseling core curriculum classroom lesson. This is especially useful for school counselors as a checklist prior to teaching, to ensure that they have everything required. The materials section can also include the type of curriculum to be used, such as whether a school counselor will be teaching *Second Step*. If a purchased curriculum is to be

Figure 4.8 Lesson Plan: Materials and Procedure

Lesson Plan Template

1. Lesson Subject and Title:

2. Grade(s):

3. Learning Objective(s):

4. Standards:

5. Materials:

6. Procedure:

7. Plan for Evaluation: How will each of the following be collected?

   • Process Data:
   • Perception Data:
   • Outcome Data:

8. Follow-Up:

Lesson plan adapted from ASCA

used, school counselors will want to secure the purchase of the curriculum by talking to their administrator and also participate in the appropriate training, if necessary.

Procedure

The procedure section of the lesson plan is where detailed instructions about how to teach the content are provided. In this section, school counselors describe, step by step, how the lesson will be taught. As school counselors write their lesson plans, details to be added include explanations of key concepts, discussion questions to ask students throughout the lesson, and engagement strategies to use (refer to Chapter 5). Consider how teachers create lesson plans for a substitute teacher. Teachers must include thorough descriptions of each portion of the lesson to ensure that the content is taught in the way the teacher intended. Similarly, when completing the procedure section of a lesson plan, school counselors are encouraged to write out detailed information, so another school counselor could teach the same content solely by reading the lesson plan.

Tips for Writing Detailed Procedures

• For lessons that include a PowerPoint or Google Slides presentation, consider writing what the school counselor will say and what the students are expected to do for each slide.
• Include student engagement strategies (discussed in Chapter 5) in the lesson plan to remind the presenter to use them.
• Add the targeted amount of time that it may take for each portion, to keep the school counselor instructor on track in teaching all the content both efficiently and thoroughly.

How to Create Effective Lesson Procedures

With lesson objectives and standards already determined, creating the lesson content, or *procedures*, is the next step. The basic structure and sequence for a lesson is as follows:*

A. Welcome

B. Behavior expectations

C. Standards and objectives

---

*Adapted from *Direct Interactive Instruction* (Action Learning Systems, 2012).

D. Accessing prior knowledge

E. Input and model ("I do")

F. Guided and independent practice ("We do" and "You do")

G. Restate objectives, assessment, and closure

Welcome. To begin classroom lessons, school counselors address the students and, depending on how often school counselors visit classes, they may also restate the school counselor's role. School counselors who visit classrooms weekly or every other week likely do not need to reintroduce their role, aside from the initial classroom visit at the beginning of the year. When school counselors visit once per month or less frequently, reminding students of the counselor's supportive role on campus is important. School counselors may ask students to brainstorm and share ways in which school counselors can help them, reinforcing and building on responses while also adding any important aspects that may be left unaddressed.

Because students often say that school counselors help students "who have problems," Danielle's school counseling team reframed the role after a student said, "School counselors make sure everyone has fun at school." Solving problems is part of helping students have fun at school, along with teaching students new skills, being there to listen if they are upset, and so on. School counselors can also remind students of other supportive adults in their life, such as teachers and family members.

Describing different situations and identifying multiple adults on campus whom students can lean on during difficult times helps solidify the school counselor role and helps prevent school counselors from being the person to whom students resort for everything. Additionally, if there are multiple school counselors per school or support staff who help in the school counseling department, displaying a photo of the team helps students become familiar and comfortable with everyone.

Behavior Expectations. At the beginning of the lesson, it is important to clearly state classroom behavior expectations. Some schools have schoolwide expectations, and

Figure 4.9 Don't Blow Your Top! Slide 1: Lesson Introduction

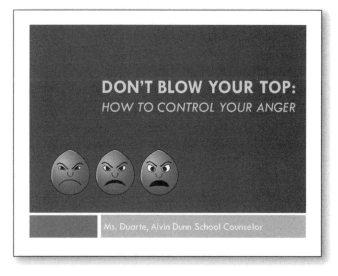

Figure 4.10 Don't Blow Your Top! Slide 2: Behavior Expectations

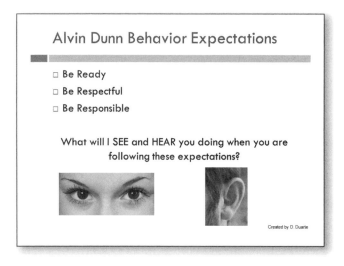

Figure 4.11   Don't Blow Your Top! Slide 3: School Counseling Program Introduction

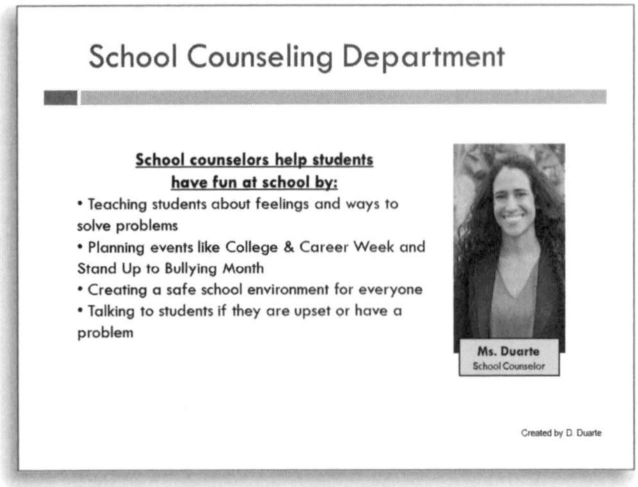

in that case school counselors are advised to use these same requirements in their lesson (such as Positive Behavior Interventions and Supports), while specifically relating the expectations to their presentation. For example, when reminding students to be ready, respectful, and responsible, school counselors can ask students to share examples of what that looks and sounds like while they are teaching (keeping their eyes on the speaker, raising their hand to share, staying on topic when talking with a partner about questions asked, etc.). Another effective method is to point out students who are already modeling appropriate behavior and list specific behaviors school counselors are expecting as they are teaching:

- "I notice you all are sitting quietly while I'm talking, which is very respectful."
- "Thank you for showing you are ready by quickly clearing off your desks, Jesus and Lily."
- "I know you all will raise your hand when you want to share an answer, which shows respect to your classmates and me."

If the school has not yet created schoolwide expectations, it is recommended that school counselors create their own, because remembering each different teacher's guidelines may be difficult. Because school counselors visit all classrooms, teaching students the way their school counselor expects them to behave creates universal expectations. Some teachers' strategies may be incorporated over time, such as giving class points or adding a marble to the jar for positive behavior, but starting with school counselor–specific rules and rewards is OK, too. By setting and restating clear expectations *every* time a school counselor starts a class lesson, students are reminded of appropriate behavior, which is a proactive classroom management strategy (for more on classroom management, see Chapter 6).

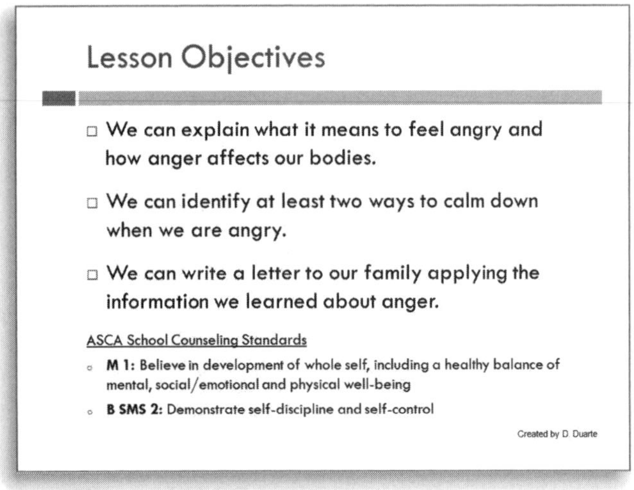

Standards and Objectives. Students are learning standards through the lesson objectives, which are what students are expected to believe, know, and do after the lesson. These learning takeaways are important, so school counselors want to share the objectives at both the beginning and the end of the lesson. Sharing the objectives with students sets the focus of the lesson and gives

Figure 4.12   Don't Blow Your Top! Slide 4: Lesson Objectives

students ownership of their learning. A recommended practice is for students to read the objectives out loud together (i.e., choral reading; see Chapter 5 for more engagement strategies). The standards that align with the lesson objectives are also shared, whether they are stated or displayed visually, to show students, teachers, administrators, and families that school counselor lessons are based on standards, just as teachers' lessons are.

Accessing Prior Knowledge. Now that the students know the school counselor, as well as his or her behavior expectations, standards, and objectives, the counselor can prompt students to think about and access prior information they have about the topic, rather than jumping into new content. This can be done by posing a discussion question and asking students to (1) share with a partner, and then with the class (i.e., "Think-Pair-Share"), or (2) quickly write down their response and then share it with the class (i.e., "Think-Ink-Pair-Share"; see Chapter 5 for more details). This allows the school counselor to establish a framework for the lesson that is connected to what students already know. By bridging students' current knowledge with the new content, students can make meaningful connections to the lesson that will assist them in learning the new information presented. Additionally, accessing prior knowledge builds interest in the topic and

Figure ... Don't Blow Your Top! Slide 5: Accessing Prior Knowledge

Table 4.5   Activity 4.4

Below are examples of elementary school counseling lesson topics. The first three include questions to access prior knowledge; fill in the others with questions to ask students at the start of a new lesson.

Lesson Topic	Suggested Question for Accessing Prior Knowledge
Kindness Matters: Learning About Respect	What are ways in which students show respect to one another?
Let's Explore Careers!	What are some careers you've thought about pursuing when you grow up?
Look Out, Middle School, Here We Come!	What excites you about starting middle school, and why?
We Can Ace That Test!	
On Time, All the Time (Attendance)	
Learning to Problem Solve	
We Are Ready for College!	

Figure 4.14 Don't Blow Your Top! Slide ... of Knowledge

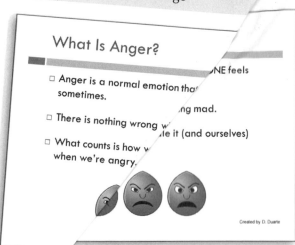

demonstrates how the new learning can be related to other experiences in students' lives.

Input and Model ("I Do"). Now that students understand the topic, it's time for school counselors to dive into the content of the lesson, which is called *input*. By definition, *input* is "the act or process of putting in" (www.merriam-webster.com/dictionary/input). Within core curriculum classroom lessons, this means that the school counselor shares important information needed to master the objective with students. There are many ways to spice up the input portion of lessons with a variety of engagement strategies, which are discussed in greater detail in the next chapter. Choral or popcorn reading of information, using visuals, pausing for students to discuss, and sharing examples are all ways to engage students in the lesson content. In addition, having students take guided notes (discussed in Chapter 5) also supports engagement and retention of material.

Modeling is a way to support input through demonstrating a new skill while students watch. In the same way a fashion model on a runway demonstrates how to wear a new outfit, school counselors model, or show students how they can use the information they are learning. For example, in the lesson on respect, school counselors can model (act out) one specific example of how to show respect to others on the playground or model (perform) using a polite tone of voice. *Non-modeling* is another way to utilize this strategy; in this case, the school counselor shows students what *not* to do and explains why. For instance, school counselors

Figure 4.15 Don't Blow Your Top! Slide 7: Input of Knowledge and Modeling

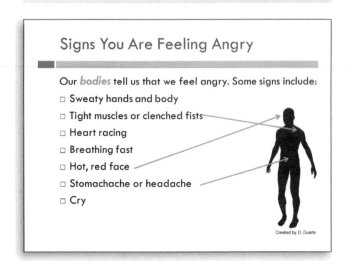

can non-model using a rude tone of voice, and then discuss with students the reasons why a rude voice can upset someone. Using non-modeling teaches students what not to do and the reasons why the behavior is not useful. Non-modeling is especially effective when discussing a common mistake or frequent problem, to help prevent student error. By modeling and non-modeling, school counselors help students remember what is being taught, feel confident in their answers, and reduce potential errors. When using technology with students, such as filling out an online survey, modeling is extremely important so that students understand what to do prior to working independently. In this case, school counselors may want to create step-by-step screenshots of ways to navigate the information.

The input and modeling portion of the lesson can also be called *"I do,"* which means that this is the part of the lesson where the school counselor is directly teaching students what they need to know and showing them how to learn this through examples (Killian, 2015). During this part of the lesson, school counselors check for understanding throughout, while delivering content. Rather than solely asking students whether they understand (because they may say they do, but this may not actually be true), the strategies listed in Table 4.6 can be incorporated into teaching content during the input phase.

Figure 4.16   Don't Blow Your Top! Slide 8: Input of Knowledge and Modeling

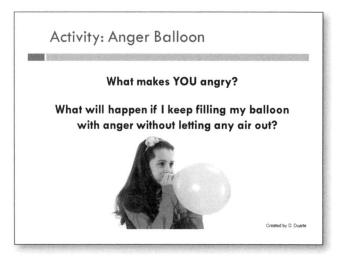

Table 4.6   Checking for Understanding

Strategy for Checking for Understanding	Suggested Question for Checking for Understanding
Thumbs Up/Thumbs Down	Ask students: "If you understand what was just taught, give me a thumbs up; if not, give me a thumbs down." Then randomly call on a student with his or her thumb up to explain what he or she learned. If the student doesn't know, ask another student. If 25% of the class or more have their thumb down, or the students you call on can't answer, explain the concept in a different way. Additionally, in order to create a safe learning environment, allow students to temporarily pass when called on, but tell them you will come back to them (and do so!).
Explain to Your A-B Partner	At the beginning of the lesson, help students find a partner sitting near them. Instruct one partner to be A and the other to be B. Periodically throughout the lesson, ask students to turn to their partner, and choose one of the partners to explain what was learned, and then randomly call on a student to share with the class. If students are having difficulty explaining, reteach the content.
Fist to Five	Ask students: "Using your right hand with a fist to mean you don't understand at all, five fingers to mean you could teach your neighbor what we learned, or three fingers to mean you halfway understand, show me how much you learned." Assess how many students show a four or five, and if approximately 75% of the class do have a four or five, randomly call on a student to explain what he or she learned. If that student doesn't know, ask another student, and if less than 75% of the class indicate a four or five, share an example or teach the material differently.

Figure 4.17 Don't Blow Your Top! Slide 9: Input of Knowledge

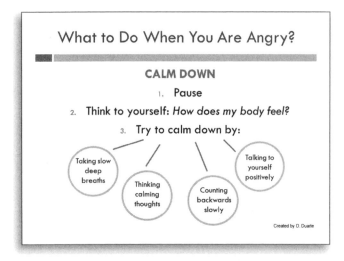

Figure 4.18 Don't Blow Your Top! Slide 10: Guided Practice

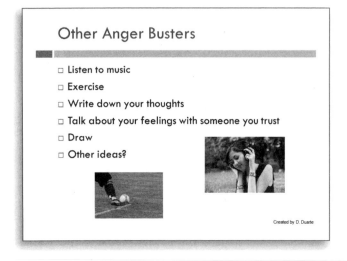

Guided and Independent Practice ("We Do" and "You Do"). Students have now been taught the content knowledge to apply to an activity. In the guided practice phase, the school counselor supports students as they use the information they have learned to compare and contrast, evaluate, organize, design, predict (or any of the level-three and beyond verbs from Bloom's Taxonomy, page 87) with their knowledge. During *guided practice*, students will often work together, and the school counselor may lead them step by step, asking questions and calling on students to share. As students answer, the school counselor praises correct responses or politely corrects answers that are off track, helping teach the rest of the group. The guided practice portion of a lesson is also referred to as *"We do."* As students work together with the school counselor and their peers ("we"), they are supported in learning the steps to gain mastery of skills.

Guided practice moves to *independent practice* when, through checking for understanding and providing group support, students appear to fully understand and can apply their learning. As students work independently, the school counselor moves around the room, monitoring students' progress, providing feedback (praising or correcting), and observing students in their attainment of mastery. Hopefully the wonderfully engaged classroom teacher is supporting the independent practice phase as well! Independent practice can also be called *"You do,"* as students retain what they have learned by practicing on their own.

Examples of guided and independent practice include the following:

- Students brainstorm ways to be respectful at school with a partner, and then the school counselor discusses the shared strategies with a group, reinforcing and correcting as appropriate (guided practice). This would be done prior to students making their own personal and individual commitment to showing respect at school (independent practice).
- The school counselor supports a group of three students as they act out a scenario using decision-making steps in front of the class (guided practice). After the group's guided practice, students work in small groups to create and act out their own scenarios (independent practice).

Figure 4.19 Don't Blow Your Top! Slide 11: Independent Practice

Figure 4.20 Don't Blow Your Top! Slide 12: Closure

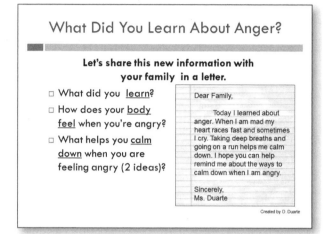

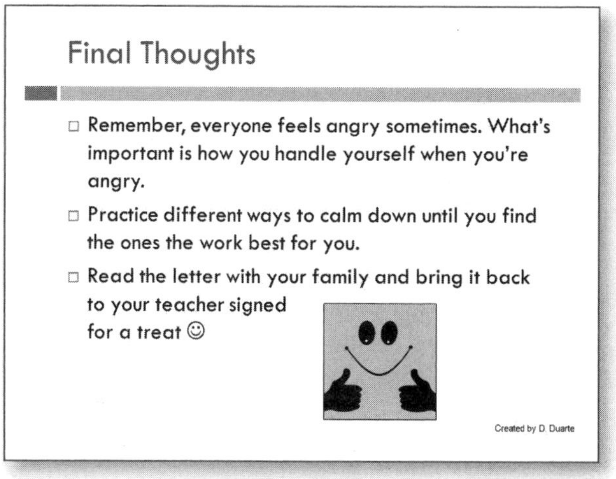

Restate Objectives, Assessment, and Closure. At the end of the lesson, it's time to refer back to the objectives as part of the lesson closure. One effective way to review the objectives is to take the objective statements and turn them into sentence frames, calling on students to answer. A *sentence frame* involves providing the beginning of a sentence and asking students to fill in the end, as shown in Figure 4.21. This is also a way to informally assess that students have learned the objectives, especially when students are called on randomly. School counselors can also review and clarify key points of the lesson as they are ending. For instance, in the lesson shown here, the school counselor will use call cards to ask students to explain anger, describe ways in which anger can affect people's bodies, and list ways to calm down. Through restating the lesson objectives and important information, students' knowledge is reinforced and integrated into their learning.

In addition to calling on students to share what they learned, counselors can use a "ticket out the door" as a straightforward and effective assessment strategy (which is described in greater detail in Chapter 5). School counselors can ask a question or use a sentence frame for students to complete and turn in at the end of the lesson. Additionally, if the lesson includes an activity, the correct completion of the activity can also be a means of assessing a skill. Pre- and post-tests, as discussed in *The Use of Data in School Counseling* (Hatch, 2013), also assess student learning of lesson content. See Chapter 8 for additional information on assessment strategies.

Figure 4.21 Don't Blow Your Top! Slide 13: Restate Objectives

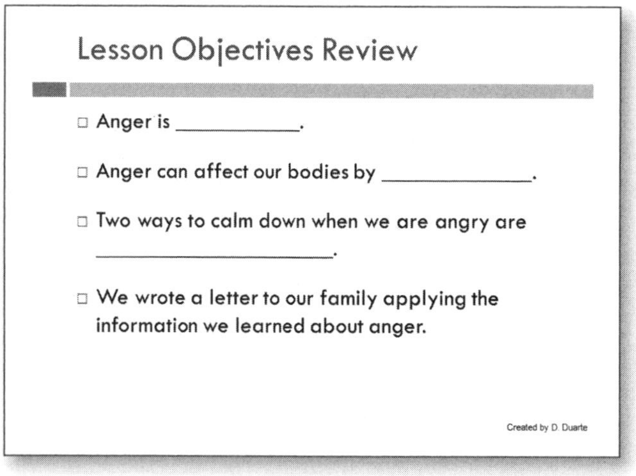

Lesson Objectives Review

☐ Anger is _____.

☐ Anger can affect our bodies by _____.

☐ Two ways to calm down when we are angry are
_____.

☐ We wrote a letter to our family applying the information we learned about anger.

Created by D. Duarte

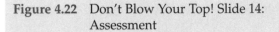

Figure 4.22 Don't Blow Your Top! Slide 14: Assessment

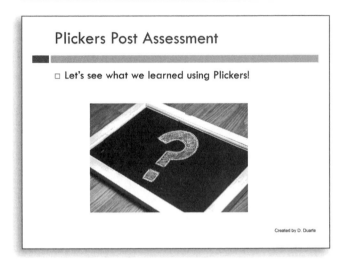

School counselors may also be assessing students more formally through a post-assessment test as part of the closure. In this lesson, Plickers was used to survey students' attitudes and knowledge about the lesson content (see Figure 4.22). More details about creating assessments and using technology tools, such as Plickers, for pre/post test administration can be found in Chapter 8.

Plan For Evaluation

In this section of the lesson plan, elementary school counselors describe how they will assess their lesson.

- *Process data:* the number of students impacted by the lesson
- *Perception data:* attitudes, knowledge, and skills gained from the lesson (through pre- and post-assessments)
- *Outcome data:* the achievement-related and achievement data

This section is important for counselors to show the impact that their lesson makes on students' attitudes, knowledge, and skills related to the lesson topic, and the way in which student behaviors can be affected based on the lesson. While not all school counseling lessons include pre- or post-assessments or other types of measurement, including the potential perception and outcome data in the lesson plan describes the ways in which the lesson *can* be assessed.

In the accompanying lesson plan, "Don't Blow Your Top!" (see Figure 4.25 toward the end of the chapter), the school counselor includes the plan for evaluation in the following way:

- *Process data:* all fourth- and fifth-grade students (approximately 180 students)
- *Perception data*
  - *Attitudes:* percentage of students who believe "it is OK for kids to feel angry."
  - *Knowledge:* percentage of students who can define anger; percentage who can identify how anger can make someone's body feel; percentage who can identify ways to calm down when feeling angry
  - *Skills:* percentage of students who can write a letter describing how anger makes them feel and explaining ways in which they can calm down

- *Outcome data:* tracking the number of behavior referrals and the number of suspensions before and after the lesson (looking for a decline)

More information about different types of assessment data is described in Chapter 8.

Follow-Up

The final section of the lesson plan discusses next steps after the lesson is completed. For example:

- After the lesson on career exploration, the first- and second-grade students will participate in Vehicle Day, where more than 10 careers on wheels will be displayed. Classes will rotate around the blacktop for 15- to 20-minute stations, listening to the presenters discuss their careers and asking questions. Students will also complete the "When I Grow Up . . ." activity, writing a sentence and drawing a picture about a career in which they are interested.

- The school counselor will monitor students during the fall "Respect and Anti-Bullying" lesson and also talk with teachers to see if any students have reported mistreatment, following up appropriately. School counselors will let students know they will be teaching another respect and anti-bullying lesson in the spring, reiterating expectations and building on the skills they have learned.

- During Red Ribbon Week, students will make end-of-day announcements about staying healthy and drug free. All families will receive a letter explaining Red Ribbon Week, with suggestions for developmentally appropriate discussions with their children and family resources. At the Friday flag assembly, seniors from the feeder high school will talk about their choice to stay drug free and share their plans for the future.

While the process of creating lesson plans is time-consuming in the beginning, school counselors who dedicate this time to making detailed plans will save themselves time in the future. Creating detailed lesson plans allows school counselors to build and franchise their comprehensive school counseling program for future consistency and program sustainability.

Figure 4.23   Lesson Plan: Plan for Evaluation

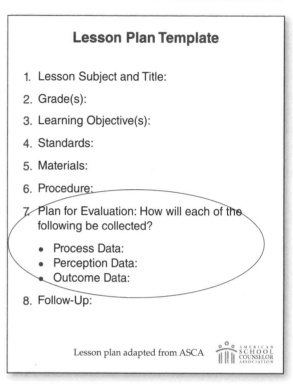

Lesson Plan Template

1. Lesson Subject and Title:
2. Grade(s):
3. Learning Objective(s):
4. Standards:
5. Materials:
6. Procedure:
7. Plan for Evaluation: How will each of the following be collected?
   - Process Data:
   - Perception Data:
   - Outcome Data:
8. Follow-Up:

Lesson plan adapted from ASCA

Figure 4.24   Lesson Plan: Follow-Up

Lesson Plan Template

1. Lesson Subject and Title:
2. Grade(s):
3. Learning Objective(s):
4. Standards:
5. Materials:
6. Procedure:
7. Plan for Evaluation: How will each of the following be collected?
   - Process Data:
   - Perception Data:
   - Outcome Data:
8. Follow-Up:

Lesson plan adapted from ASCA

CULTURAL RESPONSIVENESS AND CONSIDERATIONS WHEN LESSON PLANNING

Being mindful of students' diverse cultures and including multiculturalism within school counseling lesson plans is important to ensure that students' backgrounds are both respected and incorporated during the lesson, which helps students feel connected to the topics they are learning. Culturally responsive teaching aims to improve both engagement and motivation of diverse populations, especially students of color, infusing their culture into lessons to make meaningful connections and improve student outcomes (Gay, 2010; Vavrus, 2008). Learning about the diverse backgrounds of their school is important to help elementary school counselors address the varying needs of their students, and incorporating this knowledge into core curriculum helps students feel both respected by and connected to their counselor. In some cases, the school counselor may become the student as he or she learns about the school population and comes to understand the needs, challenges, and support that their students require socially and academically. When planning for core curriculum lessons, school counselors can incorporate multiculturalism by

1. creating a welcoming and inclusive environment that embraces diverse sharing—school counselors can explain and remind students what this looks like during their expectations at the beginning of classroom lessons. See Chapter 6 for more on creating classroom expectations.

2. incorporating students' personal and cultural perceptions into the lesson—when school counselors "activate prior knowledge" prior to teaching content, they can be mindful in seeking out diverse ideas.

3. embedding diverse student backgrounds and voices into lessons—for example, by including examples and photos that represent diverse cultures, especially those that directly apply to students in the school community.

4. including time for cooperative learning through group work—while this is not possible for every lesson, working in heterogeneous groups allows for diverse students to collaborate with and learn from one another.

In the sample lesson "Don't Blow Your Top!" (see Figure 4.25), Danielle was mindful of the ways in which different cultures may express anger. In some cultures, expressing anger outwardly is accepted, but in other cultures, it is the norm to keep feelings inside. As Danielle presented the topic, she was mindful in helping students understand that different types of expression are normal. Additionally, she helped students recognize that it's OK for others to express their anger in ways different from their own. Unless the expression of anger hurts others, all types are OK.

Additional examples of topics for specific cultural considerations include the following:

- Study skills and homework lessons

  o Teaching students to "advocate" for their learning by reaching out to teachers may be difficult for some students based on language barriers or cultural approaches to interacting with authority or questioning adults.

- o Consider the chores and other responsibilities that students may have, especially in single-parent families, where students may need to prioritize other family needs along with homework and school responsibilities.
  - o Based on students' home situations, studying in a quiet place or having their own desk may be unrealistic; instead, provide diverse options about how and where to study.

- English language learners

  - o Incorporate pictures, slow cadence of speech, and provide additional opportunities to check for understanding.
  - o Include lots of time to pair-share so that students have practice speaking and hearing others' ideas prior to sharing with the class.

- College and career exploration lessons

  - o Be mindful of incorporating diverse careers and vocational pathways that do not all require a four-year degree, including the military.
  - o Represent diverse photos of men and women from different backgrounds, in a variety of roles.
  - o When describing jobs compared to careers, be careful not to imply that one is better than the other, especially because students' family members may work in jobs; instead, focus on diverse options.
  - o Recognize and honor diverse education levels (especially with populations who will be first-generation college students; use caution to avoid minimizing their parents' education levels).

- Lessons including technology

  - o If technology is being discussed for at-home activities (such as using Google Calendar for homework and class assignments), include options for students who do not have access to technology at home.

What is the student population at your school? What cultural considerations do you need to make when planning your core curriculum classroom lessons?

Family Education Lesson Plans

As school counselors are creating lesson plans for their schoolwide curriculum, they are encouraged to also create lesson plans for their parent education workshops. In this way, parent education becomes consistent and predictable year to year. As you look back through this chapter, it will be helpful to utilize similar strategies for family education and workshops. What are some of the ideas in this chapter that most resonate with you to include in your parent education lesson plans? How might your parent education lesson plans differ from your student lesson plans?

Figure 4.25 Lesson Plan: Don't Blow Your Top!

1. **Lesson Subject and Title:** Don't Blow Your Top! How to Control Your Anger (anger management lesson)

2. **Grade(s):** 4 and 5

3. **Learning Objective(s):**

   By the end of this lesson, students will be able to

   - Explain what it means to feel angry and how anger affects their bodies.
   - Identify at least two ways to calm down when they are angry.
   - Write a letter to someone in their family applying the information they learned about anger.

4. **ASCA Domain and Mindset/Behavior Standards:**

   - *Domain:* Social/emotional
   - *Mindset 1:* Believe in development of whole self, including a healthy balance of mental, social/emotional and physical well-being
   - *Behavior Self-Management Skill 2:* Demonstrate self-discipline and self-control
   - *Behavior Social Skill 1:* Use effective oral and written communication skills and learning skills

5. **Materials:**

   - "Don't Blow Your Top!" PowerPoint
   - Laptop and projector
   - 3 × 5 cards
   - Pencils
   - Balloon (not blown up)
   - Lined paper

6. **Procedure:**

   Slide 1: Welcome students to the class and share the lesson title ("Don't Blow Your Top!").

   Slide 2: Ask all students to read the school's behavior expectations out loud together (be ready; be respectful; be responsible). Ask students to silently *think* what the school counselor will see and what he or she will hear when students are following these expectations in the class. After allowing 10 to 15 seconds of think time, ask students to *pair* with a neighbor and tell the partner what they thought about. After 2 to 3 minutes of discussion, call on students who are demonstrating the expectations to *share*, and also praise the students specifically for their on-task behavior (raising their hand, looking at the speaker, etc.).

   Slide 3: Remind students about the members of the school counseling department, including their counselor and any other counseling staff. Tell students that the counselor's job is to help students have fun at school by teaching them lessons about feelings (like they are doing today), planning events, talking to them if they have a problem, and helping everyone at school feel safe and happy.

   Slide 4: Explain the objectives for the presentation and why they are important. Have one student read the first objective and another student read the second, or ask the whole class to read each objective collectively. Explain that this is what the students will be learning today.

   Objectives:

   - We can explain what it means to feel angry and how anger affects our bodies.
   - We can identify at least two ways to calm down when we are angry.
   - We can write a letter to our family applying the information we learned about anger.

   Tell the students that the objectives are aligned to the school counseling standards at the bottom of the slide.

   Slide 5: Ask the students to think quietly about things that have made them feel angry. While they are thinking, ask two students to pass out a 3 × 5 card to each student. Tell the students they are going to write their name on the card and two to three things that make them feel angry. Explain the example on the PowerPoint (make sure to *model* what you'd like students to write on the card by updating the slide with your own name and developmentally appropriate examples of what makes you feel angry). Walk around and observe while students are writing, noticing any specific students you'd like to call on to share and any you'd want to avoid. After several minutes, regroup the class and ask for three to four students to share what makes them feel angry. After each student shares, ask the class to raise their hand if what the student said makes them angry, too. Ask one or two students to quietly and quickly collect all the cards and bring them up to you in the front as you proceed with the next slide.

Slide 6: The school counselor may want to have different students read each bullet point, calling on the first student and asking the next student to "popcorn" to a new student. Expand on the bullet points, explaining that feeling angry is normal, just as in the examples shared with the class. Explain that anger is a normal emotion that everyone feels. However, if we overreact when we are upset by saying or doing things we don't mean, that is when we can get ourselves into trouble.

Slide 7: Explain the different feelings that students may have to alert them when they are feeling angry. An arrow accompanied by different body signs will appear on the screen with each click (sweaty hands and body, tight muscles or clenched fists, heart racing, etc.). The school counselor may want to briefly act out some of descriptions, such as clenching his or her own fists and then asking students to clench theirs. Explain that different people feel differently when they are angry, and it is important to understand how your body feels because it's like a warning sign to remind you to calm down. If there is time, school counselors can ask students to share what happens to their body when they are angry with a partner.

Slide 8: Tell students that when we get angry, we feel it in our bodies, and if we don't calm down, we can stay upset. Take out the balloon and explain that it is like our body. Read one of the examples of being upset from the card (without reading the student's name), then puff into the balloon. Continue to do this until the balloon gets very large. Ask the students what will happen if you keep blowing. (Answer: The balloon will pop!) Explain that, yes, when we don't calm down, we can end up saying or doing something we don't mean.

Slide 9: Randomly call on student names from the cards to read: (1) "Stop and think," (2) "Ask yourself, *How does my body feel?*" (3) "Try to calm down by . . ." and then each of the calm-down strategies. At each one, stop and practice.

- Taking slow, deep breaths: Demonstrate how to breathe in and out deeply, without gasping or puffing loudly. Practice with the class three times.

- Thinking calming thoughts: Explain that thinking about a peaceful place or something that helps them feel happy can take their mind off what is making them upset. Give some examples (like being at the beach or laying on the couch). Ask students to close their eyes and picture a peaceful place.

- Counting backward slowly: Ask students which is more calming—counting quickly or slowly—and then ask why. Students will likely respond that counting slowly helps them relax; if not, help guide them to the answer, and then practice as a class.

- Talking to yourself positively: Explain that sometimes when we get upset, the words in our head sound like this: "I'm so mad!"; "I can't believe he did that to me!"; or "She's so mean!" However, if we let those words go on and on in our head, we will get more angry instead of less. Instead, we can think things like, "I'm mad, but I'm going to calm down"; "I'm just going to ignore him"; and "I will get through this." Saying positive, calming words will help us feel less upset so that we don't say or do something that we don't mean.

Slide 10: Discuss the other "anger busters" listed on the slide, and talk about when students can or can't use different ways to calm down. For instance, when they are in class, they can't listen to music, but that is a strategy they can use at home. Ask students to list other ideas they have that help them calm down.

Slide 11: Explain that students are going to write a letter to their family explaining what they have learned. While reading each question, pause for the class to fill in the underlined word (i.e., Counselor: "What did you . . ." [pause]; Students: "learn"?). As you are describing your example, ask two students to quietly pass

Figure 4.25 (Continued)

out lined paper. If possible, turn on classical or other calm music while students are writing. Walk around the class to answer questions and support students as they are writing. If some students are finishing earlier than others, ask them to add other calm-down ideas to their letter and/or pass out Plickers for post-assessment.

Slide 12: As students are finishing up, remind them that it is OK to feel angry and to practice different calm-down strategies until they find their favorites. Also ask students to read the letter with their family, and ask them to have an adult sign to show that he or she read the letter. When students bring back the signed letter, they will get a surprise from the school counselor (such as a pencil, five extra minutes of recess, or their name entered in a raffle), or this can be part of their homework as coordinated with their teacher.

Slide 13: Finally, review the objectives with the students and call on students randomly using the cards to fill in the sentence frames ("Anger is _____," "Anger can affect our bodies by _____," etc.).

Slide 14: Administer the post-test; thank the class and tell them that you look forward to reading their signed letters.

7. **Plan for Evaluation:** How will each of the following be collected?

- **Process Data:**

  o *Who:* All fourth and fifth graders (approximately 180 students)

  o *What:* Students receive a lesson regarding identifying feelings of anger and ways to calm down

  o *When:* Early Spring (February/March)

  o *Where:* Taught in individual fourth- and fifth-grade classes

- **Perception Data:**

  Pre-/post-assessment (pre-assessment is administered a week prior to the lesson, and post-assessment is given immediately following the lesson, using Plickers)

  o *Attitudes:* percentage of students who believe "It is OK for kids to feel angry"

  o *Knowledge:* percentage of students who can define anger, identify ways anger can make some-one feel (in their body), and identify ways to calm down

  o *Skills:* percentage of students who can apply their learning to describe how anger makes them feel and how they can calm down (through writing a letter to their family)

- **Outcome Data:**

  Tracking the number of behavior referrals and the number of out-of-school suspensions before and after the lesson (looking for a decline)

8. **Follow-Up:**

The school counselor will check in with each teacher 2 to 3 days later to collect signed letters. The counselor will briefly review the letters to determine which strategies were most commonly selected (perception data) and return the letters to students with a surprise. The school counselor will also talk with teachers and campus supervisors to ask whether students seem to be utilizing the calm-down strategies. A follow-up lesson may be implemented if additional support on the topic is needed, as evidenced by behavior referrals.

Figure 4.26 Revised Bloom's Taxonomy Action Verbs

Action Words for Bloom's Taxonomy

Sample of 176 unique words identified for a level of Bloom by 4 or more lists in a sample of 30 published lists (f = number of lists that nominate the word for a level of Bloom).

This document reformats **Table 1**, published in Stanny, C. J. (2016). Reevaluating Bloom's Taxonomy: What Measurable Verbs Can and Cannot Say about Student Learning. *Education Sciences, 6* (4), *37*; doi:10.3390/educsci6040037, for single-page printing. Used under CC-BY, licensed under CC-BY by Claudia J. Stanny.

Knowledge	f	Understand	f	Apply	f	Analyze	f	Evaluate	f	Create	f
arrange	6	articulate	4	act	19	analyze	24	appraise	22	arrange	22
choose	4	associate	4	adapt	4	appraise	11	argue	12	assemble	14
cite	17	characterize	4	apply	22	break	8	arrange	5	categorize	7
copy	4	cite	4	back / back up	5	break down	7	assess	17	choose	7
define	21	clarify	5	calculate	10	calculate	9	attach	4	collect	9
describe	14	classify	18	change	9	categorize	19	choose	10	combine	14
draw	5	compare	11	choose	11	classify	10	compare	18	compile	7
duplicate	7	contrast	7	classify	6	compare	24	conclude	13	compose	19
identify	20	convert	13	complete	5	conclude	6	contrast	8	construct	29
indicate	4	defend	12	compute	10	contrast	19	core	6	create	19
label	21	demonstrate	6	construct	13	correlate	5	counsel	4	design	24
list	27	describe	22	demonstrate	20	criticize	11	create	4	develop	18
locate	10	differentiate	8	develop	4	critique	14	criticize	11	devise	13
match	14	discuss	21	discover	8	debate	8	critique	14	estimate	5
memorize	10	distinguish	12	dramatize	16	deduce	6	decide	4	evaluate	4
name	22	estimate	11	employ	16	detect	7	defend	15	explain	8
order	5	explain	28	experiment	6	diagnose	4	describe	4	facilitate	4
outline	11	express	17	explain	5	diagram	12	design	4	formulate	18
quote	7	extend	11	generalize	5	differentiate	20	determine	6	generalize	7
read	4	extrapolate	5	identify	4	discover	4	discriminate	9	generate	11
recall	24	generalize	11	illustrate	18	discriminate	11	estimate	15	hypothesize	8
recite	12	give	4	implement	4	dissect	6	evaluate	16	improve	5
recognize	14	give examples	8	interpret	15	distinguish	21	explain	9	integrate	4
record	13	identify	14	interview	6	divide	12	grade	4	invent	10
relate	11	illustrate	9	manipulate	10	evaluate	4	invent	8	make	6
repeat	20	indicate	8	modify	12	examine	18	judge	25	manage	8
reproduce	11	infer	15	operate	17	experiment	9	manage	15	modify	10
review	4	interpolate	5	organize	4	figure	4	mediate	9	organize	21
select	16	interpret	17	paint	4	group	4	prepare	12	originate	9
state	23	locate	10	practice	15	identify	7	probe	4	plan	21
tabulate	4	match	7	predict	9	illustrate	8	rate	5	predict	8
tell	4	observe	5	prepare	11	infer	14	rearrange	19	prepare	12
underline	7	organize	5	produce	13	inspect	8	reconcile	12	produce	13
write	5	paraphrase	22	relate	12	inventory	9	release	6	propose	9
		predict	12	schedule	11	investigate	7	rewrite	4	rate	21
		recognize	11	select	4	order	5	select	5	rearrange	8
		relate	7	show	13	organize	6	set up	15	reconstruct	9
		report	10	simulate	5	outline	10	supervise	9	relate	8
		represent	4	sketch	17	point out	12	synthesize	16	reorganize	9
		restate	15	solve	19	predict	4	test	8	revise	12
		review	15	translate	5	prioritize	4	value	7	rewrite	7
		rewrite	12	use	25	question	12	verify	9	role-play	4
		select	7	utilize	4	relate	17	weigh	5	set up	9
		summarize	20	write	5	select	12			specify	5
		tell	7			separate	10			summarize	7
		translate	21			solve	8			synthesize	4
						subdivide	10			tell / tell why	5
						survey	7			write	17
						test	14				

5

Student Engagement

Juanita and Melissa both work as full-time elementary school counselors in the same school district. They collaborated with their counseling coordinator and the other K–6 counselors in the district to create franchised core curriculum lessons to deliver throughout the year (discussed in Chapter 2). This was meant provide a consistent structure for all schools. However, at the end of the first year of implementation, Juanita and Melissa's results are very different.

Looking at the results of her pre- and post-assessment, Juanita feels frustrated. When she teaches a lesson, she gives it her all! Her lesson content aligns with the pre- and post-assessments and everything else that The Use of Data in School Counseling *textbook (Hatch, 2013) told her to do. However, students don't seem to be engaged in her lessons. She struggles to get students to participate, and many are off task as she is teaching. This lack of learning is reflected in her post-assessment data, and Juanita is very disappointed.*

On the other hand, Melissa has great classroom participation and sees large gains on pre- and post-assessment knowledge, with students improving their attitudes, knowledge, and skills. Teachers praise Melissa for the variety of student engagement strategies she uses, which keep students interested in the lesson content. Students are so busy engaging in the material she is teaching that there are few disruptions, even in classes that typically experience behavior challenges.

Juanita wonders, what is Melissa doing to get such positive feedback from teachers and great results from students? Does she have a magic wand?! Why are her students performing so much better? Juanita decides to observe Melissa to see how she is teaching the same content but getting different student outcomes. As Juanita watches, she discovers that she isn't incorporating active participation strategies within her lessons and realizes the value of student engagement. She talks to Melissa afterward, and they brainstorm ways for Juanita to include a variety of new strategies within her next lesson to improve student learning.

ENGAGING STUDENT LEARNERS

Effectively engaging students throughout the beginning, middle, and end of classroom lessons is essential. Research supports strong connections between high levels of student engagement throughout the teaching and learning process and improved student performance (Action Learning Systems, 2012). By utilizing a variety of student engagement techniques, school counselors assess student learning throughout the lesson, and lesson content becomes more fun.

Within the educational environment, *engagement* is defined as "a student's persistence at a task and includes cognitive, emotional, and behavioral engagement" (Action Learning Systems, 2012, p. 145). Therefore, school counselors are encouraged to help students think deeply, connect emotionally with the content, and demonstrate engagement through their actions during core curriculum lessons. There are two kinds of engagement within classroom teaching: overt and covert.

COGNITIVE ENGAGEMENT THROUGH OVERT AND COVERT ENGAGEMENT STRATEGIES

To promote cognitive engagement, consider the following ways to incorporate both overt (observable) and covert (not observable) strategies within classroom lessons.

Overt	Covert
Observable	Not observable
Use when observable results are needed	Use when students need processing (thinking) time

Overt strategies are used when observable results are wanted or needed. They include students' sharing their response to a question with a partner, writing down the answer to a prompt, or reading a passage out loud as a class. School counselors can observe students' participation in all of these examples, making them overt.

Covert strategies allow students time to mentally process. Examples are asking students to think about their answer, silently remember a past experience, or follow along while the school counselor is reading. In these examples, school counselors cannot see students' mental processes, but paired with overt strategies, students' unobservable thinking can be assessed.

For example, after students think about their answer (covert), they can pair with a partner to discuss (overt), and then several students can be called on at random to share their answers with the class (overt again). Think-Pair-Share, as this strategy is called, is a way to hold students accountable to the unobservable covert strategy, because they will have to share their answer with a partner, and also possibly with the class. When students know that they are being held to these standards, they are more likely to be engaged in the topic, rather than thinking about what they are going to eat for lunch. Combining overt and covert strategies together allows for deeper student engagement in the lesson content.

Through utilizing both overt and covert engagement strategies during the beginning, middle, and end of core curriculum classroom lessons, school counselors engage all students throughout their teaching (see Figure 5.12 at the end of the

Activity 5.1

Covert or Overt?

Below are examples of phrases school counselors can say to engage students in the lesson content as they are teaching. Read each one and determine whether it is overt or covert, and why:

Example 1: "Think back in your mind to a time when you were angry."

- *Covert:* While school counselors hope that students are thinking about a past experience, they cannot observe what each student is actually thinking.

Example 2: "Everybody repeat the problem-solving steps with me."

- *Overt:* School counselors can both hear and watch the mouths of students as they say a phrase together.

1. "Be prepared to answer the question."
2. "Write down what you would do in the following scenario."
3. "Give me a thumbs up if you agree, or a thumbs down if you disagree."
4. "Remember to follow along in your head as I read."
5. "I'm going to pull a card with a student's name on it to answer the next question."
6. "Think about _____. Give me a thumbs up when you have it."

Answers

1. "Be prepared to answer the question."
   - *Covert:* School counselors cannot observe whether students are preparing to answer the question in their mind, but they hope so!

2. "Write down what you would do in the following scenario."
   - *Overt:* School counselors can observe students writing, and can later read what they wrote to determine whether students are on track.

3. "Give me a thumbs up if you agree, or a thumbs down if you disagree."
   - *Overt:* Watching students' thumbs allows the school counselor to observe participation and assess students' thoughts about the question. Tip 1: Wait until all thumbs are observed, allowing for processing time and setting the expectation of full class participation. Tip 2: Ask a student with his or her thumb up to explain his or her thought process, and then ask a student with his or her thumb down to do the same. Compare and contrast their answers.

4. "Remember to follow along in your head as I read."
   - *Covert:* School counselors cannot observe whether students are following along, but the following tips can help: This strategy can become overt if the counselor asks students to follow along with their fingers on the book or paper (so that the counselor can observe their actions), or if the counselor stops periodically and calls on a student at random to pick up reading where the counselor left off.

(Continued)

(Continued)

5. "I'm going to pull a card with a student's name on it to answer the next question."

   • *Overt* and *covert:* As the counselor pulls a card, students are (hopefully!) thinking about their response, which is covert. Once the called-upon student answers the question, the strategy becomes overt.

6. "Think about _____. Give me a thumbs up when you have it."

   • *Overt* and *covert:* School counselors cannot observe what students are thinking, but students are held accountable by showing that they are ready through a thumbs up. Tip: Remember to call on students at random to share their answers, to ensure that they do "have it."

chapter for the "Don't Blow Your Top!" lesson plan with engagement strategies highlighted throughout the entire lesson). As students actively participate, their attention improves, their speed of learning increases, and their retention of the information is stronger (Schunk, 1989). In addition, as students are busily engaged with the lesson content, there is less time for them to be off task or disruptive. Strong instructional practices are some of the best classroom management strategies.

There are a variety of ways to incorporate different overt and covert strategies within classroom lessons. By allowing for more mental engagement through covert strategies, paired with overt teaching practices, school counselors can actively engage students throughout the entire lesson and make learning more fun.

STUDENT ENGAGEMENT STRATEGIES

As school counselors plan their core curriculum class lessons, consideration is given to include different types of strategies, depending on the intended results. Do school counselors want students to (a) think deeply about a concept and share ideas with a partner, (b) learn and apply new information, and/or (c) stay focused on the content being taught? There's a strategy for that! Following are descriptions of the authors' favorite overt (observable) strategies, which may also include covert (unobservable) think time as well. The explanations help school counselors decide which strategy to use, with tips and reminders for effectiveness. As you are reading, first review the figure that demonstrates each strategy, then read the description of how, when, and why to use it, as well as the tips and reminders.

Pull Cards

How and When to Use

Calling on students randomly throughout a class lesson, rather than relying solely on raised hands, sets the expectation that all students will participate in the lesson. Some teachers may have pull cards or sticks with student names for school counselors to borrow, but rather than risk it, counselors can add a quick activity to create pull cards to their lesson. Students are distributed a card when they come into the classroom and are asked to write their name on the card. Additionally, by asking the student to respond to a question that aligns with the lesson topic, the school counselor can activate prior knowledge (see Chapter 4) or quickly pre-assess the class before teaching content. Once pull cards are created, school counselors collect the cards and call on students to read parts of the lesson or to answer questions after they have discussed their answers with a partner.

Why to Use

The average school counselor to student ratio is 491 students to one counselor (ASCA, n.d.), which can make it difficult for counselors to remember student names. Rather than only calling on known students or saying, "The girl in the green jacket," pull cards allow for counselors to address the whole class. As mentioned previously, using pull cards engages the entire class of students in the lesson, because they don't know who will be chosen, and it sets the expectation that all students will be participating.

Tips and Reminders

Remind students to write legibly and, if there are two students with the same name in the class, ask them to write their last name on the card as well. To save instructional time, the school counselor can ask a student or two to politely help collect the cards as he or she moves on to the next part of the lesson. School counselors can also use apps such as Class Dojo (see Chapter 6) or Stick Pick to create electronic lists of their students. See page 75 in Chapter 4 for an example of a pull card.

Think-Pair-Share

How and When to Use

When posing a question to students, first give them time to *think* to themselves about the answer (several seconds). Then ask them to find a partner to *pair* with and discuss their ideas. Finally, call on partners to *share* their ideas with the class. When using

Figure 5.1   Pull Cards

Pull Cards

1. Give each student a 3 × 5 index card as they come into the classroom and ask them to write their name on the card.
2. You can also ask them to write other information that aligns with the lesson topic (like how often they write in their planner every week before a lesson on organization) or answer questions (such as a pre-test question).
3. Collect cards and use them to randomly choose students to participate during the lesson.

Source: Illustration by Gogis Design, http://www.gogisdesign.com.

Figure 5.2   Think-Pair-Share

Think-Pair-Share

1. Identify the point of discussion
2. Allow students time to think individually.
3. Have students face a partner to share ideas.
4. Pair/student contributes to whole group.

Source: Illustration by Gogis Design, http://www.gogisdesign.com.

Think-Pair-Share, school counselors can also discuss the importance of stopping and thinking prior to answering a question (for example, by allowing the class to think more deeply about their answers and giving time for students who think at different speeds).

Ideas of when to use this strategy include the following:

- At the beginning of the lesson, when asking a question to access prior knowledge.

  "What is an example of a problem you had recently?"

- In the middle of lesson, to break up teaching content.

  "What are some good ways to calm down before trying to solve a problem?"

- At the end of the lesson, when reviewing the objectives.

  "Tell your partner the problem-solving steps we learned today."

Think-Pair-Share can easily be turned into Think-*Ink*-Pair-Share by asking students to write down their ideas on a paper or card prior to sharing with a partner.

Why to Use

This strategy can and should be built into every school counseling core curriculum classroom lesson. Rather than having full-class discussions with only a few students participating, or calling on students who raise their hand, Think-Pair-Share allows the entire class to engage in the content. By allowing students to consider their own answers first, talk with a partner, and then share and/or listen to answers from the class, Think-Pair-Share provides an opportunity for all students to be engaged.

Tips and Reminders

School counselors may want to pair up students for Think-Pair-Share, for example, by asking rows to face one another and discuss, or by telling students to talk with the student in the desk facing theirs. Directing students on how to find partners decreases confusion and gets them talking without wasting time. When using Think-Pair-Share, remember to call on students randomly to share their answers with the class. By selecting random students to respond, rather than taking volunteers, the school counselor sets the expectation that all students must be prepared to share their answers, which keeps them further engaged during independent think time and their partner discussions. Additionally, while students are talking with their partners, the school counselor can listen to a group and, upon hearing a strong answer, praise the student and tell him or her to be ready to share with the class. This builds confidence and is especially effective with students who may be less sure of their answers or need extra support (such as dual language learners, quiet students, or children with IEPs).

"Sole" Mates

How and When to Use

Another way to pair up students for partner activities is through "Sole" Mates. Ask students a question and give them about 30 to 45 seconds of think time and/or allow them to write down their answers. Then direct students to stand up and find a partner with similar shoes to the ones they are wearing (their "sole" mate!). They can find shoes that are of similar color or style, or any other way they choose. When they find a partner, students share their answers.

Why to Use

Using an activity like "Sole" Mates to partner students allows them to get up and talk with someone from the other side of the classroom. It also helps them create connections with one another in a unique and creative way.

Tips and Reminders

Prior to releasing students to find a partner, remind the class of behavior expectations, such as walking in the classroom, using indoor voices, and the signal to finish sharing. School counselors may also want to limit the time it takes students to find a partner by giving students a 10- to 15-second countdown to find their "sole" mate. In addition, an effective way to stop the partner share is by using an attention getter, such as "If you hear me, clap once. If you hear me, clap twice." (Additional attention getters are discussed further in Chapter 6.)

Choral Reading

How and When to Use

The strategy of Choral Reading can be incorporated into classroom lessons when the school counselor wants the entire class to read a phrase or passage together. Prior to use, the school counselor can teach Choral Reading by saying something like, "We are going to read this sentence together like a choir. When a choir sings, do they sing at the same time or at different times?" Hopefully students respond that choirs sing

Figure 5.3 "Sole" Mates

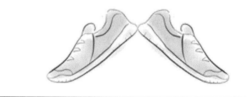

"Sole" Mates

1. Pose a question to students and allow time to think and/or write down their answers.
2. Ask students to get up and find their "sole" mate—someone with similar shoes on—to discuss their answer.

Source: Illustration by Gogis Design, http://www.gogisdesign.com.

Figure 5.4 Choral Reading

Choral Reading

1. Have a passage or phrase for all students to read together.
2. Once ready, give a signal for the group to read together chorally.

• Appropriate for school counselors to use in whole group and/or small group.

Source: Illustration by Gogis Design, http://www.gogisdesign.com.

all together. The school counselor can then say, "Yes! Just like a beautiful choir, we are all going to read this sentence together." The school counselor will want to prompt students to start at the same time, by saying a phrase like "Ready? Go," or

"1, 2, 3." The practice of Choral Reading is particularly useful for bringing classroom focus to an important concept, such as the lesson objective.

Why to Use

The strategy of reading out loud helps students form both visual and auditory links in memory pathways. Therefore, asking all students to read an important word or phrase together improves learning. Students who are less confident readers also benefit from practicing within a safe group setting, where their voice will blend in.

Tips and Reminders

Teach or remind students *how* to read together prior to prompting for Choral Reading, to gain desired results. Ensure that the sentence or phrase students are reading is not too long, otherwise students might have trouble reading it together. Additionally, if the majority of students do not read out loud or together, ask the class to try again until the entire class participates appropriately. By maintaining and following through with high expectations, the school counselor both engages students in the lesson and applies strong classroom management techniques.

Echo/Repeat Responses

How and When to Use

Similar to Choral Reading, the Echo/Repeat Responses strategy involves all students saying a word or phrase together. The difference is that the school counselor will say a word or phrase first, and the students will then repeat the word with prompting. For example, a school counselor presenting elementary-level college information may include new vocabulary such as university, degree, and scholarship. The school counselor can say these new words to students, and then ask them to repeat the words as a group.

Figure 5.5   Echo/Repeat Responses

Echo/Repeat Responses

1. Students "echo" the word, phrase, etc. school counselor states.

- Appropriate for school counselor to use with whole group, and/or with individual students.
- A useful way of ensuring that students practice the target vocabulary being taught.

Why to Use

The Echo/Repeat Responses technique is best used to emphasize important points within a lesson when the concept or words are new. Rather than having students chorally read a new word, which they may be unable to pronounce, the school counselor models through Echo/Repeat Responses.

Tips and Reminders

As with all whole-class engagement strategies, set and reinforce the expectation that

Source: Illustration by Gogis Design, http://www.gogisdesign.com.

all students will participate in Echo/Repeat Responses. If the whole class does not echo the words, ask them to try again. Additionally, school counselors can ask the students to repeat words or phrases multiple times in different ways, such as "Turn to your neighbor and say, 'University,'" "Whisper it," or "Look at your teacher and tell him the new word we are learning." As a modification, school counselors can also pause while reading a projected sentence, prompting students to fill in the missing word or phrase. For example, when reading the objective "We will learn ways to *calm down* when we are angry," the school counselor can pause before the words "calm down," so that the students can read "calm down" out loud as a class. To help students stay on track, the school counselor should explain this strategy to students and use a different color font and/or underline the word for students to say.

Figure 5.6   Sentence Frames

Sentence Frames

1. Pose a question to students and provide them with a prompt to respond that aligns with the question.
2. Allow time for students to respond.

- The framework allows students time to structure their thoughts.
- It is helpful to reframe the answer with "because" or "when."
- Example: What makes you angry?
  I feel angry when _____.

Source: Illustration by Gogis Design, http://www.gogisdesign.com.

Sentence Frames

How and When to Use

Sentences Frames are especially useful at the elementary school level, as they provide language supports to help students speak in complete sentences. School counselors can pose a question to students with an accompanying sentence frame (sentence starter) to help them structure their response.

Example Sentence Frames

- Why are drugs and alcohol dangerous?
  - Drugs and alcohol are dangerous because _____.
- What makes you angry?
  - I feel angry when _____.
- How can you plan to reach your college and career goals?
  - I can start planning to reach my college and career goals by _____.

Why to Use

By prompting students on how to respond, sentence frames scaffold learning for students at different levels. Primary students (grades K–3), dual language learners, and students with disabilities especially benefit from the supportive academic language to help them structure their thoughts into complete sentences.

Figure 5.7 Guided Notes

Guided Notes

1. **Create a set of notes with fill-in-the-blank information about the lesson you are teaching (ex: A-G requirements are ____; A growth mindset is ____).**
2. **Provide the guided notes handout to students to fill in as you are presenting the lesson content and allow time to fill in the blanks.**

Source: Illustration by Gogis Design, http://www.gogisdesign.com.

Tips and Reminders

Before sending students off into a discussion, counselors may want to prompt students with the sentence frame by saying it out loud.

Guided Notes

How and When to Use

Guided notes are a helpful addition to classroom lessons that include a lot of knowledge for students to learn. Rather than solely presenting information to students, creating a guided notes sheet for students to fill in while the school counselor speaks helps draw student attention to the most important content. To create a guided notes page, school counselors design a worksheet that aligns with their lesson content, with some words missing that students will fill in (see the example in Figure 5.8).

Why to Use

Guided notes engage students because they are looking for missing information to add to their note sheet provided by the school counselor. Additionally, creating a guided notes page for students allows them to organize and save the information they are learning. School counselors can also monitor student engagement by walking around the room while students are filling out their guided notes, and quietly remind students to fill in the blank spaces if they are not paying attention. In addition, guided notes are an introduction to students taking notes on their own, which is an essential academic skill for students to learn.

Tips and Reminders

While carefully crafted guided notes worksheets help students focus on the lesson, creating too many blank spaces can actually take away from students' ability to pay attention, as they'll be searching for words rather than listening. Therefore, be sure to make blank spaces only for the most important content (such as information from your pre- or post-assessments), and also pause as you are speaking to allow time for students to fill in the blanks. Boldface and/or underline the words on the PowerPoint or Google Slides presentation that fit into the blank spaces, and also refer students to their guided notes worksheet in order to help alert them to write down the content. Using Choral Reading or Echo/Repeat Responses (described previously), the class can read or repeat the words that fit into their guided notes. School counselors may also want to title and/or number the sections for students to fill in so that it is easier for them to follow along.

Figure 5.8 PowerPoint Slides and Guided Notes

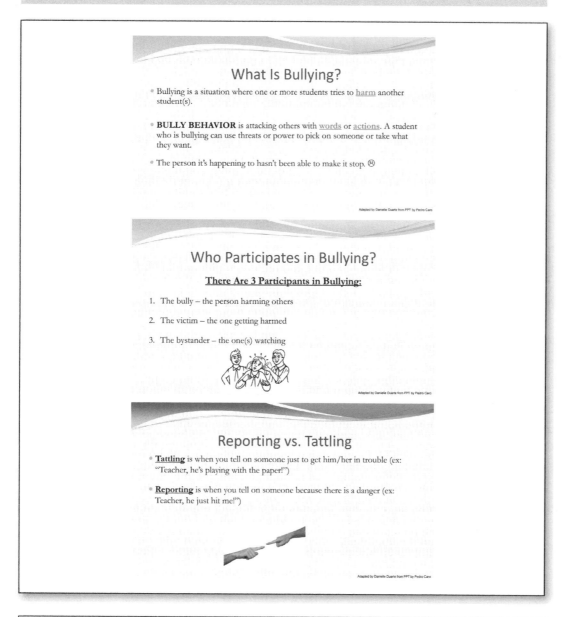

What Is Bullying?

- Bullying is a situation where one or more students tries to <u>harm</u> another student(s).

- **BULLY BEHAVIOR** is attacking others with <u>words</u> or <u>actions</u>. A student who is bullying can use threats or power to pick on someone or take what they want.

- The person it's happening to hasn't been able to make it stop. ☹

Adapted by Danielle Duarte from PPT by Pedro Caro

Who Participates in Bullying?

There Are 3 Participants in Bullying:

1. The bully – the person harming others

2. The victim – the one getting harmed

3. The bystander – the one(s) watching

Adapted by Danielle Duarte from PPT by Pedro Caro

Reporting vs. Tattling

- **Tattling** is when you tell on someone just to get him/her in trouble (ex: "Teacher, he's playing with the paper!")

- **Reporting** is when you tell on someone because there is a danger (ex: Teacher, he just hit me!")

Adapted by Danielle Duarte from PPT by Pedro Caro

Guided Notes Page

What Is Bullying?

Bullying is a situation where one or more students tries to _____ another student.

Bully behavior is attacking others with _____ or _____.

There Are 3 Participants in Bullying:

_____: the person doing something.

_____: the person who is getting harmed.

_____: the person(s) watching.

Reporting Versus Tattling:

_____: is when you tell on someone just to get them in trouble.

_____: is when you tell on someone because there is a danger.

> The pre- post-assessment aligned with this lesson can be found in Chapter 8, and the lesson PowerPoint is available in the online appendix.

Partner Jigsaw

How and When to Use

Partner Jigsaw is a strategy used to break up a large amount of lesson content, while having students investigate and become the experts in different topics, and then sharing with their peers. The school counselor will separate students into groups, and each group will receive a specific topic or a portion of the information. Jigsawing can also be used when students start responding to or acting out different scenarios based on the lesson content. Students form groups and work together based on the school counselor's directions. Examples include the following:

- The school counselor provides situations with different social problems to each group. Students use the problem-solving steps they've learned to identify the problem and create potential solutions.
- The school counselor gives each group pamphlets from different colleges. Teams also receive a handout with information to fill in, such as where the school is located, the cost of tuition, location, and so forth.
- Teams are provided packets of information about the risks of using tobacco, alcohol, and marijuana during a Red Ribbon Week lesson. Groups investigate the facts and write down risks they discover.
- Each group is given a scenario with different situations where bullying/mistreatment has occurred. Using the strategies the school counselor has taught, teams brainstorm what to do and act out the scenario to the class.

While groups are working, the school counselor (and hopefully the teacher) walks around the room to answer questions and monitor group progress. At the end of the given time, the school counselor will ask each group to share their expert knowledge with the entire class. The class can take notes or fill in an additional portion of the handout (if one is provided) while their classmates present. If a role-play or other activity is showcased where students apply the information learned from the lesson, the school counselor can reiterate what was taught after each group shares/presents.

Why to Use

Using Partner Jigsaw is a way to help students learn experientially, and it also breaks up a large amount of content. By working collaboratively, students own their learning and also learn from one another.

Tips and Reminders

School counselors may want to consider different ways to group students prior to beginning the lesson, such as by current table groups or numbering off into random groups. Consider the number of students in the group and how this impacts group dynamics.

Typically, forming groups of three to five students is ideal. If students must move to find their team members, remember to consider ways to reduce transition times, such as all students being in their new groups as the school counselor counts backward from 10 (for more on transitions, see Chapter 6).

Prior to starting group work, school counselors may want to set group protocols, such as one group member is the timer, another is the recorder, a third is the presenter, and so on. Regardless of students' role, remind them that they will all participate in the discussion. Also remind students about using an inside voice during teamwork, so that all groups can hear as they are working. Prior to beginning, tell students how much time they will have to complete the work and consider setting a timer (a timer they can see while they are working is particularly helpful; see Chapter 6, page 114).

The school counselor is also advised to assess whether groups are on track to finish by walking around, and they may need to adjust the time as necessary. Providing several countdown warnings also helps groups finish up on time. As student "expert" groups are sharing with their peers, remind students of expectations as they are listening and advise presenters to use a loud voice. The school counselor may want to repeat the most important information shared to ensure that all students gain the necessary content.

Figure 5.9   Partner Jigsaw

Partner Jigsaw

1. Each student receives a portion of the materials to be introduced.
2. Students leave their "home" groups and meet in "expert" groups.
3. Expert groups discuss the material and brainstorm ways in which to present their understandings to the other members of their "home" group.
4. The experts return to their "home" groups to teach their portion of the materials and to learn from other members of their "home" group.
5. Students can use a graphic organizer to write down notes as experts talk.

Source: Illustration by Gogis Design, http://www.gogisdesign.com.

Fist to Five

How and When to Use

Strategies like Fist to Five or Thumbs Up/Thumbs Down (described on page 77) allow school counselors to quickly assess the entire class for participation and to see how many students are on the right track. Counselors can ask students to rate, on a scale of fist (zero) to five, how much they understand a concept or how much they agree or disagree with a statement.

Fist to Five for Understanding. By scanning the room, a school counselor can instantly observe the number of students who report they understand at a high (four or five) level. If 25% or more students are reporting ones or twos, the school counselor can reteach or ask students who are displaying fours and fives to explain to the group in their own words. If a strong majority of the class report that they understand, the counselor is still advised to ask several students to explain, to deter students from mimicking the answer of their classmates when they really may not know.

Figure 5.10   Fist to Five

Fist to Five

1. Ask students to rate, on a scale of fist to five, with a fist meaning they don't know at all and a five meaning they could teach someone else, the answer to the following question, or whether or not they agree with a statement.
2. Pose the question to the students.
3. Observe the range (or lack of range) within the room and randomly call on students to explain their number.

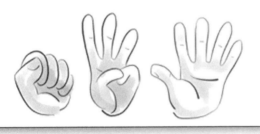

Source: Illustration by Gogis Design, http://www.gogisdesign.com.

Figure 5.11   Ticket Out the Door

Ticket Out the Door

1. At the end of the lesson, give an index card or piece of blank paper to each student.
2. Pose a question or sentence starter that relates to the lesson objective.
3. Have each student write their answer, and as they exit, they are to turn in their index card or slip of paper containing their answer.
4. School counselor can use student responses to gauge student leaning (and even as a brief post-assessment).

Source: Illustration by Gogis Design, http://www.gogisdesign.com.

Prompting students to display numbered fingers can also be used for classroom responses to a multiple-choice question. The school counselor can post a question related to the lesson topic, asking students to show their answers on their fingers. Again, the counselor is advised to call on students to share their rationale for their answers, to further evaluate students' knowledge.

Fist to Five for Agree/Disagree. When using this strategy to assess students' attitudes, the school counselor can ask students with different levels of agreement to share their opinions. The school counselor can facilitate a discussion with the diverse thoughts and ideas shared.

Why to Use

Fist to Five is a quick way to observe the range (or lack of range) within the class. Following up by calling on students to explain their rationale for their response supports deeper reflection and allows the school counselor to check for understanding.

Tips and Reminder:

Wait until all students have their hands up, allowing for students at all levels to have enough processing time and setting the expectation that everyone in class will participate.

Ticket Out the Door

How and When to Use

Assessing what students have learned and how they are applying the lesson content may come in the form of a Ticket Out the Door. One way to apply this concept is to ask students a question and/or provide a sentence frame to complete at the end of the lesson, based on the content taught. Students can write their response (preferable), or if time is limited, the counselor can chose one or two students at random to share their answers out loud. The Ticket Out the Door can also be the completion of an assignment or activity given during the lesson.

Ticket Out the Door examples:

1. Study Strategies and Organization Lesson

   Two strategies to help me be successful in school are _____.

2. College Knowledge Lesson

   Do you want to go to college? Why or why not?

3. Career Exploration Lesson

   What career would you like to further explore?

4. Anti-Bullying and Respect Lesson

   A way to show respect to my classmates is _____.

5. Problem-Solving Steps Lesson

   Share an example situation of when you can use the problem-solving steps we learned today.

6. Goal-Setting Lesson

   My academic goal for fourth grade is _____.

   Three actions I can take to achieve my goal are:

   1. _____

   2. _____

   3. _____

Activity 5.2

Consider a recent classroom lesson you presented. What type of Ticket Out the Door can you create to align with your lesson?

Why to Use

A Ticket Out the Door is a means of assessment, helping school counselors understand what students learned from the lesson. While school counselors are advised to more formally assess one or two classroom lessons with pre- and post-tests, a Ticket Out the Door is a less formal way to evaluate the attitudes, knowledge, and/or skills gained from the lesson content. Although the school counselor does not have comparison (pre-test) data, results can still be reported, which is discussed further in Chapter 9.

Tips and Reminders

When writing the Ticket Out the Door question or sentence frame, be specific. Rather than asking students, "What did you learn from the lesson?" ask a detailed question aligned with the most important concepts. If students are completing an assignment or activity, school counselors can either briefly check for completion (if the students should keep the information) or collect the tickets. Completion of a Ticket Out the Door can also be an incentive to stay on task and work efficiently if the tickets are to be turned in prior to recess, lunch, or end-of-the-day dismissal.

Using Engagement Strategies Within Family Workshops

School counselors can also use a variety of the engagement strategies listed previously when presenting to families; adult learners need engagement, too! Imagine the parents/guardians who have been up since 5:30 a.m. to get ready for work and get their children dressed, fed, and ready for school, and then dropped off their kids, worked all day, and are now at a parent meeting at 6:00 p.m. Those parents/guardians are tired and need an engaging presentation just as much as the students did earlier in the day! Below are some suggestions for ways to incorporate engagement strategies into presentations for families:

- *Think-Pair-Share:* Incorporate reflection questions pertaining to the topic into the presentation and ask parents/guardians to introduce themselves to a neighbor as they pair and exchange ideas, and then share some with the larger group.
- *Thumbs Up/Thumbs Down or Fist to Five:* Both of these strategies are a great way to assess the audience, for example, by asking how much knowledge they have on the topic (from zero to five), or to observe how much participants agree/disagree with statements (using a thumbs up or down or a fist [not at all] to open hand [strongly agree]).
- *Guided Notes:* Topics with a lot of information, such as positive parenting techniques or college readiness, can offer a good opportunity to include Guided Notes. Rather than passing out a handout with all the information in a traditional manner, school counselors can create Guided Notes for participants to fill out while they are listening, to keep parents/guardians engaged as they fill in the information.
- *"Sole" Mates:* Incorporating "Sole" Mates into the family workshop provides participants with a chance to stand up and meet someone new as they share their thoughts.
- *Partner Jigsaw:* Depending on the topic, school counselors may want to include a Partner Jigsaw, for example, by having parents/guardians split into groups to discuss different topics or respond to various scenarios. This strategy is especially impactful for multisession family workshops, as participants can dive deeper into workshop content and connect with one another.
- *Ticket Out the Door:* Asking parents/guardians to respond to a question as they leave is a great way for them to reflect on the topic they learned and for the school counselor to see what parts of the family workshop were most impactful and/or what questions still remain.

Incorporating a variety of classroom engagement strategies throughout the beginning, middle, and end of core curriculum classroom lessons involves students in the learning, which becomes interactive and fun. School counselors can include different strategies in their lessons, trying out a variety of techniques to see which work best for various situations. Through using these techniques, school counselors engage all students in the lesson, deepening their learning to create a greater impact on their attitude, knowledge, skills, and future behaviors.

Figure 5.12 Lesson Plan: Don't Blow Your Top! (With Engagement Strategies Highlighted)

6. Procedure:

Slide 1: Welcome students to the class and share the lesson title ("Don't Blow Your Top!").

Choral Reading

Slide 2: Ask all students to read the school's behavior expectations out loud together (be ready; be respectful; be responsible). Ask students to silently *think* what the school counselor will see and what he or she will hear when students are following these expectations in the class. After allowing 10 to 15 seconds of think time, ask students to *pair* with a neighbor and tell the partner what they thought about. After 2 to 3 minutes of discussion, call on students who are demonstrating the expectations to *share*, and also praise the students specifically for their on-task behavior (raising their hand, looking at the speaker, etc.).

Think-Pair-Share

Slide 3: Remind students about the members of the school counseling department, including their counselor and any other counseling staff. Tell students that the counselor's job is to help students have fun at school by teaching them lessons about feelings (like they are doing today), planning events, talking to them if they have a problem, and helping everyone at school feel safe and happy.

Choral Reading

Slide 4: Explain the objectives for the presentation and why they are important. Have one student read the first objective and another student read the second, or ask the whole class to read each objective collectively. Explain that this is what the students will be learning today.

Objectives:

* We can explain what it means to feel angry and how anger affects our bodies.
* We can identify at least two ways to calm down when we are angry.
* We can write a letter to our family applying the information we learned about anger.

Tell the students that the objectives are aligned to the school counseling standards at the bottom of the slide.

Think-Ink-Pair-Share

Slide 5: Ask the students to think quietly about things that have made them feel angry. While they are thinking, ask two students to pass out a 3 × 5 card to each student. Tell the students they are going to write their name on the card and two to three things that make them feel angry. Explain the example on the PowerPoint (make sure to *model* what you'd like students to write on the card by updating the slide with your own name and developmentally appropriate examples of what makes you feel angry). Walk around and observe while students are writing, noticing any specific students you'd like to call on to share and any you'd want to avoid. After several minutes, regroup the class and ask for three to four students to share what makes them feel angry. After each student shares, ask the class to raise their hand if what the student said makes them angry, too. Ask one or two students to quietly and quickly collect all the cards and bring them up to you in the front as you proceed with the next slide.

Creating Pull Cards

Similar to Thumbs Up/Down

Slide 6: The school counselor may want to have different students read each bullet point, calling on the first student and asking the next student to "popcorn" to a new student. Expand on the bullet points, explaining that feeling angry is normal, just as in the examples shared with the class. Explain that anger is a normal emotion that everyone feels. However, if we overreact when we are upset by saying or doing things we don't mean, that is when we can get ourselves into trouble.

Popcorn Reading

Slide 7: Explain the different feelings that students may have to alert them when they are feeling angry. An arrow accompanied by different body signs will appear on the screen with each click (sweaty hands and body, tight muscles or clenched fists, heart racing, etc.). The school counselor may want to briefly act out some of descriptions, such as clenching his or her own fists and then asking students to clench theirs. Explain that different people feel differently when they are angry, and it is important to understand how your body feels because it's like a warning sign to remind you to calm down. If there is time, school counselors can ask students to share what happens to their body when they are angry with a partner.

Think-Pair-Share

(Continued)

Figure 5.12 (Continued)

Slide 8: Tell students that when we get angry, we feel it in our bodies, and if we don't calm down, we can stay upset. Take out the balloon and explain that it is like our body. Read one of the examples of being upset from the card (without reading the student's name), then puff into the balloon. Continue to do this until the balloon gets very large. Ask the students what will happen if you keep blowing. (Answer: The balloon will pop!) Explain that, yes, when we don't calm down, we can end up saying or doing something we don't mean.

Pull Cards

Slide 9: Randomly call on student names from the cards to read: (1) "Stop and think," (2) "Ask yourself, *How does my body feel?*" (3) "Try to calm down by . . ." and then each of the calm-down strategies. At each one, stop and practice.

- Taking slow, deep breaths: Demonstrate how to breathe in and out deeply, without gasping or puffing loudly. Practice with the class three times.

Practice Activity

- Thinking calming thoughts: Explain that thinking about a peaceful place or something that helps them feel happy can take their mind off what is making them upset. Give some examples (like being at the beach or laying on the couch). Ask students to close their eyes and picture a peaceful place.

- Counting backward slowly: Ask students which is more calming—counting quickly or slowly—and then ask why. Students will likely respond that counting slowly helps them relax; if not, help guide them to the answer, and then practice as a class.

Practice Activity

- Talking to yourself positively: Explain that sometimes when we get upset, the words in our head sound like this: "I'm so mad!"; "I can't believe he did that to me!"; or "She's so mean!" However, if we let those words go on and on in our head, we will get more angry instead of less. Instead, we can think things like, "I'm mad, but I'm going to calm down"; "I'm just going to ignore him"; and "I will get through this." Saying positive, calming words will help us feel less upset so that we don't say or do something that we don't mean.

Slide 10: Discuss the other "anger busters" listed on the slide, and talk about when students can or can't use different ways to calm down. For instance, when they are in class, they can't listen to music, but that is a strategy they can use at home. Ask students to list other ideas they have that help them calm down.

Ticket Out theDoor

Slide 11: Explain that students are going to write a letter to their family explaining what they have learned. While reading each question, pause for the class to fill in the underlined word (i.e., Counselor: "What did you . . ." [pause]; Students: "learn"?). As you are describing your example, ask two students to quietly pass out lined paper. If possible, turn on classical or other calm music while students are writing. Walk around the class to answer questions and support students as they are writing. If some students are finishing earlier than others, ask them to add other calm-down ideas to their letter and/or pass out Plickers for post-assessment.

Echo/Repeat Response

Slide 12: As students are finishing up, remind them that it is OK to feel angry and to practice different calm-down strategies until they find their favorites. Also ask students to read the letter with their family, and ask them to have an adult sign to show that he or she read the letter. When students bring back the signed letter, they will get a surprise from the school counselor (such as a pencil, five extra minutes of recess, or their name entered in a raffle), or this can be part of their homework as coordinated with their teacher.

Pull Cards

Slide 13: Finally, review the objectives with the students and call on students randomly using the cards to fill in the sentence frames ("Anger is _____," "Anger can affect our bodies by _____," etc.).

6

Classroom Management

Malik did not receive training in classroom management during his school counseling graduate program. Although he previously worked as a high school counselor, he is finding that while some classroom management strategies apply to younger students at his elementary school, the high energy and range of developmental levels of the students make teaching them much different. At times Malik struggles to get students' attention and to appropriately address off-task behavior. Additionally, several teachers have asked Malik for advice about ways to structure and manage their class, but Malik doesn't feel skilled enough to give them feedback.

Malik is not alone. According to a survey by the American School Counselor Association (ASCA), 74% of school counselors reported that they did not receive training in classroom management, and only 11% definitively stated that they did receive such training ("Classroom Management Skills," 2016). However, while the large majority have not received instruction in classroom management strategies, 82% report that teachers have asked them for help in this area ("Classroom Management Skills," 2016). This mismatch highlights the need for school counselors to be effectively trained in classroom management techniques for their own implementation of classroom lessons and to support others.

MANAGING CLASSROOMS

Teaching core curriculum classroom lessons provides school counselors with the opportunity to impact a large number of students simultaneously. Therefore,

Figure 6.1 ASCA School Counselor Classroom Management Survey

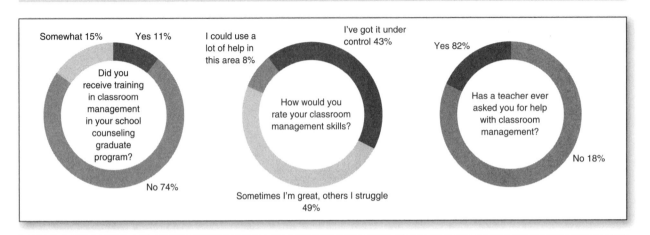

Source: ASCA School Counselor (2016). Classroom management skills: From chaos to calm, from inattentive to inspired 53(6).

utilizing classroom time effectively and efficiently is extremely important in order to maximize student learning. Proactive classroom management skills are correlated with positive school climate, improved student-teacher relationships, and high levels of achievement (Gettinger & Kohler, 2006; Mitchell & Bradshaw, 2013; Simonsen, Fairbanks, Briesch, Myers, & Sugai, 2008). Because school counselors don't have a consistent group of students for each lesson, they must be skilled in employing effective strategies to keep students focused and participating appropriately. In order to support the varying structures of different classes, school counselors will use flexibility within their management styles to adapt to the needs of the class, while consistently maintaining high expectations for all students. Students at the elementary level exhibit a broad developmental range, which requires that school counselors learn and apply different management techniques across a wide variety of ages and developmental levels to effectively support student success.

The classroom management strategies presented in this chapter are primarily focused on prevention, the key to effectiveness. Explicitly teaching and practicing behavior expectations during class lessons is an essential component of impeding off-task and other problem behaviors. The engagement strategies presented in the previous chapter support a well-managed classroom. Students who are involved in the learning during the entire lesson are less likely to demonstrate off-task behavior. Paired together, engaging lesson content and strong classroom management result in the ideal combination to produce a well-executed core curriculum lesson. Later in the chapter, strategies for ways to address minor, recurrent, or extreme problem behaviors are presented. Various approaches are also provided that school counselors can apply to appropriately and swiftly redirect and/or provide consequences to students.

PROACTIVE CLASSROOM MANAGEMENT

Explicitly Teach Expectations

Ensuring that all students understand and can perform to the school counselor's expectations is essential for successfully teaching core curriculum classroom lessons. When students are attending and participating appropriately, deeper learning occurs

(Evertson & Weinstein, 2013). Therefore, school counselors are advised to spend a fair amount of time explaining, practicing, and reinforcing procedures and routines during their first few classroom visits. The extra time spent initially will save time in the long run, as students will know what is expected when the school counselor is teaching.

Ideally, universal behavior expectations are already in place schoolwide. Common expectations aligning with schoolwide programs such as Positive Behavior Intervention and Supports (PBIS) often include three to four of the following:

- Be ready
- Be respectful
- Be safe
- Always do your best
- Be responsible
- Be a problem solver
- Care for others

When working at a school with universal behavior expectations, school counselors are advised to clearly explain what each expectation means in the context of their

Activity 6.1

Look at the behavior expectations in the column on the left side of this table. Notice the sections on the right that are filled in with explicit examples of what the school counselor will see and hear when students are following directions. In this table two behavior expectations—be ready and be respectful—are explicitly detailed as an example. Complete the table by filling in additional ideas for how school counselors can prompt students to provide specific examples of expectations for core curriculum lessons.

Behavior Expectation	What Will School Counselors See and Hear During Class Lessons?
Be ready	• Follow directions the first time they are given • Participate in the lesson • Raise your hand when you want to share an answer
Be respectful	• Quietly listen to the school counselor when he or she is talking • Keep your hands and feet to yourself • Politely listen to other students when they are sharing
Be safe	• •
Always do your best	• •
Be responsible	• •
Be a problem solver	• •
Care for others	• •

Figure 6.2 Good Listeners SLANT

Good Listeners SLANT

teaching. For instance, one example of being responsible might be turning in homework; however, if school counselors don't give homework, what does being responsible look like during a school counseling lesson? Students can brainstorm what the school counselor will see and hear when following each expectation, sharing specific examples with the class. Helping students process each of the expectations together, in a developmentally appropriate way, increases their understanding and therefore increases their compliance with the expectations.

If a school does not have universal expectations, elementary counselors generally have two options: (1) to create consistent expectations that the school counselor always uses with every class, or (2) to incorporate each teacher's expectations when visiting different classes. The first choice is recommended, because learning the variety of rules and procedures for each classroom is a lot to remember. Even if the school counselor's expectations are slightly different from a teacher's, students are generally able to code shift, especially when expectations are taught well and reinforced. School counselors may want to adopt three to four of the expectations listed previously as their universal school counseling expectations, or SLANT (discussed in the box that follows).

In addition, school counselors can still use components of teachers' classroom management systems. For example, if a teacher gives out "Scholar Dollars" for participating students or class points when all students are following directions, the school counselor can do the same when students are participating in ways that align with counselor expectations. If school counselors decide to incorporate each teacher's classroom rules (option two), they will want to work with teachers before the school year to clearly understand the expectations and consider how they will fit with core curriculum. This option is advised for school counselors with smaller caseloads and/or who visit classrooms frequently (weekly or every other week).

SLANT

The SLANT classroom management strategy has been shared by multiple educational leaders, including by Doug Lemov in *Teach Like a Champion 2.0* (2015; discussed in Chapter 4).

S: Sit up straight

L: Listen

A: Ask and answer questions

N: Nod your head

T: Track the speaker

Slightly different variations for each letter are available, but the intent of SLANT is the same—focusing students on learning. As is advised for all behavior expectations, explicitly teach students what each letter means. "Track the speaker" is likely a new phrase for students, so more depth may be needed when describing this expectation. Tracking the speaker means that students are looking at the speaker, whether it is the school counselor or a student called on to answer a question. As the counselor moves around the room, which is advised (see the section on circulating later in the chapter), students' heads follow as the counselor walks. When a student is sharing his or her response with the class, the other students' heads turn to the student speaker. Once these ideas are taught, school counselors can use this one word—SLANT—to remind students of all five behavior expectations.

Review Expectations Each Visit

Reminding students of the school counselor's classroom expectations at the beginning of each visit is a preventative strategy that helps set the tone for the lesson. Readers will recall that this was mentioned when discussing lesson plans in Chapter 4. While students may remember the expectations from the last visit, reviewing them upfront is much better than having to stop mid-lesson to attempt to redirect behavior after students are not following directions. After explicitly teaching and reviewing classroom norms during the first two visits, there are a variety of ways to quickly review procedures and expectations during subsequent visits:

- Provide a short opportunity for students to discuss what the counselor will hear when the class expectations are being followed, such as through Think-Pair-Share.
- Ask all students to read the expectations together out loud, then call on students randomly to share examples of each expectation.
- Remind students of the expectations, then positively praise students or the class as a whole for demonstrating the expectations. (Examples: "Our classroom expectation is to be respectful, and your entire class is showing me respect by listening quietly while I'm talking," or "Remember that we track the speaker, and I see Julissa and D. J. doing just that, as they are keeping their eyes on me while I walk around the room.")

Positive reinforcement increases the likelihood that students will follow directions, so school counselors are encouraged to recognize students or the class as a whole.

Reinforce Appropriate Behavior

Acknowledging students who are on-task and following directions is an effective strategy to maintain a positive classroom environment (Canter, 2010). Educational research suggests a ratio of five positive interactions (thanking students for staying on task, providing nonverbal acknowledgment for following directions, praising a correct answer, etc.) for every one negative interaction (redirecting misbehavior, disciplining a student, etc.) with the classroom. By maintaining a 5:1 ratio, school counselors develop positive relationships with their students, encouraging better behavior and decreasing classroom disruption.

Outward recognition of students who are following the school counselor's expectations signals to the class that the counselor is monitoring everyone's behavior and motivates students to follow directions and stay on task. Reinforcing appropriate behavior often corrects the behavior of students who are not following directions as well. This strategy is useful to incorporate throughout the lesson, to maintain positive energy and high expectations. Suggestions on how to reinforce behavior include the following:

- Positively acknowledge the behavior immediately after it takes place.
- Specifically state the behavior you are acknowledging.
- Use a positive, sincere tone of voice.
- Acknowledge effort and improved behaviors.
- Vary the positive reinforcement provided to individual students and the class.

In some cases, school counselors may want to use incentives to reinforce positive behavior. Counselors can build on what teachers are already doing, such as assigning table or ClassDojo points (see the ClassDojo box later in the chapter for more details), adding marbles to a jar, or moving students' clips/color cards to a more positive state. School counselors can also create their own special incentives, such as giving stickers to students with exemplary behavior, creating class raffles, or coordinating special activities. See the following story from school counselor Ashley Kruger about how she uses GoNoodle when the class is following directions and participating during core curriculum lessons.

GoNoodle

One tool that I often use as an incentive for students to follow expectations and participate during core curriculum lessons is GoNoodle. GoNoodle is a free online program that incorporates movement and mindfulness through songs, dancing, and guided mindfulness activities. Students absolutely love this reward, as it gives them the opportunity to move around, have fun, and celebrate one another for being respectful, responsible, and safe learners. At the end of my core curriculum lessons, I always ask students to raise their hands if they think they worked together as a team to follow expectations. This gives students the opportunity to reflect on their behavior and engagement throughout the lesson, and they are usually very honest and self-aware! Using this incentive also encourages students to support other students who may be having difficulty following expectations. Since introducing this program at my school, many teachers now use these activities as "brain breaks" throughout the day as well.

—Ashley Kruger

Effectively Manage Transitions

Effectively and efficiently coordinating the shift from one activity to another takes practice and well-honed skills. Although elementary school counselors generally teach for no more than 20 to 40 minutes at a time, transitions within lessons still occur, such as shifting from partner sharing to whole-group discussion, taking out coloring supplies for an activity, or standing up to sing a song and then moving back to sitting. Minimizing transition time reduces disruption and increases the efficiency of classroom lesson instruction.

Providing clear, explicit, step-by-step directions for transitions before they take place ensures that students understand what is expected. If the directions are multi-step, ask students to repeat them out loud: "First we will _____," and "Then we will _____." Remember to consider students' developmental level when giving instructions; younger students can remember only one to two steps at a time, while older students can generally process more. The school counselor may also want to model what the students will be doing to show an example of what is expected (see the section on modeling in Chapter 4, page 76).

Attention Getters

School counselors skilled in effective transitioning are able to quickly regain students' attention at the beginning of a lesson or when regrouping the class. *Attention getters* are strategies often used to refocus all students in a fun and impactful manner, for example:

School Counselor: "Class, class!"

Students: "Yes, yes!"

Figure 6.3 lists more attention getters used by school counselors to call out a word or phrase, allowing the students to respond with a different phrase and to stop talking. Remember to practice and remind students how they will be called back together *before* starting an activity or partner discussion.

Figure 6.3   Attention Getters

ATTENTION GETTERS

SCHOOL COUNSELOR	STUDENT
Ready set...	...You bet!
Hocus pocus...	...Everybody focus!
Holy moly...	...Guacamole!
Macaroni and cheese...	...Everybody freeze!
1, 2, 3, eyes on me...	...1, 2, eyes on you!
To infinity...	...And beyond!
Zip, zip, zat...	...We're all that!
Ready to rock...	...Ready to roll!
All set...	...You bet!
Flat tire...	...Shhhhh!
Are you focused?	...Yes, I am!
Hand on top...	...That means stop!
Tootsie roll, lollipop...	...We've been talking, now let's stop!

The school counselor can also instruct students to quiet down without a verbal response by using the following prompts:

School Counselor:	"Finish up in 5, 4, 3, 2, 1."
School Counselor:	"If you can hear me, clap once."
Students:	[Clap]
School Counselor:	"If you can hear me, clap twice."
Students:	[Clap, clap]
School Counselor:	"If you can hear me, clap three times."
Students:	[Clap, clap, clap]
School Counselor:	[Silently raises hand into the air]
Students:	[As they see the counselor's hand, students stop talking and raise their own hands]

Countdown Timer

Displaying a *countdown timer* is another way to manage transitions by preparing the class for the transition to come. When students are working in groups or participating in an activity, countdown timers can be included in PowerPoint presentations (you can google "countdown timer" to find step-by-step instructions on how to do this), displayed through YouTube (check this out on YouTube.com), and Google itself offers a timer (see Figure 6.4). School counselors can also give several verbal warnings to cue students, such as warnings at 5 minutes, 2 minutes, 30 seconds, and so on.

School counselors are encouraged to positively reinforce the class after all students quickly refocus their attention. If all students do not respond, practice again

Figure 6.4 Example Timer From Google

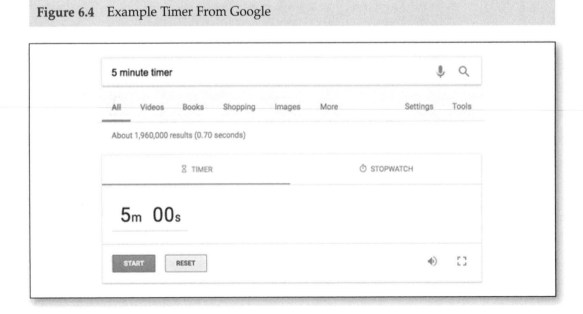

until you receive full-class participation. This holds students to high expectations and also sets the tone for full-class compliance next time. Positive reinforcement for all transitions is suggested to recognize and appreciate the class for following directions. Remember to be specific in praise—for example, "Thank you for quickly and quietly coming to the carpet," or "I appreciate how you all just stopped what you were doing and turned your attention toward me."

Differentiating Instruction

Differentiating instruction is another strategy that ensures that students at various developmental levels and with different learning abilities can access the curriculum based on their needs. Additionally, differentiating the curriculum also provides students with activities to keep them engaged and to prevent unstructured time for those who finish faster than others (which can lead to misbehavior). Whether students are taking a pre- or post-test, working on an activity, or completing a ticket out the door, they are likely to finish at different rates. School counselors can anticipate and plan for this with the following strategies:

- After students finish a pre-test, ask them to write down all the things they know about the lesson topic.
- Between activities, ask students to begin thinking about a question related to the lesson.
- If some students have finished a response to a question ahead of others, ask them to add additional answers or examples.
- When students finish an activity, ask them to help a neighbor or share their activity with another student who has finished.
- As students are completing a ticket out the door, ask several who have finished first to pick up the tickets of others and the additional students to take out a silent reading book (or transition to the next activity they will begin as the school counselor leaves the classroom).

Proactive Classroom Management in Action

Mr. Rivas was teaching a lesson on problem solving, and student groups were creating a role-play of how to respond to various scenarios using the skills they had learned. Prior to breaking into the activity, Mr. Rivas informed the students that they had 10 minutes to practice and be ready to share their role-play with the class. He also displayed a 10-minute timer for everyone to see while they were working. While students were practicing, Mr. Rivas circulated the classroom to answer questions, give suggestions, and ensure that groups were on task. When one group finished early, he asked them to think of another way they could solve the problem, so that they would have two different ways to act out the scenario. When the 10 minutes was up, Mr. Rivas used an attention getter to refocus the group. Because the class was in Ohio, the students were trained to respond to "O-H" by saying "I-O." Mr. Rivas yelled "O-H" at the end of the activity, and all the students responded with "I-O" before becoming quiet. After the class quieted down, signaling to Mr. Rivas that he had their attention, he thanked them for staying on task during the group time and reminded the class of the expectations as they watched one another's role-plays.

Student Leaders

Incorporating *student leaders* is another strategy for efficient transitioning. A school counselor can spend several minutes passing out papers, which is a loss of those instructional minutes. Instead, ask students to perform the task while the school counselor proceeds with the lesson content. Multiple students helping can also get the job completed faster. In addition, school counselors can be strategic about utilizing students who may benefit from movement and/or from being helpers.

School counselors can also intentionally minimize their own time spent transitioning between one activity and another, reducing unstructured time for students (which thereby can reduce misbehavior). For example:

- The school counselor can come into the classroom early to set up for the lesson while the teacher is wrapping up his or her instruction, so that the counselor is ready to begin at the appropriate time.
- Rather than allowing 30 seconds of silence while loading a video on the computer, the school counselor can fill that time by asking students to silently think about a question and/or tell a partner what they know about the topic being discussed.
- The counselor can ask a student to pass out materials for an activity, rather than stopping instruction to give out the items.
- School counselors can begin setting up for the next activity or discussion while students are finishing up their current activity.

Seating Arrangements

Although school counselors don't structure class seating, understanding various seating arrangements is helpful for effectively teaching different types of lessons. For some lessons, such as reading and discussing a book with primary students, the school counselor may want students to sit on the floor. In other situations, such as when students need to use supplies from their desk for an activity, sitting in their seats is preferable. Considering the classroom structure prior to entering the class, and communicating the desired formation with the teacher in advance, can reduce the time needed to make these changes to maximize success. If a major room change is needed, such as for a group activity, the school counselor will likely want to discuss this with the teacher beforehand and arrive to the classroom early.

As school counselors learn the personalities and dynamics of individual students and groups, they may want to make modifications to seating during counseling lessons. For instance:

- A third-grade teacher seats a talkative student alone while other students are in groups; however, Think-Pair-Share is incorporated into many counselor lessons. The school counselor finds a suitable partner for the solo student to sit with during counseling lessons, with the agreement that the student will appropriately participate in the lesson.
- The school counselor is reading a story to a second-grade class while students sit on the carpet. Two students in the back are poking the students in front of them, so the counselor politely asks them to move up front.

- During the last several classroom lessons, the school counselor has noticed that two students are off topic during partner activities. Before the lesson starts, the counselor quietly asks one of the off-task students and another student who is generally on topic to switch seats.

As a school counseling trainee, Ashley Hansen from Ohio State University asked the class to make name tags prior to beginning teaching. During the classroom lesson, she observed which students worked well together and who would benefit from sitting apart. In the following class lesson, Ashley placed their name tags strategically so that the students had to sit where their name tags were placed. This created an environment for students to sit by new students and not by their peers who would be distracting. Overall, Ashley found that the seat changes allowed for a better classroom lesson, and the students were active participants the whole time.

Circulate the Classroom

Moving around the classroom while teaching is an effective strategy for keeping students focused, as proximity stresses accountability. Students are more likely to be on task when they think their teacher—or, in this case, their school counselor—is watching them. Therefore, circulating while teaching both holds students' attention and refocuses the beginning of off-task behaviors. While moving around the room, the school counselor can subtly redirect students while still leading instruction by pointing to a guided notes sheet that isn't filled in, putting a hand on the shoulder of a student who is talking to a neighbor, or making eye contact with an off-task student and quickly shaking his or her head. Counselors should remember to teach students to follow the counselor with their gaze as the counselor moves around the room (which is called "tracking the speaker"; see the SLANT box earlier in the chapter).

Tip: School counselors who frequently use PowerPoint or Google Slides presentations can invest in a clicker to advance their slides. This allows school counselors the flexibility to walk around the room, rather than be tethered to their computer. School counselors can also ask a student to be the technology leader by helping move from one slide to the next. The student can sit by the computer and advance slides when cued. This is a great strategy for a student who sometimes loses focus, as this role alerts his or her attention to what is coming next.

HOW TO HANDLE STUDENTS WHO ARE OFF TASK OR MISBEHAVING

While school counselors can implement all the strategies previously listed and incorporate active participation into their lessons, they still might encounter an off-task or misbehaving student. Not to be confused with school counselors administering discipline, effectively addressing problem behavior in the class is essential to facilitating a successful lesson in which students participate appropriately. Mastering strategies to apply when swift intervention is needed, in an effective and respectful way, is an essential component of being a successful school counselor.

Culturally Responsive Classroom Management

As school counselors incorporate classroom management strategies while teaching core curriculum lessons, understanding and appropriately responding to diverse student behaviors is important. General school expectations in the United States incorporate Western, White, middle-class practices (Weinstein, Curran, & Tomlinson-Clarke, 2003), which may or may not reflect students' cultural norms. The high proportion of disciplinary action received by Latino and African American boys in school (U.S. Department of Education Office for Civil Rights, 2014) is one example of why school counselors should be mindful of their own unintentional biases and learn about students' cultural backgrounds, which may impact their behavior. Particularly at the elementary school level, when young students are adapting to the school system and possibly code shifting between expectations in their classroom that may differ from those in their home, school counselors can recognize and modify classroom management strategies to fit diverse student populations.

Adapted from Weinstein, Curran, and Tomlinson-Clarke's article "Culturally Responsive Classroom Management: Awareness into Action" (2003), the following strategies help integrate culturally responsive practices into classroom management during core curriculum counseling lessons:

- *Creating caring, inclusive classrooms:* Regardless of the cultural makeup of the classroom, a goal of school counselors when teaching core curriculum lessons is to create a safe and supportive learning environment. This is especially essential for counseling lessons, because the topics may address sensitive items, such as students sharing their feelings, discussing drugs or alcohol or bullying, and sharing hopes and dreams for the future. Setting expectations for both respect and inclusion, while also incorporating diversity into classroom lessons, helps all students feel safe, welcome, and valued. By incorporating multicultural examples and diverse content into lessons, as well as acknowledging and praising differences (such as complimenting English language learners for speaking two languages), school counselors help all students feel valued.
- *Establishing clear behavior expectations:* Clearly defined and consistently reinforced behavior expectations ensure that all students understand what is expected, which is particularly important in diverse classrooms. Different cultures view and value behaviors differently—in some cultures, students engage more interactively, such as by calling out answers without raising their hands; in other cultures, students show respect to teachers by not making eye contact. Both of these examples could be unintentionally viewed as incorrect participation, so explicitly teaching and explaining the purpose behind expectations provides clarity and prevents confusion. Additionally, understanding, respecting, and accommodating for variations in student behavior based on culture is also important.
- *Communicating with students in culturally consistent ways:* Addressing students' multicultural needs includes understanding and responding to a variety of ways in which communication is expressed and understood in different cultures. For instance, in some cultures, asking questions to authority figures is a sign of disrespect; in other cultures, straightforward directives are more clearly understood than passive strategies (e.g., "Please sit down" versus "Can you sit down for me?"). In addition, cultural differences apply to tone of voice and body language. Therefore, school counselors' understanding of their school population and adapting their communication styles to meet diverse student needs can impact student behaviors.
- *Applying multicultural awareness when addressing misbehavior:* To approach classroom management from a culturally responsive framework, school counselors are advised to

reflect on the types of behaviors they interpret as off task or problematic, considering how students' diverse backgrounds may play a role. Providing an example, Weinstein et al. (2003) explained that Black children may be more likely than White children to jump into activities without waiting their turn or to challenge school authority figures, which may be interpreted as disruptive or rude. However, if these behaviors can be reframed as signaling excitement and passion, school counselors can identify students' strengths and focus them appropriately within the classroom setting prior to implementing punishment. School counselors can appropriately modify their expectations to meet the diverse needs of the classroom, while also helping students understand the school system and act accordingly. Additionally, considering race, ethnicity, and gender within the framework of disciplinary actions can reduce inequities in the numbers of students who receive punishment.

Managing problem student behaviors can generate fight-or-flight reactions in any educator, including school counselors, and parents, too (Gesek, n.d.). In *fight* mode, a counselor might want to argue or yell at a student, and in *flight* mode, the counselor may escape the problem by ignoring it. While both responses stem from basic instincts, neither is an effective strategy for addressing and changing the problem. The following sections present multiple strategies for the elementary school counselor to consider using while remaining calm and positive. As a reminder, if several students are off task or misbehaving during a lesson, school counselors are encouraged to revisit and practice expectations with the entire class.

Proximity

Just as circulating the classroom can prevent off-task behavior, moving into close proximity to the off-task student often corrects the behavior. The school counselor can continue teaching while also putting his or her hand on the student's desk or shoulder or shaking his or her head, which generally redirects the behavior. If needed, the school counselor can quietly remind the student of the expectations, which is less obstructive than saying the same thing loudly across the room.

Quickly and Positively Redirecting Misbehavior Early On

Many types of off-task behaviors quickly change when they are immediately and effectively addressed. Predictable and consistent redirection, before the off-task behavior escalates, prevents the need for further discipline. School counselors are advised to remain calm, use a positive tone of voice, and talk to the student privately if possible. The school counselor may incorporate an engagement strategy into their lesson, such as Think-Pair-Share, or ask the class to think silently about a question while the counselor addresses the student who is misbehaving.

Students may tune out when long directions are given, so brevity and specificity are recommended. Consider using sentence starters such as "Please ____" and "I need you to ____," followed by the specific direction. For example:

- "Please start working on the activity."
- "I need you to stop talking to your neighbor."
- "Remember to raise your hand before answering."

After the direction, allow the student a minute to self-correct, then demonstrate follow-through. When the student modifies his or her behavior, the school counselor can positively reinforce the change with a nod or smile toward the student, or quietly say, "Thank you," to show that the counselor has noticed the change. This simple acknowledgment recognizes the student for his or her correction but does not distract from the lesson. If the student continues with the behavior, provide another specific reminder and watch for follow-through before taking further action (such as assigning consequences or having problem-solving conversations, as explained in the next two sections).

Assigning Appropriate Consequences Within the Classroom Setting

If consequences are necessary, make them short and to the point. For instance:

- Politely and quickly ask a student who is touching her neighbor after multiple warnings to move her seat next to you.
- Walk over to a student who is continually fidgeting with toys in his desk and put your hand out to signal that you will take and hold onto the toys until the end of the day.
- Calmly ask a student who has been reminded multiple times to stay in her seat to please sit in her seat with her head down for 3 minutes to calm down.
- Ask a student to apologize to his classmate after grabbing a pencil out of her hand.
- If appropriate and known, utilize a strategy from the classroom teacher's behavior management system, such as asking the student to move his or her name to "warning" on the behavior board, writing down the student's name to miss 5 minutes of recess, or earning a negative ClassDojo point (see the ClassDojo box later in the chapter for more details).

Remember to not argue with students but instead wait patiently until they follow through with your directions. Generally, when students are given time to calm down, they adhere to any consequences given. If school counselors are struggling with a particularly difficult student, they can also seek out the classroom teacher for support.

A Problem-Solving Conversation in Action

Third-grade student Jenny was playing with her bracelets and talking to her neighbor during the school counseling lesson. The school counselor first redirected Jenny's attention by asking her to read out loud. When Jenny was distracted again, the counselor moved in Jenny's direction while continuing to present, and quietly put out his hand to collect her bracelets. After the lesson, the school counselor asks to speak with Jenny:

School Counselor: Hi Jenny! I'm glad we're getting to talk today, because I really like coming into your class and teaching you and your classmates. You are usually focused and participating, but today was different. Can you tell me what I saw?

Jenny: I was talking to Carmen.

School Counselor: I did see you talking to Carmen. What else did I see?

Jenny: I was playing with my new bracelets.

School Counselor: Yes. Those are really nice bracelets, but I could see they were distracting you. What are some of the reasons you think I wanted you to pay attention?

Jenny: You want me to learn.

School Counselor: I do want you to learn, because I care about you, Jenny! Do you think you're able to learn as much if you're talking or playing?

Jenny: No.

School Counselor: I don't think so, either. So what can you do next time, and what can I do to help you?

Jenny: Not talk and play around.

School Counselor: I think not talking and focusing are great ideas for the next time I come into your class. Do you think those are also good ideas for when I'm not in your class?

Jenny: Yes.

School Counselor: How come?

Jenny: So I can learn from my teacher, too.

School Counselor: Your teacher and I care about you, and we want to help you learn and grow. Is there anything your teacher or I can do to help you?

Jenny: I don't think so.

School Counselor: How about we find a place to put these bracelets so that you don't get distracted?

Jenny: I'll put them in my backpack.

School Counselor: That's a great idea! I'll let your teacher know that we had a really good talk and that you are going to focus really hard and keep your bracelets in your bag.

Jenny: OK.

School Counselor: I'm really glad we talked out this problem, Jenny, and I'm looking forward to seeing how on task you will be the next time I come into your class.

Jenny: Thanks, Mr. T!

Individual (or Small-Group) Problem-Solving Conversations

If a student (or two) is misbehaving during a classroom lesson, the school counselor is advised to talk with the student about the observed actions after the lesson concludes. Remaining positive and supportive, the school counselor can ask the student about the observed behaviors and problem solve ways to improve next time. By brainstorming alternatives to the inappropriate behaviors, school counselors reteach students what is expected (see the previous box for an example). Additionally, because school counselors teach in classrooms only periodically, prior to the start of the next lesson, the counselor may want to privately and encouragingly remind the student who was off task during the last lesson about the previously made agreement to be on task.

Employing effective classroom management skills ensures that the entire class is engaged and on task during core curriculum lessons. Although many school counselors do not have training in this area, through practicing the strategies discussed in this chapter, they will likely see improved classroom behavior as students are following directions and staying on task. Through a strong preventative approach, coupled with swiftly and effectively managing off-task behaviors, school counselors will foster engaged and efficient classrooms during their lessons.

ClassDojo

ClassDojo is a classroom communication app used in many K–8 schools in the United States and in 180 additional countries (Harris, 2016). Educators create free accounts, adding all their students, and each child gets a profile and can modify his or her own avatar. ClassDojo replaces old forms of classroom management, letting teachers (and school counselors) give students positive feedback for skills such as "helping others" or "having a growth mindset." Teachers (and counselors) can share this feedback and other important moments with parents to keep them in the loop. When teaching classroom lessons, school counselors can utilize teachers' ClassDojo accounts to reinforce the on-task and collaborative behavior they observe by awarding points to individual students, groups, or even the whole class. They can also take and share photos or videos with parents through ClassDojo to demonstrate student learning of core curriculum and other exciting moments. School counselors who visit classrooms regularly can set up and use their own ClassDojo accounts (especially if a particular teacher does not have one set up). Go to http://www.classdojo.com for more information.

School counselors create detailed lesson plans, teach using a variety of engagement strategies, utilize effective classroom management strategies, and analyze data to evaluate their lessons. The School Counseling Core Curriculum Lesson Feedback Tool shown in Figure 6.6 was designed to help counselors assess and increase their skills in teaching, as they self-evaluate and/or ask others for feedback to improve their practices.

Figure 6.5 Chapter 4 Lesson Plan Highlighting Classroom Management Strategies

6. Procedure:

Slide 1: Welcome students to the class and share the lesson title ("Don't Blow Your Top!").

Slide 2: Ask all students to read the school's behavior expectations out loud together (be ready; be respectful; be responsible). Ask students to silently *think* what the school counselor will see and what he or she will hear when students are following these expectations in the class. After allowing 10 to 15 seconds of think time, ask students to *pair* with a neighbor and tell the partner what they thought about. After 2 to 3 minutes of discussion, call on students who are demonstrating the expectations to *share*, and also praise the students specifically for their on-task behavior (raising their hand, looking at the speaker, etc.).

Slide 3: Remind students about the members of the school counseling department, including their counselor and any other counseling staff. Tell students that the counselor's job is to help students have fun at school by teaching them lessons about feelings (like they are doing today), planning events, talking to them if they have a problem, and helping everyone at school feel safe and happy.

Slide 4: Explain the objectives for the presentation and why they are important. Have one student read the first objective and another student read the second, or ask the whole class to read each objective collectively. Explain that this is what the students will be learning today.

Objectives:

- We can explain what it means to feel angry and how anger affects our bodies.
- We can identify at least two ways to calm down when we are angry.
- We can write a letter to our family applying the information we learned about anger.

Tell the students that the objectives are aligned to the school counseling standards at the bottom of the slide.

Slide 5: Ask the students to think quietly about things that have made them feel angry. While they are thinking, ask two students to pass out a 3 × 5 card to each student. Tell the students they are going to write their name on the card and two to three things that make them feel angry. Explain the example on the PowerPoint (make sure to *model* what you'd like students to write on the card by updating the slide with your own name and developmentally appropriate examples of what makes you feel angry). Walk around and observe while students are writing, noticing any specific students you'd like to call on to share and any you'd want to avoid. After several minutes, regroup the class and ask for three to four students to share what makes them feel angry. After each student shares, ask the class to raise their hand if what the student said makes them angry, too. Ask one or two students to quietly and quickly collect all the cards and bring them up to you in the front as you proceed with the next slide.

Slide 6: The school counselor may want to have different students read each bullet point, calling on the first student and asking the next student to "popcorn" to a new student. Expand on the bullet points, explaining that feeling angry is normal, just as in the examples shared with the class. Explain that anger is a normal emotion that everyone feels. However, if we overreact when we are upset by saying or doing things we don't mean, that is when we can get ourselves into trouble.

Slide 7: Explain the different feelings that students may have to alert them when they are feeling angry. An arrow accompanied by different body signs will appear on the screen with each click (sweaty hands and body, tight muscles or clenched fists, heart racing, etc.). The school counselor may want to briefly act out some of descriptions, such as clenching his or her own fists and then asking students to clench theirs. Explain that different people feel differently when they are angry, and it is important to understand how your body feels because it's like a warning sign to remind you to calm down. If there is time, school counselors can ask students to share what happens to their body when they are angry with a partner.

Sidebar callouts (right margin):

Explicitly Teach/Review Expectations

What Will the Counselor SEE and HEAR?

Reinforcing Appropriate Behavior

Effectively Manage Transitions (Student Leaders)

Circulate

Attention Getter

Clear Directions

Effectively Manage Transitions (Student Leaders)

Incorporating Activities and Engagement Strategies Into Lessons Is a Form of Proactive Classroom Management

(Continued)

Figure 6.5   (Continued)

Slide 8: Tell students that when we get angry, we feel it in our bodies, and if we don't calm down, we can stay upset. Take out the balloon and explain that it is like our body. Read one of the examples of being upset from the card (without reading the student's name), then puff into the balloon. Continue to do this until the balloon gets very large. Ask the students what will happen if you keep blowing. (Answer: The balloon will pop!) Explain that, yes, when we don't calm down, we can end up saying or doing something we don't mean.

Slide 9: Randomly call on student names from the cards to read: (1) "Stop and think," (2) "Ask yourself, *How does my body feel?*" (3) "Try to calm down by . . ." and then each of the calm-down strategies. At each one, stop and practice.

> Incorporating Activities and Engagement Strategies Into Lessons Is a Form of Proactive Classroom Management

- Taking slow, deep breaths: Demonstrate how to breathe in and out deeply, without gasping or puffing loudly. Practice with the class three times.

- Thinking calming thoughts: Explain that thinking about a peaceful place or something that helps them feel happy can take their mind off what is making them upset. Give some examples (like being at the beach or laying on the couch). Ask students to close their eyes and picture a peaceful place.

- Counting backward slowly: Ask students which is more calming—counting quickly or slowly—and then ask why. Students will likely respond that counting slowly helps them relax; if not, help guide them to the answer, and then practice as a class.

- Talking to yourself positively: Explain that sometimes when we get upset, the words in our head sound like this: "I'm so mad!"; "I can't believe he did that to me!"; or "She's so mean!" However, if we let those words go on and on in our head, we will get more angry instead of less. Instead, we can think things like, "I'm mad, but I'm going to calm down"; "I'm just going to ignore him"; and "I will get through this." Saying positive, calming words will help us feel less upset so that we don't say or do something that we don't mean.

Slide 10: Discuss the other "anger busters" listed on the slide, and talk about when students can or can't use different ways to calm down. For instance, when they are in class, they can't listen to music, but that is a strategy they can use at home. Ask students to list other ideas they have that help them calm down.

Slide 11: Explain that students are going to write a letter to their family explaining what they have learned. While reading each question, pause for the class to fill in the underlined word (i.e., Counselor: "What did you . . ." [pause]; Students: "learn"?). As you are describing your example, ask two students to quietly pass out lined paper. If possible, turn on classical or other calm music while students are writing. Walk around the class to answer questions and support students as they are writing. If some students are finishing earlier than others, ask them to add other calm-down ideas to their letter and/or pass out Plickers for post-assessment.

> Effectively Manage Transitions (Student Leaders)

> Circulate

Slide 12: As students are finishing up, remind them that it is OK to feel angry and to practice different calm-down strategies until they find their favorites. Also ask students to read the letter with their family, and ask them to have an adult sign to show that he or she read the letter. When students bring back the signed letter, they will get a surprise from the school counselor (such as a pencil, five extra minutes of recess, or their name entered in a raffle), or this can be part of their homework as coordinated with their teacher.

> Differentiate Instruction/ Student Leaders

Slide 13: Finally, review the objectives with the students and call on students randomly using the cards to fill in the sentence frames ("Anger is _____," "Anger can affect our bodies by _____," etc.).

> Incorporating Incentives and Collaborating With Teacher

Figure 6.6 School Counseling Core Curriculum Lesson Feedback Tool

School Counseling Core Curriculum Lesson Feedback Tool

One aspect of school counseling program delivery is teaching core curriculum classroom lessons. School counselors can use this feedback tool to help them evaluate their teaching strategies. You can use this tool for self-reflection and/or to receive feedback from a teacher, fellow school counselor, or administrator. The intention is to learn and improve your teaching practices. Please note that perfection is not necessary and also not likely...everyone is learning and improving! Responses reflecting future growth are highly encouraged.

Name: _____ **Date:** _____

Lesson Topic: _____ **Grade Level:** _____

Standards and Objectives

Standards/lesson objectives are clearly explained to students, referenced throughout the lesson, and referred back to at the end of the lesson.

5	**4**	**3**	**2**	**1**
Outstanding		Adequate		Weak

REASONS:

Lesson topic is relevant and meaningful, connecting with students' academic, college and career, and/or social/emotional needs, interests, and concerns.

5	**4**	**3**	**2**	**1**
Outstanding		Adequate		Weak

REASONS:

Standards addressed in lesson are developmentally appropriate and are reasonable to learn within the classroom presentation time (not too few, not too many).

5	**4**	**3**	**2**	**1**
Outstanding		Adequate		Weak

REASONS:

Lesson Structure and Sequence

Lesson is organized and proceeds in a sequential, logical order.

5	**4**	**3**	**2**	**1**
Outstanding		Adequate		Weak

REASONS:

Created by Danielle Duarte with support of Direct Interactive Instruction Materials

(Continued)

Figure 6.6   (Continued)

Prior knowledge is accessed and built upon during the lesson.

5	**4**	**3**	**2**	**1**
Outstanding		Adequate		Weak

REASONS:

School counselor checks for understanding throughout the lesson.

5	**4**	**3**	**2**	**1**
Outstanding		Adequate		Weak

REASONS:

Students demonstrate their learning at the end of the lesson.

5	**4**	**3**	**2**	**1**
Outstanding		Adequate		Weak

REASONS:

Delivery and Student Engagement

School counselor engages the entire class in the lesson through discussions and activities.

5	**4**	**3**	**2**	**1**
Outstanding		Adequate		Weak

REASONS:

School counselor appropriately incorporates a variety of interaction strategies throughout the lesson, both covert and overt (such as think-ink-pair-share, choral reading, random response cards, anticipatory sets of questions, choral response, etc.).

5	**4**	**3**	**2**	**1**
Outstanding		Adequate		Weak

REASONS:

Lesson delivery is clear, as the school counselor speaks audibly, maintains positivity, makes eye contact with students, etc.

5	**4**	**3**	**2**	**1**
Outstanding		Adequate		Weak

REASONS:

Created by Danielle Duarte with support of Direct Interactive Instruction Materials

Proactive Classroom Management

Behavior expectations are clearly explained and routines to maximize learning time are established.

5	4	3	2	1
Outstanding		Adequate		Weak

REASONS:

School counselor quickly and positively refocuses off-task behavior with minimal disruption to the entire class.

5	4	3	2	1
Outstanding		Adequate		Weak

REASONS:

Lesson maintains momentum as the school counselor moves around the room, alerts students for what will happen next, and smoothly transitions from one activity to another.

5	4	3	2	1
Outstanding		Adequate		Weak

REASONS:

Additional Sections (as Appropriate)

Lesson was developed based on developmental standards and/or data-driven need.

5	4	3	2	1
Outstanding		Adequate		Weak

REASONS:

The pre- and post-assessment are clearly written and effectively administered.

5	4	3	2	1
Outstanding		Adequate		Weak

REASONS:

Technology facilitates active participation and engagement practices (if available).

5	4	3	2	1
Outstanding		Adequate		Weak

REASONS:

Created by Danielle Duarte with support of Direct Interactive Instruction Materials

7

Schoolwide Programs and Activities

Tier 1 initiatives led by school counselors for all students at the elementary level include delivery of core curriculum and districtwide/schoolwide programs and activities. In this chapter, we will discuss the school counselor's role in schoolwide activities and how, when appropriate, to align them to core curriculum and parent education.

WHAT ARE SCHOOLWIDE ACTIVITIES?

While classroom lessons are a large component of Tier 1 services, school counselors also play a role in implementing districtwide/schoolwide activities aligned with the three school counseling domains—academic, college/career, social/emotional—within MTMDSS. Note how in the MTMDSS pyramid shown in Figure 7.1, districtwide/schoolwide activities are indicated in all domain areas within Tier 1. Figure 7.2 displays the pyramid with some examples of activities an elementary counselor may participate in or lead at his or her site within each domain area and the additional tiers, although those are not covered here. Table 7.1 provides additional examples. Throughout this chapter, multiple examples will be shared—some briefly and others in greater detail. Extensive support materials are also provided in the online appendix.

Figure 7.1 Multi-Tiered, Multi-Domain System of Supports (MTMDSS)

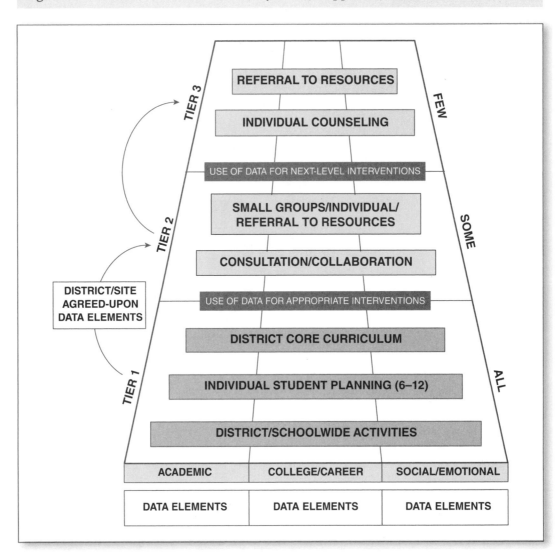

Table 7.1 Examples of District Schoolwide Programs and Activities by Domain

Academic	College/Career	Social/Emotional
• Transition Programs: Pre-K → K and Elementary → Middle • Attendance • New Student Welcome Programs	• Career Fairs and College and Career Day/Week • College Field Trips • Junior Achievement and BizTown • College Signing Day (K–5)	• Schoolwide Expectations, PBIS, and Positive Incentives • Conflict Resolution Programs • Red Ribbon Week (Drug/ Alcohol-Free) Activities • Great Kindness Challenge • Character Education

Figure 7.2 Sample MTMDSS at the Elementary Level

MULTI-TIERED, MULTI-DOMAIN
SYSTEM OF SUPPORTS (MTMDSS) EXAMPLE

TIER 3

FEW

Referral to Resources

Individual Counseling

- Crisis

DISTRICT/SITE AGREED-UPON DATA ELEMENTS
- Report Card (Study Habits)
- Homework Completion

USE OF DATA FOR NEXT LEVEL INTERVENTIONS

TIER 2

Small Groups

- Work Skills
- Study Habits

- Anger Management
- Conflict Resolution
- Impulse Control

SOME

DISTRICT/SITE AGREED-UPON DATA ELEMENTS
- Attendance
- Discipline Referrals
- Report Card (Citizenship)

USE OF DATA FOR APPROPRIATE INTERVENTIONS

District Core Curriculum (K–5)

- Organization Skills
- Study Skills
- Responsibility

- Career Development
- College Knowledge

- Second Step
- Boys Town Social Skills
- Conflict Resolution

TIER 1

ALL

District/Schoolwide Programs and Activities

- Transition to Middle School
- College and Career Day
- Peace Patrol/Playground

ACADEMIC	COLLEGE/CAREER	SOCIAL/EMOTIONAL
DATA ELEMENTS • Academic Testing/ Assessments	**DATA ELEMENTS** • College-Going Rates	**DATA ELEMENTS** • Healthy Kids/School Climate Survey

DISTRICTWIDE/SCHOOLWIDE PROGRAMS AND ACTIVITIES

Within this chapter, the samples and examples presented align with the three school counseling domains. Some are schoolwide *programs*, while others are *activities*. Depending on factors such as the ratio of students to school counselor, areas of expertise, and the amount of support provided for serving in a leadership capacity, the school counselor's role may vary from directing the entire activity, such as the Great Kindness Challenge, to being an integral part of a schoolwide program, such as Positive Behavior Intervention and Supports (PBIS).

Figure 7.3 Example of Alignment Between Schoolwide Activities and Core Curriculum Action Plan

School Spirit Days Friday Assembly	5	Second Step Unit 1 Empathy & Skills for Learning (4 lessons)	Social/Emotional M 3, B-LS 4, B-SMS 10, B-SS 1, B-SS 5	Second Step Violence Prevention Program	September – December
		Second Step Unit 2 Emotion Management (7 lessons)	Social/Emotional B-SMS 1, B-SMS 2, B-SMS 6	Second Step Violence Prevention Program	January – March
		Second Step Unit 3 Problem Solving (7 lessons)	Social/Emotional B-LS 9, B-SMS 7, B-SS 2, B-SS 5	Second Step Violence Prevention Program	April – June
College & Career Day *When I Grow Up* Career Essay Contest 4th Grade College Trip 5th Grade BizTown Trip		School Counselor Welcome & Respect Lesson	Social/Emotional M 3, B-SS 4, B-SS 7	School Counselor – Generated Lesson	September
		Red Ribbon Week	Social/Emotional M 1, B-LS 1, B-SMS9, B-SS 9	Counselor-generated anti-drug/alcohol lesson	October
		College & Career Readiness	Career M 4, B-LS 7, B-SMS 5	Counselor-generated college lesson; College & Career Presenters Day	January
Stand UP to Bullying Day Friday Assembly		Stand UP to Bullying Month	Social/Emotional M 3, B-SS 4, B-SS 9	Book: *My Secret Bully*; 4 Corners Lesson; Daily Calendar	March
Middle School Field Trip Parent Night		Transition to Middle School	Academic & Social/Emotional M 2, B-LS 8, B-SMS 10, B-SS 9	Counselor Generated; Trip to Feeder MS	April – May

When coordinating and supporting schoolwide programs and activities, the school counselor is advised to consider the amount of time spent in this area to ensure that it doesn't take away from other Tier 1 services nor inhibit delivery of Tier 2 or 3 supports. Additionally, counselors also want to align schoolwide activities with their comprehensive core curriculum action plans to supplement learning, rather than planning "random acts of schoolwide activities." There is no schoolwide prescription or recipe other than for school counselors to pay attention to their role within schoolwide programs and activities and to balance services provided across the three domains.

Figure 7.3 presents an example of accompanying schoolwide activities from the Alvin Dunn Action Plan for fifth grade.

ACADEMIC DOMAIN PROGRAMS AND ACTIVITIES

The elementary school counselor implements strategies and activities to support and maximize each student's ability to learn. At the Tier 1 level, these may include support for student transitions (e.g., welcome to kindergarten, elementary to middle school orientation), schoolwide attendance improvement incentives, and new student welcome programs (if offered as part of the schoolwide expectations program or in an effort to familiarize all new students who may have missed new school year orientation events or curriculum).

Transition Programs: Pre-K → K and Elementary → Middle

School counselors offer students opportunities to have a successful transition experience as they move into and out of elementary school. By both supporting students and parents and collaborating with teachers and other school staff, school counselors can help students gain knowledge and reduce their anxiety and stress during this process. For example, school counselors can do the following:

- Present strategies for successfully starting school during a kindergarten orientation
- Support upset students (and parents) on the first day of school
- Ensure that the core counseling curriculum is taught at the fifth- or sixth-grade level and include related parent presentations
- Collaborate with middle school counselors to present to outgoing students and/or to coordinate a field trip to the new school

Attendance Programs

Students who attend school regularly do better than students who do not (Easton & Engelhard, 1982). Therefore, school counselors are served well to be involved in schoolwide attendance improvement efforts.

Involvement doesn't necessarily mean performing clerical and administrative responsibilities. Rather, it is recommended that school counselors support schoolwide attendance and intervention programs, facilitate parent workshops, and intervene with students. Counselors can provide a variety of schoolwide supports to improve attendance. See the following example of how a school counselor conducted Tier 1 activities for attendance improvement.

One School Counselor's Various Attendance Improvement Initiatives

In 2014, I was invited by my district's Director of Student Support to attend a chronic absenteeism conference to create an intentional system focused on improving attendance through supportive, rather than punitive, means. While at the conference, I realized what a huge problem had been lurking on our campuses, with little targeted intervention to support students and families with getting to school. Missing only 2 days a month cumulatively adds up to 18 missed days and 108 hours of lost instruction in a school year.

After the conference, I began looking at my site data, trying to understand what were common reasons for students' not being at school (i.e., vacation, appointments, and tummy ache). I then created an attendance team that included myself, the attendance clerk, and the assistant principal. In year one, we met monthly to discuss current trends and ways to educate parents and students, utilizing the invaluable resource of attendanceworks.org. We developed a schoolwide chant—"On Time . . . All the Time!"—that we echo every morning with students while giving them a high five with a large foam hand.

During year one, we implemented a few proactive interventions, including the following:

- We promoted September as Attendance Awareness Month, with morning announcements, skits, and chants at our Friday Flag Assembly, and a monthly traveling

(Continued)

(Continued)

trophy for each grade-level class with the best attendance and a brag door banner for the class with best overall attendance in the school (the winning class earned an additional activity with the counselor).

- Because our data show that students in kindergarten through third grade have the highest rate of being chronically absent, we teamed up to educate parents at Back to School Night about research directly related to excessive absences and academic struggles, stressing that school is where students begin building life skills for the future, such as being punctual. We created a "Night Before School Checklist" for parents to hang on the refrigerator—using the list allows students to build the skill of being responsible for themselves.
- We addressed attendance in the monthly school newsletter and during the morning message.
- In the spring, we notified parents about the upcoming school year calendar and the importance of planning vacations and appointments during scheduled breaks, extended weekends, or early-out days.
- We gave presentations at the incoming kindergarten parent information session to make sure parents understood how much learning takes place and how missing school equals missing out.
- We held weekly Student Attendance Review Team (SART) meetings for students with excessive absences.
- We contacted parents via phone and e-mail to follow up about attendance concerns.

In year one, our chronically absent student rate decreased at site one, but increased at site two, so in our second year, we added a schoolwide challenge called "Challenge 8." I visited each class at both sites and challenged them to miss fewer than eight days of school. We used the acronym HERO—H = here, E = everyday, R = ready, and O = on time—to support the challenge through showing our HERO qualities each and every day. We added Superhero Spirit Wear days to our September Attendance Awareness Month. We campaigned all year through our website, newsletters, attendance skits at our Friday Flag Assembly, banners on fences, morning messages, administration members' wearing attendance capes, and new class challenges for daily perfect attendance. Administrators would stop in classes that posted their perfect attendance door badges to sing and dance a celebratory song. When a class achieved 10 days of perfect attendance, the counselor planned 10 to 15 minutes of class celebrations (such as a game of charades, a bubble dance party, freeze dance, or a short Pixar video clip), along with giving students HERO stickers to announce their accomplishment. Murrieta Valley Unified School District was also extremely supportive with website, Twitter, and Facebook infographics and postings encouraging the importance of being at school "On-Time . . . All the Time!" The HERO lesson plan and ideas were found on Teachers Pay Teachers. It is an entire yearlong plan that supports attendance proactively, and we saw great results!

—Jodi Spoon-Sadlon, school counselor in the
Murrieta Valley Unified School District

Table 7.2 Chronic Absenteeism at Two Elementary Schools in the Murrieta Valley Unified School District

School	2014–2015 (No System)	2015–2016 (Year 1)	2016–2017 (Year 2)	Percentage Change Over Two Years
Site 1 (Population 950)	7.5% (71 students)	5.9% (56 students)	3.4% (32 students)	–55%
Site 2 (Population 750)	8.9% (67 students)	9.5% (71 students)	4.8% (36 students)	–46%

New Student Welcome Programs

School counselors can support the success of students who transfer from other schools by creating new student welcome programs. Whether the new students transfer at the beginning of a school year or midway through, familiarizing them with the school, teaching them about expectations, and linking them with their peers can help them feel welcome and connected. Below are two examples of how school counselors created schoolwide support programs for new students.

When co-author Lisa was an elementary school counselor at a school with high mobility, she implemented a new student orientation program that included grade-level appropriate bulletin board displays welcoming new students and an orientation assembly with the principal, school counselor, and other key staff. Besides introductions, the presentation covered schoolwide expectations for behavior, policies for attendance, and the "Passport to Success" program, where new students were partnered with a "Passport Buddy," typically an older student, who showed them around the school and served as a peer mentor to aid the new student in filling the passport with stamps from the staff.

Figures 7.4 and 7.5 provide examples from Lisa's new student orientation program. A reproducible passport template can be found in the online appendix. Figure 7.6 shows the slides of a "Meet Your School Counselor" PowerPoint template for intermediate-age students that can easily be modified for a student orientation session or a core curriculum lesson. The full template, with guidance for completion given in the notes of the slides, is available in the online appendix, along with a full PowerPoint version for primary-age students.

online resources

COLLEGE/CAREER DOMAIN PROGRAMS AND ACTIVITIES

College and career development begins in elementary school (NOSCA, 2011). Early messages sent to students can profoundly affect their belief about college as a future option. College and career development activities correlate to students' understanding the connection between school and the world of work. As students gain knowledge and skills in this area, they can plan for and make a successful transition to postsecondary education and/or the workplace and experience self-fulfillment across the lifespan. At the Tier 1 level, this can include delivery of a program with a career development focus, career fairs, and college days/weeks with journal writing

Figure 7.4 New Student Welcome Program Parent Letter

BURNHAM/ANTHONY MATHEMATICS AND SCIENCE ACADEMY

1903 E. 96TH STREET, CHICAGO, ILLINOIS 60617; (773) 535-6530
9800 S. TORRENCE AVENUE, CHICAGO, ILLINOIS 60617; (773) 535-6526

Dr. Linda J. Moore, Principal ● *Ms. Sheryl Freeman, Assistant Principal* ● *Ms. Lisa. Krotiak, School Counselor*

"New Student Welcome Program!"

Dear Parent/Guardian:

You have enrolled a **new student** at our school so allow us to **"WELCOME!"** you and your family to Burnham/Anthony Academy, the Home of the Falcons! We are so glad that you are a part of our school community. As you will soon see, Burnham/Anthony is a **GREAT** place to be!

Over the next few weeks, all new students will attend a New Student Orientation where Administration and Staff will discuss important policies and expectations. At that time, primary-aged students in Burnham Branch will be given a **PASSPORT TO YOUR NEW SCHOOL** to fill with cool stamps or stickers as they are introduced to new people and shown around the school by their assigned 3rd grade **'PASSPORT BUDDY.'** In addition, an age-appropriate **special bulletin board display in each building recognizes all new falcons to our school**. Upper grade students at Anthony Branch will complete an activity where they complete a poster about themselves, including information about who they are and what they like. This is done anonymously so that others passing by can 'meet the new falcons' and play 'guess who'!

To make this a success, we ask that your son/daughter bring a **recent photograph** (or color copy) of his/her self for display on our bulletin board. Please note that we will make every effort to return the photo at the end of the program—just write your **child's name and room number** on the back of it. Also, we ask that the picture <u>not</u> be larger than 4x6 in size. If no picture is available, your child may create a collage with magazine images and words that describe them. Note: As this is a hallway display, we cannot guarantee the return of photos or the condition that photos will be returned in.

ALL PHOTOS ARE DUE TO THE CLASSROOM TEACHER BY FRIDAY, SEPTEMBER 21st.

Burnham/Anthony Academy . . . Where We Live Every Day with Character

Figure 7.5   New Student Welcome Program Student "Passport Buddy" Assignment

BURNHAM/ANTHONY MATHEMATICS AND SCIENCE ACADEMY
1903 E. 96TH STREET, CHICAGO, ILLINOIS 60617; (773) 535-6530

NOTICE OF
Passport Buddy Assignment

Dear _____ :

Here is a chance for YOU to be a PASSPORT BUDDY
to a NEW STUDENT! Be sure to put a smile on your face and give your
best FRIENDLY greeting to our new student:

_____ in Room _____ .

Remember your responsibilities as a PASSPORT BUDDY:
- Be a friend and an example of a Burnham/Anthony student with character!
- Help the student understand the passport booklet and read any questions or information.
- Introduce the student to School Staff. Make sure they get a stamp or sticker in their passport booklet when they meet!
- Show the student around our school building—the cafeteria, Main Office, etc.
- Answer any questions and explain our school rules and expectations.

Figure 7.6   Sample Slides From the "Meet Your School Counselor" PowerPoint Template

(Continued)

Figure 7.6 (Continued)

All About Me

[INSERT PHOTO OF SELF]

- **MY EXPERIENCE**
  - Graduated from [Insert University]
  - [Insert]
- **MY FAMILY [OR FAVES]**
  - [Insert]
  - [Insert]
- **MY HOBBIES**
  - [Insert]
  - [Insert]

My Goals

- To give you the academic, social-emotional, and college and career development skills you need to progress to [Xth] grade and graduate.
- To provide a supportive and fun classroom environment.
- To help you be a good friend and citizen and discover new things about your self.

Counselors Help Kids Help Themselves With . . .

- Getting to school
- Following school and classroom expectations
- Making new friends
- Solving problems
- Finding information
- Exploring careers
- Developing character

- Making safe and healthy choices
- Respecting differences
- Expressing feelings
- Improving learning and work habit skills
- Setting goals
- Being successful in school!

Teach Class Lessons

Like your teacher, we have classroom lessons that we teach based on standards.

Some topics will include:

- Respect
- Responsibility
- Goal-setting
- [Insert]

Individual Advising

School counselors serve as a listener and mentor to students and their families in times of need. We offer extra help with school or friends.

Small Group Counseling

School counselors conduct small groups for students who share a common issue or event that has occurred in their lives such as divorce or death of a loved one.

Career Counselor

We help students understand the world of work and their personal interests and strengths. We introduce them to career paths available and help with the transition to high school.

Crisis Counselor

We serve students and their families during times where critical issues occur unexpectedly such as natural disasters like tornadoes or fires

Data Analyst

School counselors analyze their school's data results and needs. We evaluate our counseling program and make necessary changes. We know the latest research and keep our resources up-to-date!

How Can I See the School Counselor?

(Continued)

Figure 7.6 (Continued)

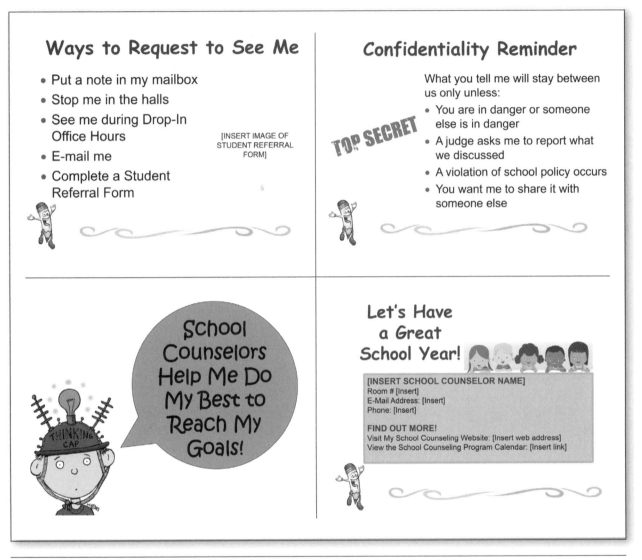

Source: "Thinking Cap" illustration by Mark A. Hicks. Used with permission. Retrieved from http://www.MARKiX.net.

prompts, "Big 10" fight songs played over the intercom as students enter the building, and college spirit wear.

Career Fairs and College and Career Day/Week

Coordinating a Career Fair or a College and Career Day includes inviting guests from the community to the school campus to share their college experiences or their career field. Their stories help increase students' awareness and knowledge of diverse options and required qualifications as they set goals for their future. School counselors can get creative and turn this into a week of activities, with students and staff wearing college gear; they can plan assemblies and provide activities for teachers (such as journal writing topics and college trivia). The following story is from a school counselor's first Career Day, which aligned with core curriculum and parent education. Pictures of the event are shown in Figure 7.7.

La Granada Elementary's Career Day

Our first annual Career Day at La Granada was held on Friday, March 17, 2017. Collaboration was a key factor—students, parents, community members, and teachers played an essential role in making the day successful.

Students in kindergarten and first grade explored and learned from local agencies, including the Forest Fire Department with Smokey the Bear, the City of Riverside Fire Department, and members of our Riverside SWAT team with their vehicles. Students in grades 2 through 5 had the opportunity to learn from various guest speakers who rotated classrooms every 30 minutes. The variety and quality of the guest speakers was essential for this event, as they reflected the demographics of our students and represented professionals from a variety of areas—dentist, pilot, FBI agents, doctor, educators, lawyer, physical therapist, entrepreneurs, scientists, and a nonprofit organization.

Families are essential to the educational development of our students at La Granada, and the Career Day was no different. While students gained knowledge in different careers, parents were invited to a separate presentation designed specifically for them. The topic of building positive relationships with their children and the effects of positive parenting was presented by one of the counselors from our local middle school. At the conclusion of the presentation, all parents were invited to a meet-and-greet with the guest speakers.

Our Career Day event was successful due to the involvement of all stakeholders. Parents, students, community members, teachers, and administrators all played a vital role. We are looking forward to continuing Career Day in future years and building on our first year's success.

—*Sandra Ruiz, La Granada elementary school counselor*

College Field Trips

Trips to local universities and community colleges provide elementary school students with the opportunity to step onto a college campus, often for the first time. In addition to the admissions/campus tours office, most campuses have departments that support early outreach and may plan special activities for younger students, which may include modified age-appropriate information, athletics experiences, and lunch on campus. Technical education schools, such as Universal Technical Institute (UTI), often provide tours that expose students to diverse career pathways. School counselors are highly encouraged to invite parents/guardians to join students, especially in communities with high percentages of first-generation students who will be the first in their families to graduate from college, as this helps demystify and increase excitement for postsecondary exploration and attainment.

Junior Achievement, BizTown, and Other Career Exploration

The Junior Achievement program supports career development through standards-based curriculum that teaches students about work readiness, entrepreneurship, and financial literacy. In some cities, Junior Achievement includes a BizTown location, where students put their new knowledge to the test by applying for and

Figure 7.7   La Granada Elementary School Career Day Photos

Sandra Ruiz, Alvord Elementary School Counselor.

"working" in a variety of jobs at the BizTown mini-city. This hands-on program allows students to learn experientially and can be found in cities including York, Pennsylvania; Houston, Texas; and San Diego, California. Counselors are encouraged to check out their local Junior Achievement office for more information

Figure 7.8   Junior Achievement BizTown

Alvin Dunn 5th Graders Take On BizTown

The 5th graders from Alvin Dunn Elementary School in San Marcos, CA participated in the Junior Achievement BizTown Program during the 2011-2012 academic year. This hands-on program teaches students about economics, career opportunities, and money management through:

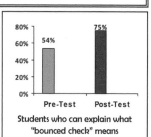

+ **Learning** *the standards-based curriculum on* _financial planning_, _work readiness_, *and* _good citizenship_.

+ **Researching** *and applying for* _jobs_ *of interest.*

+ **Practicing** *using a checkbook, balancing a bank account, and opening a savings account.*

+ **Visiting** *BizTown during which students* **worked** *in one of the* _21 businesses_ *such as Best Buy, City Hall, Cox Communications, Associated General Contractors, NBC Studios, Jack in the Box, U.S. Bank, Kaiser Permanente, SDG&E, Sea World, and State Farm Insurance.*

+ **Processing** *their experience through* _follow-up lessons_ *about what they learned, in what ways their business was successful, and what they would do differently.*

Our students can apply what they learned to the future!

American School Counselor Association Career Domain Standard C
Students will understand the relationship between personal qualities, education, training and the world of work.

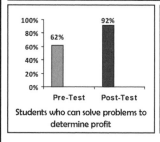

Students who can solve problems to determine profit

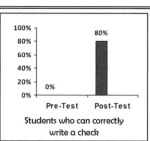

Students who can correctly write a check

Students who can explain what "bounced check" means

Thank you to the *Current Wisdom Foundation & Junior Achievement of San Diego County* for funding & coordinating this great program!!!

(www.juniorachievement.org). If this program is not available in your area, you can arrange field trips to work sites in the community or a high school with a career and technical education program, or you can collaborate with other teachers to simulate a world of work with "jobs" assigned to students in the school building.

College Signing Day

Former First Lady Michelle Obama transformed the term "College Signing Day" to not only celebrate high school athletes signing agreements to participate in sports at the university level, but also to recognize all high school seniors who are committing to postsecondary education. On or before May 1 each year, which is the day when students must submit a Statement of Intent to Register, schools across the nation celebrate their seniors and their postsecondary or military plans. While the focus is typically at the high school level, the 2017 Reach Higher College Signing Day Toolkit includes ways to incorporate the elementary and middle school levels. Through the activities listed in Figure 7.9, elementary students can be exposed to and explore a variety of colleges and get excited about the postsecondary process.

What would you like to implement at your school for College Signing Day? What are the steps you need to take to coordinate the activity? What other ideas do you have?

Figure 7.9 Reach Higher College Signing Day Toolkit—How to Celebrate in Elementary and Middle Schools

HOW TO CELEBRATE IN ELEMENTARY AND MIDDLE SCHOOLS

This is a great opportunity to promote college exploration!

1. Design a "Commitment to My Future" pledge for students to include actions that will keep them on the path to college
2. Coordinate a college field trip for students and families
3. Host a family college night with information about early ways to prepare for college
4. Take photos of students in a cap and gown with signs of what they want to be when they grow up
5. Teach a college exploration classroom including students researching colleges they are interested in attending (middle school)

HOW TO CELEBRATE IN ELEMENTARY AND MIDDLE SCHOOLS

This is a great opportunity to promote college exploration!

6. Organize a student-led college fair
7. Host a college student to speak about their path to college during an assembly
8. Design a bulletin board with school staff photos and a map of where they attended college
9. Read students "Mahalia Mouse Goes to College" by John Lithgow (elementary)
10. Host a door decorating contest for classrooms to signs college themes on their classroom doors
11. Teach students college chants and perform them together at an assembly

Source: http://www.whitehouse.gov/sites/whitehouse.gov/files/images/Documents/College_Signing_Day_Kit_01.pdf.

SOCIAL/EMOTIONAL DOMAIN PROGRAMS AND ACTIVITIES

Social/emotional supports improve school climate and academic success (Greenberg et al., 2003). At the Tier 1 level, social/emotional learning may include assemblies, participation in national awareness and celebration weeks (such as the Great Kindness Challenge or Red Ribbon Week), peer mediation programs, and school-wide programs such as PBIS and character education.

Schoolwide Behavior Expectations, PBIS, and Positive Incentive Programs

Establishing universal behavior expectations for all students is a well-researched and widely adopted strategy to support clarity of school rules for all students, school staff, and families and promote good conduct. PBIS is a proactive and systemwide approach for an entire school or district. The underlying theme is teaching behavioral expectations in the same manner as any core curriculum subject would be taught. Typically, a team of approximately 10 representative members of the school (administrators, counselor, and classified, primary/upper-grade, and special education teachers) attend two to three days of professional development provided by skilled trainers. The school team develops three to five behavioral expectations that are positively stated and easy to remember. A matrix is then built to show what each of the expectations looks like, sounds like, and feels like in all areas, including non-classroom spaces. Key in the process is focusing on preferred behaviors, rather than telling students what not to do, as depicted in Figure 7.10. See page 108 in Chapter 6 for examples of expectations that may be set schoolwide.

The PBIS team determines how the behavioral expectations and routines will be taught in classroom and non-classroom settings with guided opportunities for practice. For example, a bus may be brought to the school and the children will practice lining up, entering the bus, sitting on the bus, and exiting the bus using hula hoops to denote proper body space distance in lining up to enter the bus. "Caught You Being Good" programs can also be created, prompting adults to acknowledge students' appropriate behavior (rather than scolding them for engaging in inappropriate behavior). Plans to review and reteach expected behavior throughout the year are also included, along with modifying the office discipline referral form and data collection process. As PBIS is being rolled out on campus, the school counselor should strive to align lessons with PBIS content and refer to the schoolwide behavior expectations.

Figure 7.10 provides an example of the PBIS matrix and reinforcement system led by Lisa at her K–8 school, which referred to its program as "The Falcon Four— The Way to Be" based on the school mascot. Notice the focus on positive behaviors by using "I" statements.

While most agree that intrinsic motivation is more meaningful than incentives, many schools incorporate some extrinsic reward systems within PBIS at the elementary level. Schools use whatever tool that they can (bonus time, prizes, raffle tickets) to incentivize and motivate children to put in more effort. Some prefer a combination of social praise and tangible incentives either infrequently, randomly, or at decreased frequency over time as positive behavior becomes the norm, thus raising the bar. Reinforcing a behavior increases the likelihood that the behavior will occur again and become a habit.

Figure 7.10   PBIS Sample Code of Conduct Matrix

BURNHAM/ANTHONY MATH & SCIENCE ACADEMY CODE OF CONDUCT MATRIX

THE FALCON FOUR—THE 'WAY TO BE'!

SCHOOL EXPECTATION	IN THE CLASSROOM	IN THE HALLWAY	IN THE CAFETERIA	IN THE BATHROOM	IN THE BUS	IN OUTDOOR SCHOOL GROUNDS	DURING ARRIVAL & DISMISSAL	DURING FIELD TRIPS & ASSEMBLIES
BE Safe	-I stay in my assigned seat -I ask permission -I use materials and equipment properly -I keep my hands, feet, and objects to my self -I don't fight -I use all tech equipment gently and appropriately -I practice Internet safety	-I walk on the correct side of the hall in a single line -I don't push, bump, shove, or cut in line -I go directly to my destination	-I stay seated unless given permission -I immediately inform an adult about spills -I eat only the food that is mine -I wait my turn -I place trash in trash bins	-I don't play around in the restroom -I wash my hands with soap & water -I throw away my trash in trash can	-I am on time -I keep my hands, feet, and objects to my self -I stay in my seat -I wear my seatbelt -I don't horseplay or fight -I keep aisles clear	-I stay in approved areas only -I don't throw items -I listen for directions and whistles -I keep my hands, feet, and objects to my self -I don't push, shove, or kick -I look both ways before crossing streets	-I have my guardian write a note/call to change transportation arrangements -I stay on the sidewalks -I report a strange occurrence -I listen to the adult in charge -I walk directly to/from school without any stops	-I enter and exit in an orderly manner -I remain seated, keeping aisles clear -I stay with my group or assigned partner -I follow directions
BE Respectful	-I appreciate differences -I listen when others are speaking -I follow the directions given by the adult in charge -I value the learning of others by not disrupting -I use kinds words rather than put-downs -I use an appropriate voice level -I respect the belongings of the school and others -I take care of my environment -I treat others how I want to be treated	-I am considerate of classes in progress -I walk quietly -I maintain my personal space -I walk without touching displays and the walls -I don't have open food and drinks -I take care of my environment -I treat others how I want to be treated	-I use manners by saying "please" and "thank you" -I practice good table manners -I follow the directions given by the adults in charge -I use an appropriate voice level -I am considerate of others sitting around me -I take care of my environment -I treat others how I want to be treated	-I give others privacy -I respect the property of the school -I clean up after my self -I take care of my environment -I don't vandalize school property -I treat others how I want to be treated	-I use appropriate language -I use an appropriate voice level -I follow the instructions of the bus driver -I respect school property -I am an active listener -I take care of my environment -I treat others how I want to be treated	-I invite others to join me in play -I play fair -I apologize for accidents -I encourage others rather than putting them down -I share any school equipment -I demonstrate good sportsmanship -I follow the directions given by the adults in charge -I use an appropriate voice level -I take care of my environment -I don't vandalize -I treat others how I want to be treated	-I enter and exit the building quietly and orderly at the appropriate doors -I follow the directions given by the adults in charge -I use an appropriate voice level -I take care of my environment -I treat others how I want to be treated	-I remain focused on the speaker or guest by not talking with my friends -I sit facing forward with my hands and feet to my self -I applaud appropriately -I follow the directions given by the adults in charge -I use an appropriate voice level -I use kind words and actions -I take care of my environment -I treat others how I want to be treated

SCHOOL EXPECTATION	IN THE CLASSROOM	IN THE HALLWAY	IN THE CAFETERIA	IN THE BATHROOM	IN THE BUS	IN OUTDOOR SCHOOL GROUNDS	DURING ARRIVAL & DISMISSAL	DURING FIELD TRIPS & ASSEMBLIES
BE Responsible	-I think before I speak or act -I respond to questions when asked and participate -I take care of my textbooks -I come to class prepared with needed supplies -I come to school on time -I attend school every day -I use a planner to keep me organized -I turn in absence notes & completed assignments on time -I make good choices -I use all tech equipment appropriately	-I stay with my class/group -I have a pass with me -I return to class promptly	-I only take the food that I plan to eat -I avoid spills on the serving line by carefully placing items on my tray -I keep my space and table clean -I help others	-I report any problems -I flush the toilet after I have used it -I throw out my trash	-I make good choices -I pay attention to safety standards -I take all of my belongings when exiting the bus -I go directly home or to school -I follow the instructions of the bus driver	-I use the equipment appropriately -I clean up after myself and don't litter on school grounds -I don't engage in graffiti -I try to be an effective problem solver -I return all equipment that I use -I dress appropriately for the weather -I line up quickly -I walk away from fights	-I know how I am supposed to get home from school each day -I know what clubs & extra-curricular activities I am enrolled in -I turn in all notes to my teacher about transportation -I listen closely for announcements about dismissal or transportation -I don't leave school until dismissed -I come to school neatly wearing the required school uniform	-I use the restroom prior to the event -I behave so that everyone can enjoy the event -I am attentive -I applaud to show my appreciation & enjoyment -I show school spirit -I dress appropriately -I recognize the privilege of attending
BE Your Best!	-I am accountable for my actions -I resolve conflicts with maturity -I use time wisely -I study and complete all assigned homework -I don't waste paper & resources -I do my best work at all times -I seek improvement and challenge my self -I am an active listener -I work with integrity -I practice good hygiene	-I go directly to my destination -I carry items appropriately -I turn off all cell phones, music players, and non-approved electronic devices and keep them out of sight -I use appropriate and non-offensive language -I walk & don't run! -I don't act inappropriately	-I pick up after myself -I am accountable for my actions -I resolve conflicts with maturity -I use time wisely -I make healthy eating choices -I assist my neighbor -I take turns -I Reduce, Reuse, & Recycle	-I conserve paper and water -I use the restroom only when I need to -I use the restroom quickly, returning to class promptly -I respect my environment	-I am accountable for my actions -I resolve conflicts with maturity -I stay seated in one place until exiting the bus -I use appropriate and non-offensive language -I don't vandalize or damage the bus	-I show good sportsmanship -I keep our campus clean by cleaning up even when others don't -I am accountable for my actions -I resolve conflicts with maturity -I treat others how I want to be treated	-I go directly to my destination -I am accountable for your actions -I resolve conflicts with maturity -I use time wisely -I use kind words & actions	-I am accountable for your actions -I resolve conflicts with maturity -I am a good representative of the school -I refrain from silliness -I think before I act or speak -I show good character & integrity -I practice proper social skills

School counselors who know their student population and community can select rewards that will be meaningful and age-appropriate. If unsure, counselors can go straight to the source by asking the students! Form a focus group, create a survey, or meet with the student council to allow them to weigh in with their suggestions on what would be most valuable to them. Ideas include the following:

- *Monopoly money system:* Students earn dollars that they can redeem or "spend" at a school store for school supplies, school spirit T-shirts and products, and so on.
- *Classroom competition:* Classes earn points that are calculated once per month. The class with the highest number of points gets to display the grade-level trophy or school spirit stick in their room for the next month or can win some class reward, such as extra recess or a pizza party. Classrooms love to win a trophy, which keeps their achievement levels high and is a visual daily reminder of their efforts. Plus, it is something that has to be purchased only once because it travels from room to room.
- *Student of the Month awards or assemblies:* Honor students for displaying positive citizenship or other character traits. If presented in an assembly format, each grade level can perform a skit related to positive behavior or the monthly character trait. See Figures 7.11 and 7.12 for sample Student of the Month award sheets for both students and teachers.

Figure 7.13 shows an example of the corresponding PBIS schoolwide reinforcement "gotcha" program. Lisa created a system where all staff members were given a "Way to Be" lanyard with an attached clear pocket full of easily accessible student raffle slips. A staff member would give a slip to a student and say, for example, "Way to be respectful! I noticed that you picked up the garbage on the ground, and that shows that you care about our community." The student would then check off the corresponding star per the PBIS matrix, enter his or her name and room number, and submit the slip to the main office for a monthly raffle. The winner received a certificate stating "Way to Be" along with a prize, which was typically a hardcover book focused on a character value or life lesson obtained through donations from Lisa's DonorsChose.org grant.

Conflict Resolution Programs

Whether called Peace Patrol, Conflict Managers, or any other name, schoolwide conflict resolution programs are often led by elementary school counselors to support an improved school climate. Some common programs include the following:

- Peer Mediators
- Peace Patrol
- Safe School Ambassadors
- Peer Assistance and Leadership

Red Ribbon Week (Drug/Alcohol-Free) Activities

Beginning in 1985 and still celebrated today, during the last full week of October, Red Ribbon Week addresses the need to reduce the demand for drugs through prevention and early intervention. Schools promote prevention education to help

Figure 7.11   Example of a Student of the Month Award Sheet for Students

BURNHAM/ANTHONY MATH & SCIENCE ACADEMY

STUDENT OF THE MONTH
AWARD WINNERS

Dear _____,   Room: _____

CONGRATULATIONS!!!!

You have been nominated by your teacher, _____, as a STUDENT OF THE MONTH in your classroom. Your teacher has consistently observed you excelling or having notable improvement in the Second Step Program, demonstrating the FALCON FOUR— "THE WAY TO BE"—at our school, exhibiting strong character values and life skills, outstanding academic performance or improvement, and/or good or improved conduct and behavior.

As **STUDENT OF THE MONTH**, you will:

- Receive a certificate of achievement!

- Be awarded with a coupon for your very own Dress Down Day!! Just come to school "dressed down" on any day that you choose and turn in your coupon to be excused from the school uniform that day.

- Be featured on the SEL Bulletin Board in your school. We want others to learn from your example and get to know you better. You will complete an "ALL ABOUT ME" poster that will be displayed all year long!

- Be honored at a special awards breakfast at the end of the year for all Students of the Month.

WHAT DO YOU NEED TO DO NOW?

- Bring in a favorite photograph of yourself from home to use on your poster or see Mrs. De Gregorio, School Counselor, to take a polaroid picture.

- TOMORROW come to school at 8:30 a.m. and report directly to your teacher to begin decorating and completing your ALL ABOUT ME poster! Your teacher may give you special instructions to meet with Mrs. De Gregorio (in Burnham) or Mrs. Pondexter (in Anthony).

KEEP UP THE GOOD WORK SHOWING OTHERS "THE WAY TO BE" AT OUR SCHOOL!!

Figure 7.12   Example of a Student of the Month Award Notice for Teachers

BURNHAM/ANTHONY MATH & SCIENCE ACADEMY

STUDENT OF THE MONTH
TEACHER NOMINATIONS

MONTH: **October**

TEACHER NAME: **Ms. Langdon**   ROOM: **#105**

CONGRATULATIONS!!!!

STUDENT OF THE MONTH	STUDENT OF THE MONTH
Name: **VINCENT JONES**	Name: **ANGELA THOMAS**
This student excels or has demonstrated marked improvement in: ✓ Second Step Program ___ Demonstrating the "Falcon Four" ___ Understanding character values & life skills ✓ Academic performance ___ Conduct/behavior	This student excels or has demonstrated marked improvement in: ___ Second Step Program ✓ Demonstrating the "Falcon Four" ✓ Understanding character values & life skills ___ Academic performance ✓ Conduct/behavior
Brief description of why this student is awarded STUDENT OF THE MONTH:	Brief description of why this student is awarded STUDENT OF THE MONTH:
Vincent demonstrates THE WAY TO BE by demonstrating that he can be a team leader in the Second Step program. He has excelled in classroom group activities and has increased his Reading grade!	**Angela demonstrates THE WAY TO BE by showing empathy and concern for others. She also excels and demonstrates the "Falcon Four" code of conduct every day!**

Figure 7.13 PBIS Schoolwide Reinforcement "Gotcha" Program

Burnham/Anthony Math & Science Academy
TEACHING LESSONS FOR SCHOOL & FOR LIFE

Name: _____

Date: _____   Room: _____

THE FALCON FOUR: THE WAY TO BE

Mark the star below of the school expectation YOU followed that showed others that you know "THE WAY TO BE." Then write about where you were and what you did. Submit to the Main Office to be entered for a prize raffle!

☆ **BE Safe**   ☆ **BE Responsible**

☆ **BE Respectful**   ☆ **BE Your Best**

Description: _____

_____

_____.

Staff Initials:

_____

students learn about the risks of alcohol and drug use and teach about making good choices and standing up to peer pressure. School counselors can join Red Ribbon Week planning committees to create lesson plans for teachers, coordinate school spirit dress-up days, plan assemblies, and organize a number of other activities during the week. Counselors can also involve families in Red Ribbon Week (and other schoolwide celebrations), for example, by sending home parent letters like the one in Figure 7.14. For more information on Red Ribbon Week, visit redribbon.org.

Figure 7.14 Red Ribbon Week Family Letter

Dear Parents & Guardians,

Next week our school and community will participate in the annual **Red Ribbon Week Celebration**. The Red Ribbon Celebration began in 1985, when people began wearing Red Ribbons to symbolize the need to reduce the demand for drugs through prevention and early intervention. This awareness campaign is the kick off to a year of prevention in our schools and in our communities. This year, Red Ribbon week will be observed October 25 to October 29.

Our Red Ribbon Week Theme is **Dream, Achieve, Believe, Succeed!** We have integrated this theme into each day and have planned a fun week that incorporates prevention strategies into the activities. This Red Ribbon Calendar lists the themes for the week and spirit days taking place at Alvin Dunn. **Alvin Dunn's Parent Academy is featuring a Gang Awareness Presentation from the County Office of Education on Tuesday, October 26th from 6-7pm in the Alvin Dunn Multipurpose Room**. Additionally, you will find a Red Ribbon Resource Online Directory that features websites to help you and your children get further informed and involved in prevention.

Monday, October 25 **Dream**	Learn the Red Ribbon Week Pledge
Tuesday, October 26 **Achieve**	Turn Your Back on Drugs: Wear Your Shirt Backwards Parent Academy: Gang Awareness Presentation 6-7pm at Alvin Dunn
Wednesday, October 27 **Believe**	Sock it to Drugs - Wear Mismatched Socks
Thursday, October 28 **Succeed**	Red Ribbon Pride - Wear Red Shirts
Friday, October 29 **Dream, Achieve, Believe Succeed!**	Alvin Dunn Pride - Wear Your Alvin Dunn Shirt or Alvin Dunn Green

Your participation in Red Ribbon Week will reinforce the positive messages that your student is hearing at school all week. *Ask your students what they did each day to celebrate and have conversations about healthy lifestyles to promote their development.* Please also join us at Friday Flag on October 29 for the final celebration ending Red Ribbon Week. Thank you for your support and participation in this program.

Kind regards, *Alvin Dunn Red Ribbon Week Committee*

Featured Websites: The Anti-Drug - www.theantidrug.com
Supports parents and other adults who want to help young people avoid alcohol, tobacco, and other drugs. Information, advice for parents, and more available in English, Spanish, and other languages.

Great Kindness Challenge

Celebrated during the last week of January, the Great Kindness Challenge is a positive and proactive program focused on increasing student engagement and improving school climate. Students and staff perform as many acts of kindness as possible at their school site. Using a free checklist and other materials found online, elementary school counselors can help coordinate schoolwide activities at their site. School counselor Ashley Kruger presented information about the Great Kindness Challenge to her staff to garner their buy-in (see Figures 7.15–7.20), taught core curriculum lessons schoolwide, and planned daily activities to celebrate the week. For more information and to download the toolkit, go to http://www.greatkindnesschallenge.org.

Figure 7.15 Great Kindness Challenge Staff Presentation: Slide 1

Figure 7.16 Great Kindness Challenge Staff Presentation: Slide 2

Figure 7.17 Great Kindness Challenge Staff Presentation: Slide 3

Figure 7.18 Great Kindness Challenge Staff Presentation: Slide 4

Character Education Programs

Yearlong character education programs can be built into the school calendar and aligned with school counseling core curriculum to teach and reinforce important skills. One example of a character education program developed by Lisa when she was an elementary school counselor was "Live Every Day with Character." Each month focused on a character value and a theme or life skill, which were incorporated into monthly school counseling lessons. Teachers were provided with two to three additional lesson plans to further extend the learning, and the topics could easily be integrated into the class subject matter. In addition to the monthly lesson, the character education program included weekly morning announcements, a family workshop, and staff in-service. See Figure 7.21 for an overview of the program. A downloadable version is available in the online appendix.

Figure 7.19 Great Kindness Challenge Staff Presentation: Slide 5

Figure 7.20 Great Kindness Challenge Staff Presentation: Slide 6

School Counselors and School Climate

School climate is defined by the National School Climate Council as the "norms, values, and expectations that support people feeling socially, emotionally and physically safe" (cited in O'Brennan & Bradshaw, 2013, p. 1). It is the responsibility of all stakeholders, which poses unique leadership opportunities for school counselors. Research shows that when all students feel socially, emotionally, and physically safe, the results include reduced bullying, increased student engagement, and enhanced student outcomes. Utilizing the latest research on school climate, counselors can develop an understanding of the impact of school culture on individual experiences, equitable social and academic opportunities for all students, risk prevention and health promotion, academic achievement, teacher retention, and overall school improvement.

Studies show that a positive school climate is recognized as an important target for school reform and for improving behavioral, academic, and mental health outcomes for students, as schools with positive climates tend to have reduced exposure to risk factors for students, fewer student absences, and higher student academic motivation and engagement, leading to improvements in academic achievement across grade levels. A positive school climate also has benefits for teachers and education support professionals, because research shows that when educators feel supported by their administration, they report higher levels of commitment and more collegiality (O'Brennan & Bradshaw, 2013).

The 2016 ASCA Ethical Standards for School Counselors (ASCA, 2016) indicate an increased focus on the collaborative nature of the work and on the responsibility to the school environment with some new standards—for example, standard B.2, Responsibilities to the School, states:

School counselors: (a) Develop and maintain professional relationships and systems of communication with faculty, staff and administrators to support

(Continued)

(Continued)

students.... (d) Provide leadership to create systemic change to enhance the school.... (j) Strive to use translators who have been vetted or reviewed and bilingual/multilingual school counseling program materials representing languages used by families in the school community.... (m) Promote cultural competence to help create a safer, more inclusive school environment.

School counselors contribute to the widely available universal instruction, preventative services, and resources that are part of Tier 1. Motivational speakers for schoolwide assemblies, career or college fairs, positive incentive programs, national awareness campaigns, and schoolwide anti-bullying programs are designed to foster a positive school climate and address school-level risk factors.

NATIONAL AWARENESS CAMPAIGNS

A national or international awareness day, week, or month is a date (or range of dates) usually set by a major organization or government to commemorate an important public health, education, or ethical cause at a greater level. Based on knowledge of the school community and the climate, the school counselor can utilize nationwide awareness campaigns to evoke school spirit or a sense of community, draw attention to initiatives and movements, inspire dialogue, encourage students' commitment to actions such as choosing a drug-free lifestyle, and promote student attainment of the ASCA mindsets and behaviors standards through core curriculum.

What's particularly useful about nationwide awareness efforts is that they typically include free toolkits and downloadable resources containing curriculum for educators, flyers and informational sheets, videos, and student-led activities. They also lend themselves to a sense of increased positivity and community due to the element of fun and novel interest they add to the school year. Just as teachers may infuse awareness campaigns into their general curriculum (e.g., the Hour of Code for math), school counselors can do the same with core curriculum. For example, October is National Bullying Prevention Month, and elementary school counselors may consider making bullying and cyberbullying the focus of their lessons that month. Perhaps the first day is kicked off by transforming the walkways into school with "No Bullying" graffiti created by the Art Club or student volunteers. The school counselor can make weekly announcements during the month that discuss current statistics on bullying or quote celebrities' stories about their personal bullying experiences; the counselor also can call on all staff and students to participate in "Stand Up to Bullying Day" by dressing in school colors to show their commitment to having a bully-free climate in school.

In the previous example of the "Live Every Day with Character" program, October's focus was on respect, which is one of the six pillars of character celebrated during worldwide CHARACTER COUNTS Week! (also in October). Lisa easily incorporated this campaign into the core curriculum for that month.

Figure 7.21 "Live Every Day with Character" Program Overview

'Live Every Day with Character' Program
Monthly Values and Life Skills Calendar

"The measure of a person's character is what he would do if he were never found out."
—Thomas Macaulay

SEPTEMBER

Character Value: **Responsibility***— Moral, legal, or mental accountability; reliability. It is based on obligation; it prompts individuals to be accountable for who they are and what they do. Responsibility involves being dependable and accountable for your words and actions, doing your best, and making sure that work is done correctly and on time.
Theme: Academic Skills (i.e. Study skills, Test-taking skills, etc.)

Week 1 Quote: "I believe that every right implies a responsibility; every opportunity, an obligation; every possession, a duty."—John D. Rockefeller, Jr.
Week 2 Quote: "You cannot evade the responsibility of tomorrow by evading it today."—Abraham Lincoln, U.S. President
Week 3 Quote: "Remember always that you not only have the right to be an individual, you have an obligation to be one."—Eleanor Roosevelt
Week 4 Quote: "The world is a dangerous place, not because of those who do evil, but because of those who look on and do nothing."—Albert Einstein
Additional Quote: "The price of greatness is responsibility."—Winston Churchill

OCTOBER

Character Value: **Respect***— To consider worthy of high regard; esteem. This trait centers on the Golden Rule—treat others the way that you want to be treated. This involves using good manners; practicing nonviolence; taking care of property, people, the environment, and oneself; respecting those who are different.
Theme: Self-Concept

Week 1 Quote: "Respect yourself if you would have others respect you."—Baltasar Gracian
Week 2 Quote: "Respect for ourselves guides our morals; respect for others guides our manners."—Laurence Sterne
Week 3 Quote: "Respect commands itself and it can neither be given nor withheld when it is due."—Eldridge Cleaver
Week 4 Quote: "They cannot take away our self-respect if we do not give it to them."—Mahatma Gandhi
Week 5 Quote: "The more things a man is ashamed of, the more respectable he is."—George Bernard Shaw
Additional Quote: "If I have lost confidence in myself, I have the universe against me."—Ralph Waldo Emerson

(Continued)

Figure 7.21 (Continued)

NOVEMBER

Character Value: **Caring***— To sincerely feel interest, consideration, or concern for others. Rather than giving to others to get something in return, caring people give because it makes others feel good and/or makes their life better. It involves having compassion and putting other people's needs before your own; doing kind and thoughtful deeds for people in need.
Theme: Community/Global Awareness

Week 1 Quote: "The most important thing in any relationship is not what you get but what you give."—Eleanor Roosevelt, First Lady and Activist
Week 2 Quote: "No act of kindness, however small, is ever wasted."—Aesop
Week 3 Quote: "I expect to pass through this world but once; any good thing therefore that I can do, or any kindness that I can show to any fellow creature, let me do it now; let me not defer or neglect it, for I shall not pass this way again."—Etienne de Grellet
Week 4 Quote: "I have found the paradox that if I love until it hurts, then there is no hurt, but only more love."—Mother Teresa
Additional Quote: "Love is all we have, the only way that each can help the other."—Euripides, Orestes (408 B.C.)

DECEMBER

Character Value: **Trustworthiness***—Worthy of confidence; dependable. A trustworthy person is honest, reliable, and loyal. This involves telling the truth, keeping promises, being honest, following through on commitments, and doing what is right even if it is hard to do.
Theme: Friendship

Week 1 Quote: "Trust one who has gone through it."—Virgil
Week 2 Quote: "A lie told often enough becomes the truth."—Lenin
Week 3 Quote: "This above all; to thine own self be true."—William Shakespeare
Additional Quote: "You can make more friends in two months by becoming interested in other people than you can in two years by trying to get other people interested in you."—Dale Carnegie

JANUARY

Character Value: **Fairness***— An elimination of one's own feelings, prejudices, and desires so as to achieve a proper balance of conflicting interests. Fairness means doing what is right to make sure others are not treated badly. Sometimes fairness means equal, but fairness does not always mean the same. This trait values equality, impartiality in making decisions, and willingness to correct mistakes. It applies to taking turns, sharing, rightful consequences, and not blaming others.
Theme: Conflict Resolution

Week 1 Quote: "Injustice anywhere is a threat to justice everywhere."—Martin Luther King, Jr.
Week 2 Quote: "We must all hang together, or assuredly we shall all hang separately."—Benjamin Franklin
Week 3 Quote: "A man has honor if he holds himself to an ideal of conduct though it is inconvenient, unprofitable, or dangerous to do so."—Walter Lippman
Week 4 Quote: "I dream of the day when all Americans will be judged not by the color of their skin but by the content of their character."—Martin Luther King, Jr.
Additional Quote: "A problem is a chance for you to do your best."—Duke Ellington, U.S. Composer/Jazz Musician

FEBRUARY

Character Value: **Citizenship***— Member in a community. Citizens have a moral obligation to do their share to honor and improve on traditions of freedom, democracy, and independence. Citizenship involves making a community, school, neighborhood, and home better by cooperating, respecting authority, obeying rules and laws, voting, and protecting the environment.
Theme: Leadership

Week 1 Quote: "And so, my fellow Americans, ask not what your country can do for you. Ask what you can do for your country. My fellow citizens of the world, ask not what America will do for you, but what together we can do for the freedom of man."—John F. Kennedy, U.S. President
Week 2 Quote: "No matter what language we speak, we all live under the same moon and stars."—John Denver, U.S. Singer and Songwriter
Week 3 Quote: "Never doubt that a small group of thoughtful, committed citizens can change the world. Indeed, it is the only thing that ever has."—Margaret Mead
Week 4 Quote: "One generation plants the trees; another gets the shade."—Chinese proverb
Additional Quote: "Being powerful is like being a lady. If you have to tell people you are, you aren't."—Margaret Thatcher, Former Prime Minister of England

MARCH

Character Value: **Self-Discipline**—Correction or regulation of oneself for the sake of improvement. Self-discipline is making good choices, having control over your thoughts, feelings, and actions, being patient, taking responsibility for your actions, and practicing good habits.
Theme: Goal Setting

Week 1 Quote: "With self-discipline, most anything is possible."—Theodore Roosevelt, U.S. President
Week 2 Quote: "Whatever you can do or dream you can, begin it. Boldness has genius, power, and magic in it."—Johann von Goethe, Poet and Dramatist
Week 3 Quote: "If it is to be, it is up to me."—Shirley Nelson Hutton, U.S. Businesswoman
Week 4 Quote: "Even if you are on the right track, you'll get run over if you just sit there."—Will Rogers, U.S. Cowboy/Philosopher/Comedian
Additional Quote: "What people say, what people do, and what they say they do are entirely different things."—Margaret Mead, Anthropologist

APRIL

Character Value: **Integrity**—Firm adherence to a code moral or ethical values. It implies sincerity and honesty. Integrity means being strong enough to do what you know is right, knowing the difference between right and wrong, and choosing the right thing even when it is difficult.
Theme: Decision-Making

Week 1 Quote: "My life is my message."—Mahatma Gandhi, Nationalist Leader
Week 2 Quote: "Aim above morality. Be not simply good; be good for something."—Henry David Thoreau, Writer
Week 3 Quote: "Generations to come will scarce believe that such a one as this ever in flesh and blood walked upon this earth."—Albert Einstein (in a quote about Gandhi)
Week 4 Quote: "Some people fall for everything and stand for nothing."—Aristotle
Additional Quote: "Never give in except to convictions of honor and good sense."—Winston Churchill

(Continued)

Figure 7.21 (Continued)

MAY

Character Value: **Humility**—The quality of being humble. Not being proud or arrogant; being grateful for what one has.
Theme: Career Readiness Skills

Week 1 Quote: "Humility does not mean thinking less of yourself than of other people, nor does it mean having a low opinion of your own gifts. It means freedom from thinking about yourself at all."—William Temple, Statesman
Week 2 Quote: "The farther a man knows himself to be free from perfection, the nearer he is to it."—Gerard Groote, Reformer
Week 3 Quote: "Half of the harm that is done in this world is due to people who want to feel important. . . They are absorbed in the endless struggle to think well of themselves."—T.S. Eliot, Poet
Week 4 Quote: "Humility is the foundation of all other virtues."—Confucius
Additional Quote: "If I have seen farther than other men it is by standing on the shoulders of giants."—Isaac Newton, English Mathematician and Physicist

JUNE

Character Value: **Perseverance**—To persist despite opposition or discouragement. Perseverance helps someone stick with an activity until it is finished. It means not giving up and not quitting.
Theme: Vision

Week 1 Quote: "I never failed once. It just happened to be a 2,000 step process."—Thomas Edison, Inventor
Week 2 Quote: "The only real voyage of discovery consists not in seeking new landscapes but in having new eyes."—Marcel Proust, French Novelist
Additional Quote: "Right is always right, even if everyone is against it. And wrong is always wrong, even if everyone is for it."—William Penn

Elementary School Counselors. . . We Care About Kids

Figure 7.22 "Character Counts!" Week Flyer

BURNHAM/ANTHONY MATHEMATICS & SCIENCE ACADEMY

Dr. Linda J. Moore, Principal ● *Ms. Sheryl Freeman, Assistant Principal* ● *Social & Emotional Learning Committee*

Character Counts! Week
October 16th—20th

CHARACTER COUNTS! WEEK INFORMATION

This week is a NATIONAL event that more than three million young people are celebrating across the country. Events focus on the "Six Pillars of Character":

- **TRUSTWORTHINESS**—This means being honest, reliable, loyal, and a person of integrity. Think 'blue' as in "true blue."
- **RESPECT**—This means courtesy, tolerance, acceptance, and treating others the way that you want to be treated. Think 'yellow/gold' as in the Golden Rule.
- **RESPONSIBILITY**—This means duty, accountability, self-control, and the pursuit of excellence. Think 'green' as in being responsible for a garden.
- **FAIRNESS**—This means justice, openness, and treating people equally. Think 'orange' as in dividing an orange into equal parts.
- **CARING**—This means concern for others and charity. Think 'red' as in love or a heart.
- **CITIZENSHIP**—This means doing your share, obeying, and respecting authority and the law. Think 'purple' as in regal purple or the Purple Heart Award.

"Show Your True Colors"

CHARACTER COUNTS! WEEK ACTIVITIES

- **Daily Announcements** providing information about the national initiative and the Six Pillars of Character.
- **Character Education Art Activity!** Ms. Fulkman, Art Teacher, will make beautiful 'character quilts' in each classroom. Each student will create his/her own square to contribute to the quilt.
- **True Colors Shining Through Good Deed Rainbow!!** All week long, students and staff will have the opportunity to report the good deeds others in school have done for them. Students will be given reporting slips according to their grade level assigned color; as the good deeds accumulate, the squares will collect and gradually fill in each color of our rainbow in the hallway throughout the week.
- **Outstanding Character Awards**. Teachers will each award THREE students who have exemplified all or most of the pillars of character (i.e. trustworthiness, respect, responsibility, fairness, caring, and citizenship). The nominations will be on display as the clouds of our True Colors Shining Through Good Deed Rainbow. All nominees will be honored at a special breakfast hosted by the SEL Committee and entered in a raffle to receive an electronic speller/dictionary! One winner in each building and ALL awardees will be announced over the intercom on October 20th.
- **Grade Level Pride Colors Day**—Students are encouraged to wear their Tie-Dye school pride t-shirts on Friday, October 20th. Note, this is NOT a Dress Down Day fundraiser. If the student is not wearing their grade level color, they MUST be in uniform.
- **Listening & Writing Activity**—Students will listen to the words of "True Colors" by Cyndi Lauper and reflect on the song's meaning to them.

Figure 7.23 "Character Counts!" Week Communication to Teachers and Staff

BURNHAM/ANTHONY MATH & SCIENCE ACADEMY
Dr. Linda J. Moore, Principal • Ms. Sheryl Freeman, Assistant Principal • Social & Emotional Learning Committee

Introducing our very FIRST Character Counts! Week

"Character Counts--Show Your True Colors!"

OCTOBER 16th through 20th

Dear Teachers and Staff,

As part of our "Live Every Day with Character" program, we are participating in CHARACTER COUNTS! WEEK, a <u>national</u> movement to celebrate character education! Attached you will find info on the Six Pillars of Character, mnemonics, and synonyms. Feel free to incorporate these into instruction with word webs, for example. Please review this sheet for details about what is planned . . .

GRADE LEVEL PRIDE COLORS DAY: On <u>Friday, October 20th</u>, students are encouraged to wear their grade level pride tie-dyed t-shirt that they made in art class. If students did not participate, they can wear a shirt in their assigned color—K and 4th= orange, 1st and 5th= green, 2nd and 6th= yellow, 3rd and 7th = purple, and 8th= blue. This is **NOT** a Dress Down Day fundraiser where students must pay $1.00 to participate. However, if they don't wear their assigned color, they must be in uniform.

DAILY MORNING ANNOUNCEMENTS: Certain students have been selected to read announcements over the intercom. Please send the following students to the Main Office on the designated day by 9:05am: Monday, Oct. 16h—3rd grade Keziah O. (#105) and 8th grade Caleb G., Oct. 17th—3rd grade Brian M. (#103) and 7th grade Gregory H.; Wednesday, Oct. 18th—2nd grade Ryan W. and 6th grade Deontae B.; Thursday, Oct. 19th—1st grade Cassandra T. and 5th grade Taiwo J.; Friday, Oct. 20th Heaven P. and 4th grade Natalie P. Your student's announcement is included.

"TRUE COLORS SHINING THROUGH GOOD DEED RAINBOW": Each building will have an outline of a rainbow on display. According to your assigned grade level color, students will have the opportunity during the last 10 minutes of P.E. and Art Classes throughout the week to report good deeds that others have done for them. They will fill out their forms and return to Ms. Morton and Ms. Fulkman in class. All week long, we will see our good deeds accumulate and fill in an outline of a rainbow. For purposes of this activity, <u>staff will also report good deeds done to them using RED slips</u>. These are enclosed; submit to Ms. Fulkman.

OUTSTANDING CHARACTER AWARDS: Every teacher can award **THREE** students who exemplify all or most of the Six Pillars of Character—trustworthiness, respect, responsibility, fairness, caring, and citizenship. Please complete the cloud-shaped award form and submit to Ms. Krotiak by Wednesday, October 18th at 3pm. The clouds will be part of our rainbow hallway displays. The students will be announced over the intercom and will be entered in a raffle. A winner in each building will be selected to receive a grand prize on Friday, October 20th. All students awarded will be given a breakfast (8:30 to 8:55am) by SEL in their honor during the week of October 23rd. Date is to be determined. Award forms are provided in this packet.

"TRUE COLORS" LISTENING & WRITING ACTIVITY: "True Colors" will be played over the intercom on <u>Thursday, October 19th</u>. You are asked to either conduct a discussion or set aside some time for students to reflect on and write about the meaning of the song. A CD with the song and a copy of the words are included in this packet. Remember, this is an early dismissal day for students. 7th and 8th grade classes will also enjoy motivational speaker presentations from the Black Star Project.

Selecting Awareness Campaigns

There are hundreds of awareness campaigns available that align with school counseling programs—how does an elementary school counselor choose? To keep from feeling overwhelmed, start from a place of intentionality and prioritize what is most important to your student population and school community based on your school's data, vision and mission, and goals. Follow these recommendations to conduct a successful schoolwide campaign:

1. Conduct a needs/satisfaction survey of weeklong events or campaigns you've done in the past. Ask staff for their feedback to decide whether an existing program just needs to be enhanced or what is being done already is satisfactory. Don't take for granted that staff know what each event is—be sure to include dates and a clear, brief description. For instance, rather than simply stating, "Character Counts! Week," and asking staff to rate their level of perceived impact or success, write "Character Counts! Week, 10/16–10/22, Pillars of Character Rainbow in hallways with daily morning bell work activities related to being a good citizen to aid their recollection."

2. Review data to assess whether a new program needs to be developed. If so, consider taking the lead to ensure that it happens.

3. Review the annual calendar of school counseling events to look at the level of balance each month in your time and delivery of the three counseling domains. Are there certain months that are already so heavy that they may not be a good time to offer additional activities? If so, consider conducting the campaign on a totally different day or week. What really matters is that the students get the information and activities, regardless of when an event happens.

4. Work with a team! Solicit stakeholders to help coordinate plans, make decisions, and disseminate information. Discuss this during a School Counseling Advisory Council Meeting or collaborate to form a committee by recruiting faculty, students, parents, or community organizations/leaders who share your concerns and interests about establishing schoolwide awareness programs to help determine the curriculum and activities. At the elementary level, there is often only one school counselor, so consider developing lesson plans or clear activities for classroom teachers to conduct with their students, if possible. This may require greater preparation and communication through a brief in-service training or meeting with teachers.

5. Talk with your school administration to explore the current program and opportunities for classroom education, rallies, assemblies, parent and student education events, poster and T-shirt or video contests, and so forth. Seek permission for these options if necessary.

6. Engage parent/teacher organizations or the school board to support your planned events, possibly by requesting their involvement or presence.

7. Include students who are on student leadership teams or in community service–oriented clubs, such as Student Council or Key Club. They can plan to participate to heighten awareness or provide valuable feedback and validation of your ideas.

See Figure 7.24 for a table listing online resources (with brief descriptions) for potential awareness campaigns relevant to elementary school counseling. This table is by no means all-inclusive but serves as a resource to begin your planning. A more extensive list is available in the online appendix. ASCA also provides its own online School Counseling Awareness Dates calendar (the dates for the 2017–2018 school year can be found at http://www.schoolcounselor.org/asca/media/asca/home/2017-18 AwarenessCalendar.pdf).

Figure 7.24   National Awareness Campaigns Related to Elementary School Counseling

online resources

Raising Awareness: National Campaigns Throughout the Year

AUGUST

August	Description	Website and Applicable Resources
National Immunization Month	National Immunization Awareness is an annual observance held in August to emphasize the importance of vaccination. It was established to encourage people of all ages to ensure they are up to date on all recommended vaccines.	www.cdc.gov/vaccines/events/niam.html healthfinder.gov/nho/PDFs/AugustNHOtoolkit.pdf **Toolkits:** www.nphic.org/niam www.nphic.org/niam-resources
Women's Equality Day August 26th	Founded in 1971 to commemorate the passage of the 19th Amendment and calls attention to women's continuing efforts toward full equality. Calls for women to be commended and supported in their organization and activities.	www.nwhp.org/resources/commemorations/womens-equality-day www.nwhm.org/blog/celebrate-equality-day **Resources:** shop.nwhp.org/womens-rights-and-womens-equality-day-resources-c198.aspx www.nwhp.org/resources/commemorations/womens-equality-day/10-ideas-for-womens-equality-day

SEPTEMBER

September	Description	Website and Applicable Resources
Attendance Awareness Month	A nationwide event to recognize the connection between school attendance and academic achievement.	awareness.attendanceworks.org **Resources:** www.educationworld.com/attendance-awareness-month-resources-making-attendance-priority
Hispanic Heritage Month Sept. 15- Oct. 15	Observation began in 1968 which celebrates the histories, cultures and contributions of American citizens whose ancestors came from Spain, Mexico, the Caribbean and Central and South America.	www.hispanicheritagemonth.gov/about **Resources:** www.timeforkids.com/minisite/hispanic-heritage-month-1 www.smithsonianeducation.org/educators/resource_library/hispanic_resources.html www.nea.org/tools/lessons/hispanic-heritage-month.html
National Suicide Prevention Week Monday thru Sunday surrounding World Suicide Prevention Day, Sept. 10th	A week-long campaign to inform and engage health professionals and the public about suicide prevention and warning signs of suicide.	www.suicidology.org/about-aas/national-suicide-prevention-week **Resources:** suicidepreventionlifeline.org & www.sprc.org https://www.schoolcounselor.org/asca/media/asca/Resource%20Center/Suicide-Suicide%20Prevention/Sample%20Documents/suicide-prevention.pdf

OCTOBER

October	Description	Website and Applicable Resources
Bullying Prevention Month	Founded in 2006 by PACER's National Bullying Prevention Center. The campaign unites communities nationwide to educate and raise awareness of bullying prevention.	www.pacer.org/bullying/nbpm Resources: stompoutbullying.org/index.php/campaigns/national-bullying-prevention-awareness-month www.schoolcounselor.org/school-counselors-members/professional-development/asca-u/bullying-prevention-specialist-training
LGBT History Month	Founded in 1994, the event celebrates the achievements of 31 lesbian, gay, bisexual or transgender icons.	http://lgbthistorymonth.com Resources: https://gsanetwork.org/lgbthistorymonth www.schoolcounselor.org/asca/media/asca/PositionStatements/PS_LGBTQ.pdf
National Depression and Mental Health Screening Month	Designed to raise awareness of behavioral and mental health issues and working to reduce the stigma.	https://mentalhealthscreening.org/programs/initiatives Resources: https://nacchovoice.naccho.org/2015/10/08/national-depression-and-mental-health-screening-month-provides-opportunities-for-local-health-departments/
World Mental Health Day October 10th	A day for global health education, awareness, and advocacy against social stigma.	http://www.who.int/mental_health/world-mental-health-day/en/ Resources: https://www.schoolcounselor.org/asca/media/asca/PositionStatements/PS_StudentMentalHealth.pdf
America's Safe School Week Third Full Week of October	Established by the National School Safety Center in 1984 to motivate key education and law enforcement policymakers, students, parents, and community residents to advocate for school safety.	http://www.schoolsafety.us/safe-schools-week Resources: https://nationalsave.org/what-we-do/save-events/americas-safe-schools-week/ http://www.nea.org/tools/lessons/56917.htm http://www.dare.org/school-safety/
Character Counts Week Third Week of October	Event about the universal values we share, despite differences in political or religious affiliation.	https://charactercounts.org/cc-week/ Resources: http://images.pcmac.org/Uploads/BaldwinCounty/BaldwinCounty/Departments/DocumentsCategories/Documents/Activities%20for%20National%20Character%20Counts!%20Week.pdf https://resources.charactercounts.org/free-resources/cc-week-resources/
Mix it Up at Lunch Day Last Tuesday of October	Seeks to break down barriers between students, improve intergroup relations, and help schools create inclusive communities by sitting with different students.	www.tolerance.org/mix-it-up/what-is-mix Resources: educationforjustice.org/events/mix-it-lunch-day-1
Red Ribbon Week Last Week of October	Established by National Family Partnership to lead and support our nation's families and communities in nurturing the full potential of healthy, drug free youth.	redribbon.org Resources: confidentcounselors.com/2016/10/17/red-ribbon-week-resources www.elementaryschoolcounseling.org/red-ribbon-week.html

(Continued)

Figure 7.24 (Continued)

NOVEMBER

November	Description	Website and Applicable Resources
Military Family Appreciation Month	Celebration to honor the commitment and sacrifices made by the families of the nation's service members.	www.military.com/military-family-appreciation-month
National Career Development Month	Created by the National Career Development Association to promote career awareness and development.	ncda.org/aws/NCDA/pt/sp/OLD_ncdmonth Resources: www.schoolcounselor.org/asca/media/asca/Resource%20Center Career%20Development/Lesson%20Plans/Career.pdf
Native American Heritage Month	A time to celebrate rich and diverse cultures, traditions, histories, and to acknowledge the important contributions of Native Americans.	nativeamericanheritagemonth.gov www.ncai.org/initiatives/native-american-heritage-month Resources: www.ncai.org/initiatives/native-american-heritage-month

DECEMBER

December	Description	Website and Applicable Resources
Special Education Day December 2nd	Marks the anniversary of the nation's first federal special educational law (IDEA) signed into law on December 2, 1975. It is a day to reflect and reform.	specialeducationday.com Resources: tpcjournal.nbcc.org/the-school-counselor-and-special-education-aligning-training-with-practice
Human Rights Day December 10th	The date honors the United Nations General Assembly's adoption and proclamation in 1948 of the Universal Declaration of Human Rights.	http://www.ohchr.org/EN/AboutUs/Pages/HumanRightsDay.aspx

JANUARY

January	Description	Website and Applicable Resources
Get Organized Month	Dedicated to raising awareness of the benefits of getting organized.	www.napo.net/page/NAPOGOMonth
No Name Calling Week Fourth Week of January	Provides students and educators with the tools and inspiration to create an ongoing dialogue about ways to challenge bullying and name-calling in their communities	www.glsen.org/nonamecallingweek Resources: www.niot.org/nios/nncw/stopbullying www.adl.org/education/resources/tools-and-strategies/no-name-calling-week

FEBRUARY

February	Description	Website and Applicable Resources
African American History Month	A time to pay tribute to the generations of African Americans who struggled with adversity and their many accomplishments throughout American history.	www.africanamericanhistorymonth.gov Resources: http://www.smithsonianeducation.org/educators/resource_library/african_american_resources.html www.nea.org/tools/lessons/black-history-month.htm
Career and Technical Educational Month	Campaign to celebrate the value of career and technical education and the achievements and accomplishments from programs across the country	acteonline.org/ctemonth/#.WNw5tdEzVnk Resources: khake.com www2.ed.gov/about/offices/list/ovae/pi/cte/index.html
National School Counseling Week First Full Week of February	Highlights the tremendous impact school counselors can have in helping students achieve school success and plan for a career.	www.schoolcounselor.org/school-counselors-members/about-asca-(1)/national-school-counseling-week

Random Acts of Kindness Week Second Full Week of February	An opportunity to unite through kindness, make a difference, and bring smiles to the community.	www.randomactsofkindness.org **Resources:** info.character.org/blog/bid/204198/Get-Ready-for-Random-Acts-of-Kindness-Week

MARCH

March	Description	Website and Applicable Resources
Read Across America Day School Day Closest to March 2nd	Reading motivation and awareness program that calls for every child in every community to celebrate reading on March 2, the birthday of Dr. Seuss.	www.nea.org/grants/read-across-background.html **Resources:** http://www.readacrossamerica.org www.readingrockets.org/calendar/readacross
National School Breakfast Week Second Week of March	Celebration of the school breakfast program and a time to bring attention to your breakfast program.	schoolnutrition.org/Meetings/Events/NSBW/2017
International Women's Day March 8th	A day to celebrate the social, economic, cultural and political achievements of women and to support a more inclusive, gender equal world.	www.internationalwomensday.com

APRIL

April	Description	Website and Applicable Resources
Community Service Month	Emphasizes the importance of volunteering in the community.	dailyconcepts.com/community-service-month www.nationalservice.gov community.starbucks.com/en_us/home
National Autism Awareness Month	Campaign to increase understanding and acceptance of autism spectrum disorder, promote inclusions and self-determination, and support opportunity for highest possible quality of life.	www.autism-society.org/get-involved/national-autism-awareness-month **Resources:** www.autismspeaks.org
World Health Day April 7th	Celebrated to mark the anniversary of the founding of World Health Organization and provides opportunities for individuals to get involved in activities that lead to better health.	www.who.int/campaigns/world-health-day/2017/event/en **Resources:** www.paho.org/world-health-day
Earth Day April 22nd	Worldwide various events held to demonstrate support for environmental protection.	www.earthday.org **Resources:** www.epa.gov/earthday www.nea.org/tools/lessons/earth-day-curriculum.html

MAY

May	Description	Website and Applicable Resources
Asian-Pacific Heritage Month	A day to pay tribute to the generation of Asian and Pacific Islanders who enriched America's history and are instrumental in its future success.	asianpacificheritage.gov **Resources** www.teachervision.com/holidays/asian-pacific-american-heritage-month

(Continued)

Figure 7.24 (Continued)

| National PTA Teacher Appreciation Week
One Week in May | A time to celebrate teachers and other educators, expressing gratitude for their support of students. | www.pta.org/parents/content.cfm?ItemNumber=3270

Resources:
www.nea.org/grants/teacherday.html |
| Screen Free Week
(TV Turnoff Week)
First Week of May | Event in which children, families, school and communities are encouraged to turn off screens and 'turn on life.' | www.screenfree.org

Resources:
www.commercialfreechildhood.org/resource/screen-free-week-organizers-kit |

JUNE

June	Description	Website and Applicable Resources
National Safety Month	Focuses on reducing leading causes of injury and death at work, on the roads, and in our homes and communities.	www.nsc.org/act/events/Pages/national-safety-month.aspx Resources: safetycenter.org/top-5-free-resources-for-national-safety-month healthfinder.gov/NHO/PDFs/June2NHOToolkit.pdf
International Children's Day June 1st	Global celebration of the rights and well-being of children around the world, and to appreciate the role children play in the future of our communities.	www.nationalchildrensday.us

Activity 7.1

Selecting and Aligning Your Schoolwide Programs and Activities

Based on the information presented in this chapter, consider the following questions and fill in the charts below.

1. For each counseling domain, what national awareness campaign(s) or other schoolwide activities do you currently implement? Are there additional activities you would like to include in the future? Look at your school/district calendar to see if there are any events to add from there as well.

SCHOOLWIDE ACTIVITIES		
Academic	College/Career	Social/Emotional
• •	• •	• •

2. How does each of the schoolwide activities align with the core curriculum lessons you will be teaching?

Schoolwide Activities	Alignment to Core Curriculum

3. For each schoolwide activity, what parent education and events might you include?

Schoolwide Activities	Alignment to Family Education/ Events

4. As a school counselor, what will your role be in each activity? Who will lead? Who will support?

Schoolwide Activities	School Counselor's Role

8

Pre- and Post-Tests and Assessments

As a third-grade teacher, Malia regularly assessed student learning through a variety of informal and formal assessments throughout the year. She knew the reading level of her students, their knowledge of math facts, and much more. However, when she became an elementary school counselor, Malia stopped assessing students before and after her school counseling lessons. When questioned about her decision to not assess her students, Malia stated that she simply hadn't thought of doing so and that she got out of the habit of assessing students when she switched roles. Now realizing the importance of collecting data, Malia has set a goal to create, administer, and review the results of one core curriculum lesson for a primary and upper grade during the next school year.

C reating pre- and post-assessments is a well-developed skill that requires an understanding of the purpose of the assessment and the differences between assessments designed to measure attitudes, knowledge, skills, and behaviors.

This chapter supports school counselors as they obtain the knowledge and skills needed to assess activities delivered to all students in Tier 1: core instruction, school-wide events, and parent education. Teachers assess the impact of their instruction on their students, and as active members of the educational community, school counselors do, too. School counselors deliver material and core content in the same way teachers do. Assessing students' progress provides valuable and immediate feedback on the effectiveness of the instruction and the likelihood that the knowledge, attitudes, and skills gained will lead to behavior change.

REVISITING THE ART, SCIENCE, AND WONDER OF SCHOOL COUNSELING

Did you receive a Master of Arts (MA) or a Master of Science (MS) degree? Generally, the main method of teaching within a Master of Arts (MA) degree (focused on humanities and liberal arts) is via seminars with discussion heavily based on subject matter. Master of Science (MS) degree programs tend to have a stronger focus on the research and the science behind the brain and behavior; students are often involved in lab work, research, analysis, and evaluation. Within school counseling, both MA and MS programs (leading to licensing and/or credentialing, depending on the state) cover counseling as a subject but in very different ways. Additionally, the amount of coursework devoted specifically to school counseling varies greatly from program to program. It is not surprising, therefore, that many practicing school counselors receive little or no training within their graduate program on evaluation methodologies, the use of data to drive evidence-based interventions, and how to evaluate activity or program results. This consideration is highly relevant for elementary school counselors, as they are more likely to come from a liberal arts background.

Regardless of whether a school counselor receives an MA or MS degree, the professional field has shifted to balance the "art" and the "science" of counseling—particularly as this relates to delivering evidence-based programs and practices in schools. ASCA calls for school counselors to evaluate the impact of their lessons (ASCA, 2012). School counselors are all taught the "art" of counseling (e.g. listening, empathy, respect, genuineness, unconditional positive regard, self-disclosure, interpretation, open-ended questions, etc.) and the skills to utilize them (solution-focused counseling, etc.). In today's educational world, however, counselors must also become proficient in the science of evaluating their activities and their impact on the students they serve.

Figure 8.1 The Art, Science, and Wonder of School Counseling

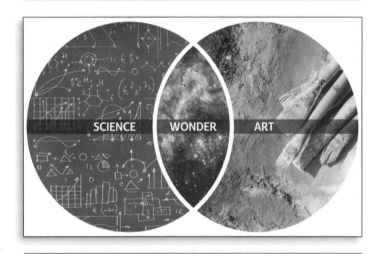

Source: Illustration by Gogis Design, http://www.gogisdesign.com.

The "Wonder" of School Counseling

You might ask: How much of the work of a school counselor each day is focused on the art of counseling as opposed to the science? When counselors focus exclusively on the art and ignore the science, they might be left "wondering" what difference they make every day. Part of the "wonder" of mixing the art and science of school counseling is the ability to take out the "wondering" by measuring the impact of the activities. When this occurs, school counselors often realize that the true "wonder" of the profession is the difference that counselors make in the lives of the students they serve each day.

CONCEPTUAL DIAGRAM FOR ELEMENTARY SCHOOL COUNSELING CURRICULUM

The conceptual diagram for a school counseling curriculum (see Figure 8.2) provides a practical model that elementary school counselors can use to guide their assessment of data in alignment with school counseling core curriculum. Adapted from the Hatching Results Conceptual Diagram (Hatch, 2013) for elementary-level and core curriculum, this visually outlines the relationship between the types of data (standards and competency, achievement-related, and achievement) and the ways to evaluate the data (process, perception, and outcome; Dimmitt, Carey, & Hatch, 2007; Hatch, 2005, 2013).

The diagram in Figure 8.2 reads left to right, representing an action framework connecting what the elementary school counselor is teaching (measured with process data) to the attainment of specific student standards and competencies (measured with perception data) and behavior change, leading to an improvement in outcomes, which is reflected in achievement-related data and subsequently in achievement data.

For example, when the elementary school counselor teaches a classroom lesson to fourth graders, the process data constitute the recipe (the who, what, when, and how often) that explains how the curriculum was delivered.

Process data:
Core curriculum

- Fourth-grade students
- October
- Three lessons in each fourth-grade classroom on study skills, including

    o Organizing classwork
    o Using a planner
    o Study strategies

Figure 8.2 Hatching Results Conceptual Diagram—Elementary Level

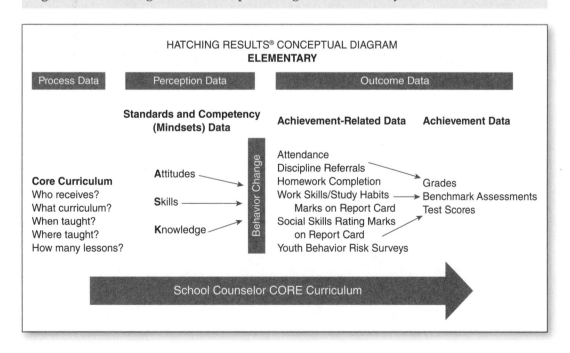

Next, the school counselor collects perception data on work skills and study habits to assess whether students acquire the following:

1. The attitude that it is important to write down classroom assignments

2. The skill of entering assignments into their planner

3. The knowledge of effective study strategies

When elementary school counselors teach their curriculum in the classroom or provide skills-based group counseling sessions, it is also appropriate for them to assess whether students have learned what was taught. Assessment answers the following questions:

- Was this a good use of instructional learning time?
- Was this a valuable use of school counselor time?
- Did students learn what was taught?
- In which areas are students competent?
- Is more instruction needed?

Collecting pre- and post-assessment data helps answer these questions.

Finally, the school counselor looks to connect the lesson content to measurable student outcomes—particularly in terms of achievement-related data. In this scenario, the goal of the lesson would be to support improvement in completing classroom assignments, homework completion rates, and marks on the "work skills and study strategies/work habits" portion of the report card. Improvements in these achievement-related outcomes lead to increased student academic performance (i.e., achievement data).

Figure 8.3 Sample Hatching Results Conceptual Diagram—Fourth-Grade Study Skills Lessons

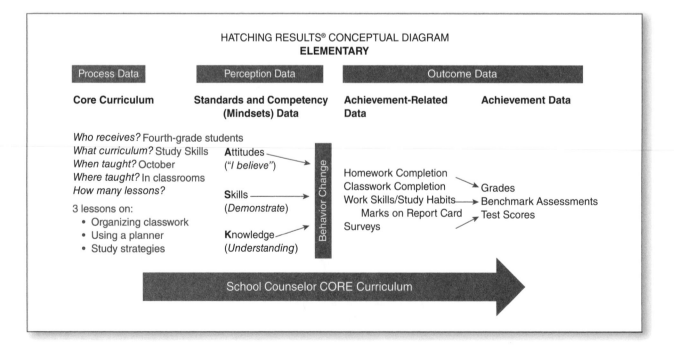

Activity 8.1

Refer to the "Don't Blow Your Top!" lesson plan from Chapter 4 (pages 84). Write the process, perception, and outcome data for this lesson, utilizing the information presented in the lesson plan and your understanding of the Hatching Results Conceptual Diagram.

CREATING PRE- AND POST-ASSESSMENTS

ASK (ASK Students What They Learned)

As professional educators, it is appropriate for elementary school counselors to assess the impact of their teaching in much the same way teachers do. One way to do this is through assessments provided prior to and following the lesson/unit. When developing pre- and post-tests, counselors are encouraged to assess areas called for in the ASCA national standards: knowledge, skills, and attitudes.

The acronym "ASK" is a reminder that when the school counselor is finished teaching a lesson, he or she should *ASK* the students what they learned (Hatch 2013). *ASK* stands for *Attitudes, Skills,* and *Knowledge.* Though this acronym reminds us to measure all three areas, arranging questions in the order of attitudes, knowledge, then skills is suggested when constructing the actual pre- and post-tests.

To develop an assessment, consider the following:

- What do you want students to *believe* that you don't already think they believe?
- What do you want students to *know* that you don't already think they know?
- What *skill* do you want students to demonstrate that you don't already think they possess?

Attitude Questions

Attitude questions measure the students' beliefs or opinions. The Likert (pronounced "lick-ert") scale is most commonly used when creating surveys to assess opinions. When students answer these items, they are stating the degree to which they agree or disagree with the statement. Typically, a five-point item is written, measuring a bipolar positive or negative response to the item.

Figure 8.4 Logic Model for Assessments

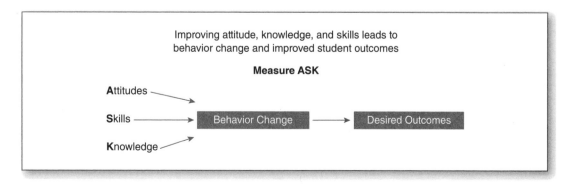

For example:

1. Strongly agree

2. Agree

3. Neither agree nor disagree

4. Disagree

5. Strongly disagree

While this scale includes a middle value representing a neutral or undecided position, it is also possible to use a forced-choice scale by removing that option. In this way, the respondents are forced to decide whether to lean more toward the "agree" or "disagree" end of the spectrum. This can be helpful if there is concern that students may not take the survey seriously and choose to opt out via the middle ground rather than commit to an opinion. For younger students, it may be more helpful to use the terminology "not sure" instead of "neither agree nor disagree."

Questions to assess attitudes can be scaled in different ways, depending on what is being assessed. The University of Connecticut has created the chart shown in Table 8.1 with the most common Likert questions in the areas of agreement, frequency, importance, quality, and likelihood (Siegle, 2010).

In elementary school, it is particularly important that students understand how to respond to measures of attitudes and beliefs. It will be helpful to model and practice with them prior to administering the assessment.

Table 8.1   Likert-Type Scale Sample Ratings

Likert-Type Scale Sample Ratings		
Agreement		
Strongly disagree Disagree Neither agree nor disagree Agree Strongly agree	Disagree Neither agree nor disagree Agree	Completely disagree Mostly disagree Slightly disagree Slightly agree Mostly agree Completely agree
Occurrences		
Very rarely Rarely Occasionally Frequently Very frequently	Never Seldom About half the time Usually Always	Not at all Little Occasionally Often All the time
Not really Somewhat Quite a bit	Never Rarely Sometimes Often Always	Never Seldom Sometimes Often

Occurrences		
Not much Some A great deal	A little Some A lot	Not much Little Somewhat Much A great deal

Importance		
Not important Moderately important Very important	Unimportant Of little importance Important Very important	Unimportant Of little importance Moderately important Important Very important

Quality		
Poor Fair Average Good Excellent	Very poor Not good All right Good Excellent	Extremely poor Below average Average Above average Excellent

Content		
Too elementary Okay Too technical	Too fast Just right Too slow	Poor Not good Good Excellent
Did not understand Understood a little Understood most of it Understood very well	No help at all Slightly helpful Fairly helpful Very helpful	Quite unsuccessful Somewhat unsuccessful Somewhat successful Quite successful

Implementation		
Definitely will not Probably will not Probably will Definitely will	Absolutely no Mostly no Neither yes nor no Mostly yes Absolutely yes	Never true Sometimes true Often true
Not at all Very little Somewhat To a great extent	Not at all true Slightly true True about half the time Mostly true Completely true	Probably not Maybe Quite likely Definitely

Overall Impression	
Very dissatisfied Somewhat dissatisfied Neither satisfied nor dissatisfied Somewhat satisfied Very satisfied	Not at all satisfied Slightly satisfied Somewhat satisfied Very much satisfied
Didn't get what I wanted Got a little of what I wanted Got a lot of what I wanted Got everything I wanted	Very uncomfortable Uncomfortable Comfortable Very comfortable

Source: Used with permission from University of Wisconsin-Extension, Cooperative Extension, Program Development and Evaluation, *Building Capacity in Evaluating Outcomes, 2008,* modified and adapted by Julie Pigott Dillard, UF IFAS Washington County Extension, 2013, http://templatelab.com/likert-scale.

Juan and Elizabeth are school counselors in the same district who often collaborate on implementing school counseling lessons. They are both unsure whether their third-grade students know the difference between "agree" and "strongly agree" and also understand that students who report that they "strongly agree" as opposed to "agree" are more likely to perform the behaviors. Therefore, one counselor decides to use emoticons, and the other opts to use thumbs up/thumbs down to assess students.

To explain the differences, the counselors ask students to share which picture represents how much they like each thing listed in Table 8.2.

Table 8.2 Ways to Describe a Likert Scale at the Elementary Level

Sample Meanings	Strongly Agree	Agree	Unsure	Disagree	Strongly Disagree
Likert Responses (Emoticons)					
Likert Responses (Thumbs Up/Down)					
Brussels Sprouts	LOVE IT! I eat it every day and ask for it on my birthday!	I eat it and enjoy it but not every day.	Not sure what this is.	Dislike it. I don't want to eat it, or I try not to eat it.	HATE it! Makes me throw up!
Pizza	LOVE IT! I eat it every day and ask for it on my birthday!	I eat it and enjoy it but not every day.	Not sure what this is.	Dislike it. I don't want to eat it, or I try not to eat it.	HATE it! Makes me throw up!
Science	LOVE IT! Very best part of the day!	Like it, but I like other subjects more.	Not sure what this is.	Don't like it and prefer not to do it.	HATE it! It's my worst subject.
Soccer	LOVE IT! I Can't wait for soccer practice!	Like it but I like other sports better.	I don't have any opinion because I've never played.	Don't like it and prefer not to play it.	HATE it! I never want to go to soccer practice again!

Both Juan and Elizabeth make sure to explain to students that there is no right or wrong answer; rather, people just have different opinions and preferences. Whereas some people like Brussels sprouts and answer with a smiley face or a thumbs up (agree), others may dislike this food and answer with a frown face or a thumbs down (disagree). The counselors then use exaggerated yucky sounds to demonstrate "strongly disagree" and jump up and down, clapping, to represent "strongly agree." Finally, they explain that some people might feel unsure because they have never eaten Brussels sprouts before, so they would select the straight face or sideways thumb response option. Juan and Elizabeth share various examples from Table 8.2 with their students. Once students understand the differences between all response options, the counselors are ready to provide the pre-test with confidence.

Icons by iStock.com/MonikaBeitlova.

Knowledge Questions

Knowledge questions measure what students know about a lesson topic both before and after the lesson is delivered. Knowledge items check the accuracy of factual content learned by students during the lesson and are either correct or incorrect. Knowledge questions are best provided in multiple-choice format, as opposed to true/false (T/F) format, which has a 50% guessing factor, compared to 33% for three multiple-choice responses (a, b, and c). Additional response items reduce the likelihood of guessing even further (see Table 8.3). The goal is to reduce student guessing and to assist in measuring actual learning, not chance. With five multiple-choice items, the baseline correct response is lower than true/false. It is important to consider the developmental level of students when determining multiple-choice responses, as fifth graders are less likely to be overwhelmed by a higher number of choices than third graders would be.

Skills Questions

The next step is to determine whether students have learned the skills taught within the lesson. Creating skills questions can be more complex than creating knowledge questions, because it requires application, or utilizing the knowledge that has been gained (Bloom, Englehart, Furst, Hill, & Krathwohl, 1956). Students think about what they learned, identify the knowledge, and apply the knowledge to a new situation or scenario (Dimmitt, Carey, & Hatch, 2007).

Table 8.3 Guessing Percentages for Pre- and Post-Assessments

Type of Question	Guessing Factor	Pre-test Sample Correct %	Post-test Sample Correct %	% Increase*
True/False	50%	50%	80%	60%
3-Item MC	33%	33%	80%	142%
4-Item MC	25%	25%	80%	220%
5-Item MC	20%	20%	80%	300%

*Learn how to calculate percentage increase/change in Chapter 9, page 219.

Note: MC = multiple-choice.

Phillip, a school counselor, was teaching fifth graders a lesson on the dangers of smoking and how to respond to peer pressure. He wanted to assess his fifth-grade students to see if they knew the dangers of using cigarettes and that cigarette smoking is responsible for killing more than 480,000 people every year. He decided to use a true/false test in classroom 1. Here is the question he asked, along with the student responses he received:

True/False: Cigarette smoking is responsible for killing about 480,000 people every year.

- 60% responded True (correct)
- 40% responded False

He then gave students in classroom 2 a five-point multiple-choice questionnaire:

Cigarette smoking is responsible for killing about _____ people every year:

a. 200,000
b. 350,000
c. 430,000
d. 480,000
e. 550,000

Responses were as follows:

a. 12%
b. 18%
c. 22%
d. 25% (correct)
e. 23%

Essentially, his students were guessing. They didn't *know* the actual number—how could they? They had not been taught the lesson!

After completing the lesson, Phillip gave students in classroom 1 a true/false assessment again and provided a multiple-choice assessment to classroom 2.

By using multiple-choice instead of a true/false question, Phillip was better able to see what students really had learned and measure growth of their knowledge more accurately. This illustrates why we recommend using multiple-choice questions rather than true/false.

Table 8.4 Example Pre- and Post-Assessment Chart Using True/False Questions Compared to Multiple-Choice

Type of Question	Pre-test Sample Correct %	Post-test Sample Correct %	% Increase
True/False	60%	95%	58.3%
5-item MC	25%	95%	280%

Note: MC = multiple-choice.

One way to differentiate a knowledge from a skill question is to compare it to math. In math, 2 + 2 = 4, which is knowledge. However, if a word problem asks, "If Jade has two apples and Maureen gives her two more, how many apples does she have now?" then the student must extract the equation from the word problem and apply his or her knowledge to solve it. In the same way, a scenario that asks students what comes next or what step a student missed in conflict resolution is the application of knowledge—a skill.

The following are sample ways in which school counselors can assess student skills:

- Provide a sample scenario within the pre- or post-assessment questions (see the following section for more details)
- Demonstrate conflict resolution skills through role-play
- Complete a career interest inventory
- Identify the location of classes on a school map
- Locate a missing part of an assignment planner
- Write a short-term or long-term goal
- Use a ticket out the door (see Chapter 5, page 102)

Writing Good Questions

Teach what you assess; assess what you teach. To begin creating your own questions, look closely at the curriculum you plan to teach. What is the core knowledge the curriculum wants the students to know? What is the core belief in the messaging? What skills are being taught within the lesson? Remember that no matter how valid the question is, students must know what is expected of them, so be sure to always include clear instructions, too. What follows are sample slides from an elementary presentation to demonstrate the formation of good pre- and post-assessment questions.

"Don't Blow Your Top! How to Control Anger"
Lesson Pre- and Post-Assessment Questions

Figures 8.5 through 8.9 show sample slides from the "Don't Blow Your Top!" classroom lesson from Chapter 4 (pages 84). Notice that the questions are created directly from the content presented on the slide. Additionally, the skill learned in this lesson is assessed through the letter written by students, which demonstrates application of their knowledge through a writing piece rather than through a pre- or post-assessment question. It would be helpful to review Chapter 4 on lesson plans prior to reading further.

"Don't Blow Your Top!"—Pre-/Post-Assessment

1. It's OK for kids to feel angry.

   a. Strongly agree

   b. Agree

   c. Disagree

   d. Strongly disagree

2. It's wrong for grownups to be angry.

   a. Strongly agree

   b. Agree

   c. Disagree

   d. Strongly disagree

3. Anger is a

   a. Feeling that means you are a bad person

   b. Feeling only some kids have

   c. Normal emotion

   d. Negative emotion

   e. Feeling that means you are a mean person

4. What can happen to our bodies when we are angry?

   a. Crying

   b. Sweaty hands

   c. Racing heart

   d. Breathing fast

   e. All of these can happen.

5. Which of the following are good ways to calm down?

   a. Taking three deep breaths

   b. Counting backward

   c. Thinking of calm things

   d. Talking to myself

   e. All of these are good ways

6. Which of the following is <u>NOT</u> an anger buster?

   a. Listening to music

   b. Exercise

   c. Eating something

   d. Writing my thoughts

   e. Drawing

The pages shown in Figures 8.5 through 8.8 are provided to assist in understanding how the pre-/post-assessment questions were created. Pay particular attention to how the questions from the pre-/post-assessment are taken directly from the lesson's slides. This is a vital skill for the school counselor to learn for creating assessments. The question must directly align to the lesson content presented. While some school counselors may state that they will "say the content" when they deliver the

Figure 8.5   "Don't Blow Your Top!" Pre-/Post-Assessment Questions 1–3

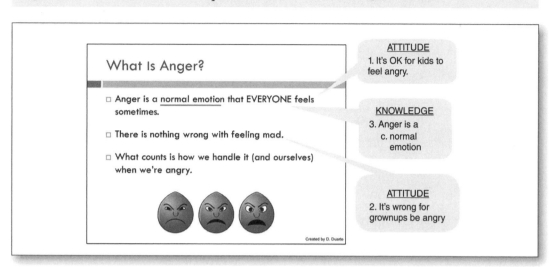

Figure 8.6   "Don't Blow Your Top!" Pre-/Post-Assessment Question 4

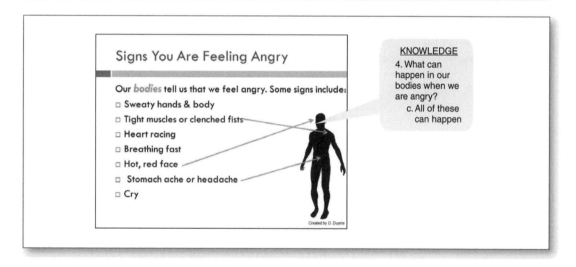

lesson, experience teaches us that we can't control or predict whether we will remember to say what is needed to ensure that students learn the material. Therefore, it is essential for the school counselor to align the questions with the visual content from the lesson. Additionally, students are more likely to learn by both seeing and hearing the information, which is another reason to be sure to include it in the visual presentation.

Note that in question 4, the answer is e (all of the above). It would be helpful when reading the PowerPoint slides and questions to review the "Don't Blow Your Top!"—Pre-/Post-Assessment questions that were listed previously.

In question 6, note that the word "not" is capitalized and underlined to ensure that students read that word. We suggest using "not" for upper grades (fourth and above) rather than lower grades, as the goal is not to see if students know how to read a question but rather to determine whether they learned the material they were taught.

Figure 8.7 "Don't Blow Your Top!" Pre-/Post-Assessment Question 5

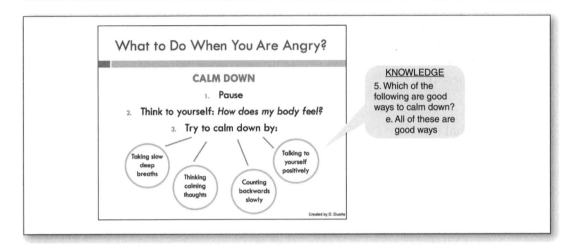

Figure 8.8 "Don't Blow Your Top!" Pre-/Post-Assessment Question 6

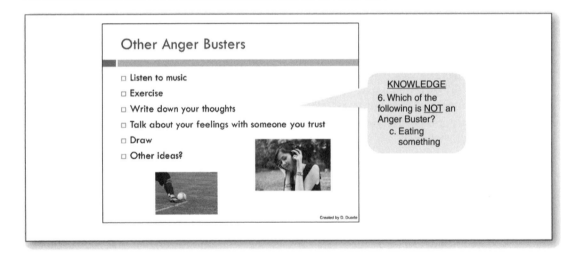

Figure 8.9 "Don't Blow Your Top!" Assessment of Skill

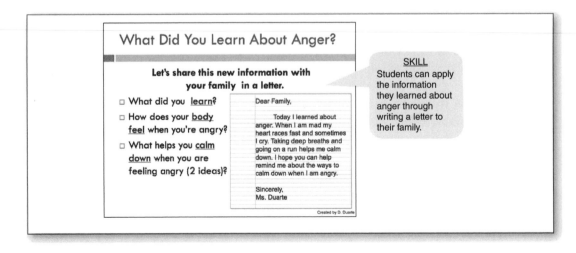

Activity 8.2

Refer to the anti-bullying lesson slides used to create guided notes in Chapter 5, page 99. What type of attitude, knowledge, and/or skills questions could be created from the information presented on the slides? Example questions are presented below. Locate the information on the slides used to create the pre- and post-assessment questions. The entire lesson and pre-/post-test can be found in the online appendix.

I believe that it is important to help stop bullying in my school.

a. Strongly agree
b. Agree
c. Disagree
d. Strongly disagree

I believe I should tell an adult every time someone calls me a name.

a. Strongly agree
b. Agree
c. Disagree
d. Strongly disagree

What is bullying?

a. An action meant to harm someone else
b. An abuse of power
c. Attacking someone with words
d. Attacking someone with actions
e. All of the above

What is a person who watches the bullying called?

a. The lookout
b. A bully
c. The victim
d. A bystander
e. An upstander

When you tell on someone you want to get into trouble, it is called:

a. Being assertive
b. Being a bully
c. Tattling
d. Whining
e. Reporting

When you tell on someone because there is danger, it is called:

a. Being assertive
b. Being a bully
c. Tattling
d. Whining
e. Reporting

Creating Pre- and Post-Assessment Questions From Prepackaged Curriculum

Many elementary school counselors teach prepackaged curriculum, such as *Second Step*. In this case, the assessment tools provided in the prepackaged curriculum may not align with attitudes, knowledge, and skills from the specific lessons being taught. If a school counselor wants to assess the impact of the curriculum he or she is teaching students, the best way is to match the content to the questions. In many *Second Step* lessons, for instance, additional skill components are built into the lesson. Using the skill components or worksheets as the "ticket out the door," the school counselor can still check for accuracy of completion and report that 100% of students were able to accurately demonstrate assertive responses.

In the next section, a sample fourth-grade *Second Step* lesson and corresponding self-created pre-/post-assessment is shared. Note how the ASK links to the curriculum and the questions.

Second Step Grade 4, Lessons 16 and 17—Pre-/Post-Assessment

1. I believe that walking away when I have a problem will help me get along better with others.

   a. Strongly agree   b. Agree   c. Disagree   d. Strongly disagree

2. I believe that calming down will help me solve my problems.

   a. Strongly agree   b. Agree   c. Disagree   d. Strongly disagree

3. I believe that it's OK to blame someone if it's their fault.

   a. Strongly agree   b. Agree   c. Disagree   d. Strongly disagree

4. "You always" and "you never" are what kind of words?

   a. Mean

   b. Problem-solving

   c. Calming-down

   d. Blaming

   e. All of the above

5. Using the word **STEP** can help us remember the steps to solving problems. What does "**S**" stand for?

   a. **S**olve the problem

   b. **S**top the bad behavior

   c. **S**ay the problem

   d. **S**eek out help from an adult

   e. **S**top the problem

6. Using the word **STEP** can help us remember the steps to solving problems. What does "**T**" stand for?

    a. <u>T</u>ry to solve the program

    b. <u>T</u>hink of solutions

    c. <u>T</u>ake your time

    d. <u>T</u>ell an adult

    e. <u>T</u>reat others better

7. Using the word **STEP** can help us remember the steps to solving problems. What does "**E**" stand for?

    a. <u>E</u>xamine the choices

    b. <u>E</u>nd the fighting

    c. <u>E</u>nd the arguing

    d. <u>E</u>xplore the consequences

    e. <u>E</u>veryone wins

8. Using the word **STEP** can help us remember the steps to solving problems. What does "**P**" stand for?

    a. <u>P</u>ick the best solution

    b. <u>P</u>romise to solve the problem

    c. <u>P</u>ractice solving the problem

    d. <u>P</u>ick new friends

    e. <u>P</u>lay nice

9. Which of these is <u>NOT</u> an example of a *blaming statement*:

    a. "You made me!"

    b. "You're always cheating at handball."

    c. "They never pick me to play."

    d. "I want a turn on the swing."

    e. "He never plays fair."

10. Which of the following is an example of a *blaming statement*?

    a. "I wish I could have a turn at handball!"

    b. "We both disagree about who is out in handball."

    c. "She never plays fair."

    d. "We disagree about who should be first in line."

    e. "I want a turn on the computer."

11. When thinking of solutions, the **two** *most important things* to remember are that they must be:

    a. Honest and fair

    b. Clear and short

    c. Safe and respectful

    d. Quick and easy

    e. Open and fun

12. Consequences

    a. Are positive

    b. Are negative

    c. Can be both positive and negative

    d. Are neither positive nor negative

13. If the solution you pick to solve the problem doesn't work, what should you do?

    a. Walk away

    b. Think of other options

    c. Tell the teacher

    d. Give up

    e. Go back to the list and choose another option

14. Axel received a "No Homework Pass" for turning in all of his homework for the month. Chloe stayed in during recess for not completing her classwork. These are examples of:

    a. Right and wrong

    b. Things teachers do

    c. What happens in school

    d. Positive and negative consequences

    e. Fair and unfair

15. Bobby knows that not keeping his hands to himself at recess is a problem. He thought of possible solutions, and explored the consequences for each solution. What should he do next?

    a. Pick the best solution

    b. Explore consequences

    c. Calm down

d. Tell himself to keep his hands to himself

e. Ask his friend for advice

16. Lulu and Fibby both want to use the iPad. Lulu wants to tell Fibby she is not being fair. Fibby was already on the iPad for 20 minutes. Instead of blaming, Lulu can say:

a. "You always want to use the iPad!"

b. "You are not being fair; it is my turn!"

c. "I'd like a turn on the iPad."

d. "You never like to share!"

e. "You can't hog the iPad!"

Figure 8.10 Creating Pre-/Post-Assessment Questions—*Second Step* Grade 4, Lesson 16 and 17, Page 1, Questions 1–5

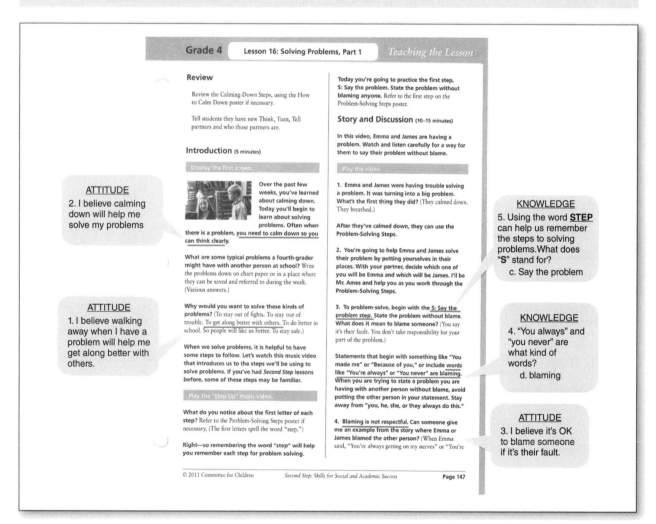

Figure 8.11   Creating Pre-/Post-Assessment Questions—*Second Step* Grade 4, Lesson 16 and 17, Page 2, Questions 9–10

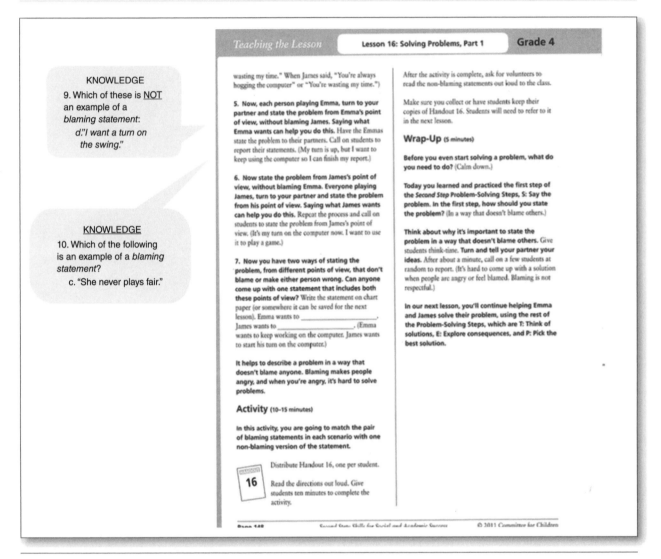

Source: Material excerpted from the Second Step Program © 2011 Committee for Children. Reprinted with permission from Committee for Children, Seattle, WA. www.cfchildren.org.

When creating assessments for core curriculum, counselors are encouraged to match the art of instruction to the science of assessments. Much like their teacher counterparts, school counselors seek to improve their instructional practice as well as outcomes for students. By learning from the results of their assessments whether their students have gained the knowledge and skills needed for success, school counselors improve their craft and practice. This wisdom is at the center of the art and the science of school counseling.

Activity 8.3

Create a pre-/post-assessment with attitude, knowledge, and skills questions for one of your core curriculum classroom lessons.

Figure 8.12 Creating Pre-/Post-Assessment Questions—*Second Step* Grade 4, Lesson 16 and 17, Page 3, Questions 6, 7, 11, 12, 14

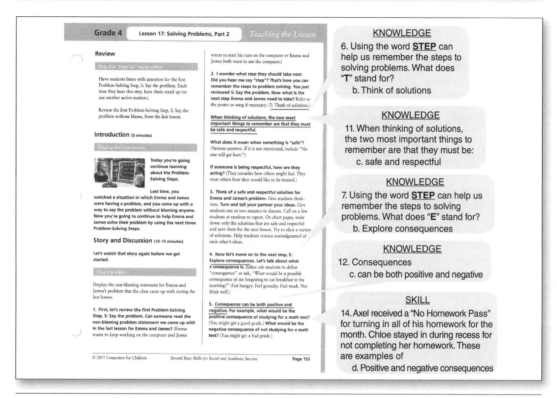

Source: Material excerpted from the Second Step Program © 2011 Committee for Children. Reprinted with permission from Committee for Children, Seattle, WA. www.cfchildren.org.

Figure 8.13 Creating Pre-/Post-Assessment Questions—*Second Step* Grade 4, Lesson 16 and 17, Page 4, Questions 8, 13, 15, 16

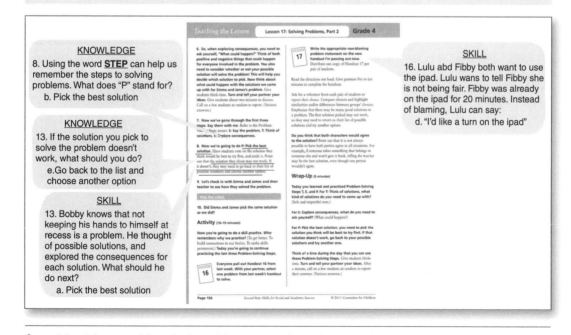

Source: Material excerpted from the Second Step Program © 2011 Committee for Children. Reprinted with permission from Committee for Children, Seattle, WA. www.cfchildren.org.

Using Technology Tools Such as Google Forms and Plickers to Support Pre- and Post-Assessments

Finding an efficient way to measure students' attitudes, knowledge, and skills is extremely important for busy elementary school counselors. Gone are the days of hand scoring pre- and post-tests because of the many technology tools available to easily collect and analyze data. Google Forms and Plickers are two tools for administering pre- and post-assessments to students but can also be used for needs assessments and other surveys. Additionally, both are user-friendly and free. See the following descriptions for more details.

Figure 8.14 *"Don't Blow Your Top!" Assessment Using Google Forms*

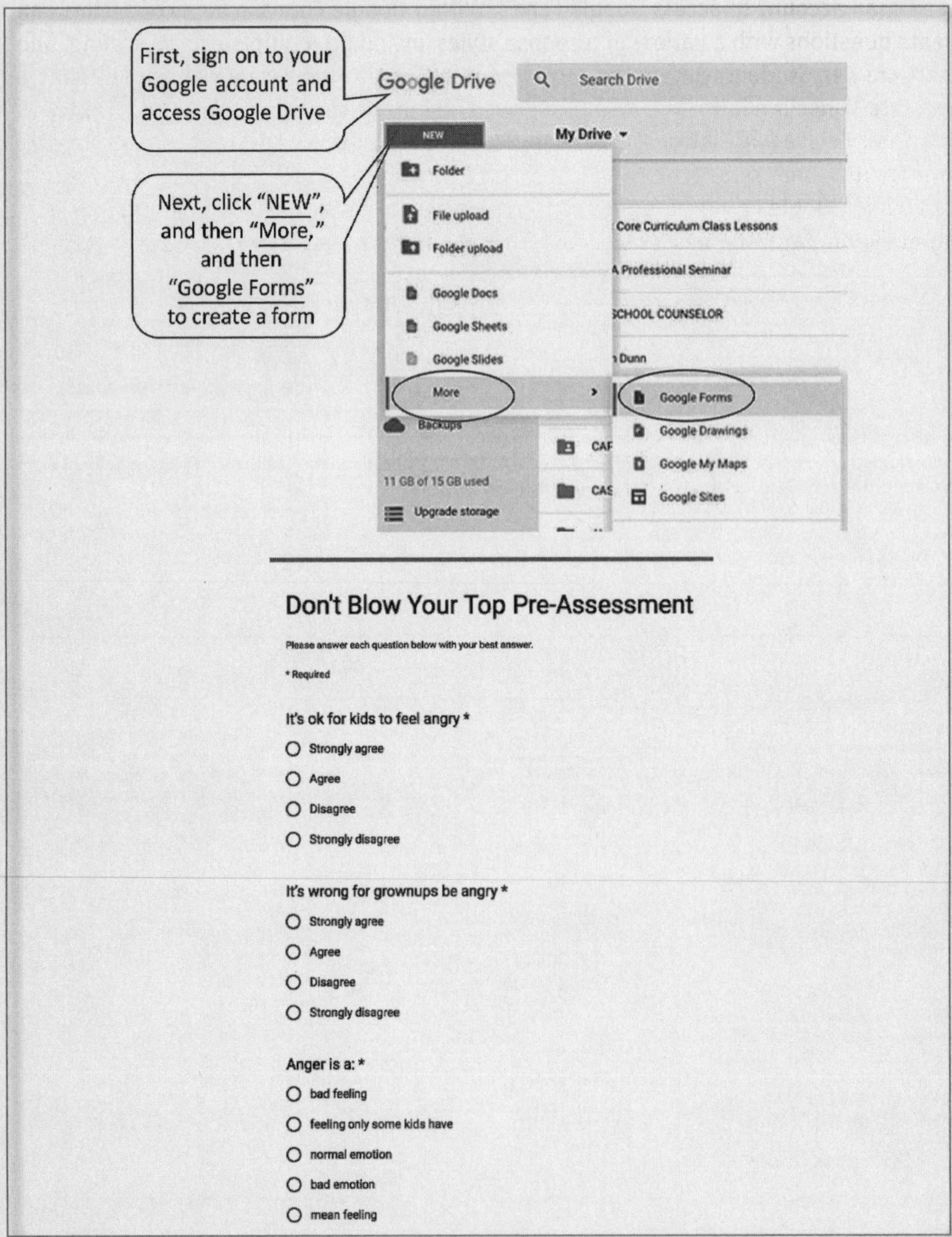

Google Forms

Google Forms is a free technology tool that allows school counselors to make an assessment or survey to collect results in an easy, streamlined fashion. After students fill out an assessment through Google Forms, their information is collected in an online spreadsheet within the creator's Google Drive folder. As Google Forms automatically creates simple charts and graphs of the data, further analysis can be completed by using the raw data in the spreadsheet. School counselors can also easily share the form with others as they are creating the questions and/or analyzing the results, making collaboration easy—so much so that many districts are using Google for their e-mail and storage platforms. School counselors working in districts without Google can create a free Gmail account to access Google Forms. Within Google Forms, school counselors can create questions with a variety of response styles, including multiple-choice, scaling, and short-answer. Students access the assessment in Google Forms via a website link that is generated once the form is complete; they can fill out the survey on a computer, tablet, or any other device with internet access. See the example survey and results using Google Forms with some questions from the "Don't Blow Your Top!" lesson. Also remember that while Google Forms automatically creates pie charts with multiple-choice and scaling question data, the best way to present pre- and post-assessment results is through

Figure 8.15 "Don't Blow Your Top!" Assessment Results Using Google Forms

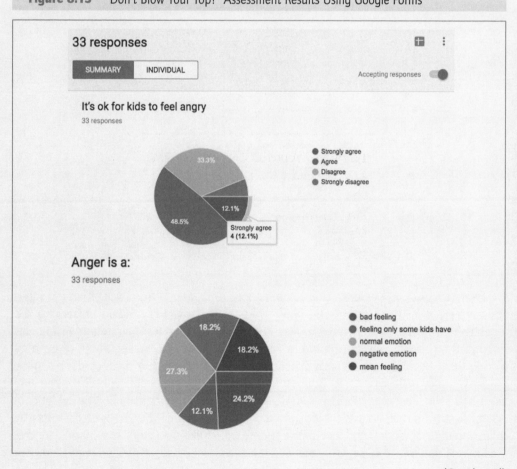

(Continued)

(Continued)

side-by-side bar graphs. School counselors are encouraged to create their own graphs using the data that Google Forms collects in a spreadsheet.

Plickers

Plickers is a way to collect assessment data without students' needing to access electronic devices. Students are given a "Plicker" (rhymes with "clicker") card with a unique visual code. The code has four sides, each lettered A, B, C, and D. The student holds the card so that the letter he or she chooses to respond to the multiple-choice, scaling, or true/false question (remember that true/false questions are not actually recommended for assessments—see page 177) is at the top of the card. The counselor uses the app on his or her smartphone to slowly scan the room and capture the answers that the students have chosen. The app will record each student's answer only once, so there is no need to worry about skewing your data. The results appear live and in real time on the teacher's device, or they can be projected on a large screen for the whole class to see via the Plickers' website if required. Plicker cards can be printed from the Plickers' website for free, or a laminated set of 40 can be ordered on Amazon for a small cost ($20 per set at time of publication).

Figure 8.16   Using Plickers for School Counseling Core Curriculum Lesson Assessment

Prior to assessing students, the school counselor creates a free Plickers account and adds the pre-/post-assessment questions to his or her saved file. When presenting the assessment to students, the school counselor can display the question and answer choices through the Plickers website, through a PowerPoint/slideshow presentation, or even by writing them on the board. As each question is asked, students turn their cards to display the answer they believe is correct at the top (A, B, C, or D). The school counselor is the only one who needs technology to assess student results—using a smartphone or a tablet connected to the internet, he or she scans the room as students hold up their cards, instantly collecting data of correct and incorrect responses. Just like Google Forms, graphs are created in real time and can be easily shared with the class. Go to http://www.plickers.com for more information or to create an account and download Plickers cards.

Figure 8.17 "Don't Blow Your Top!" Assessment Results Using Plickers (View From Smartphone)

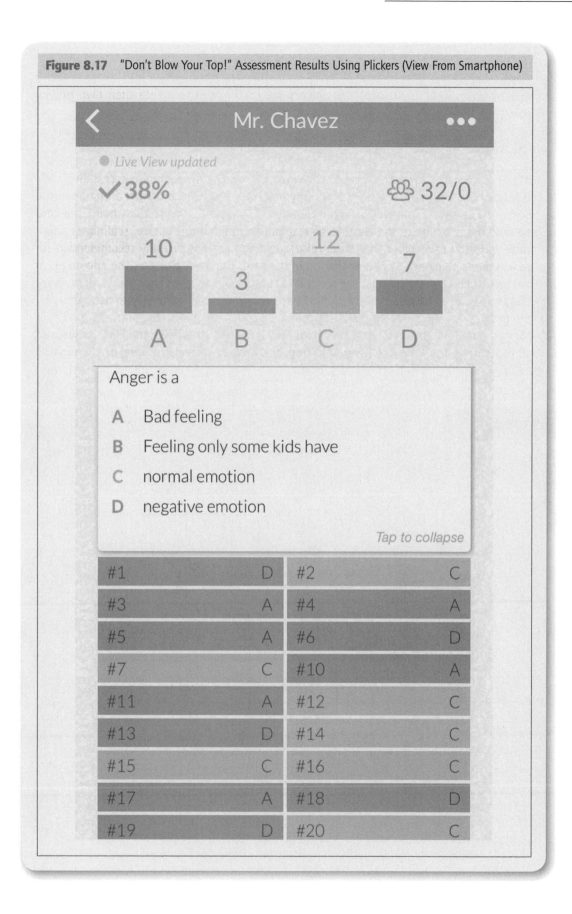

9

Sharing School Counseling Program Results

Joy was a school counseling trainee interning at an elementary school during her last semester of graduate school. One day she asked her school counseling supervisor, "What should I really focus on learning to become a highly skilled counselor?"

Her supervisor paused and then responded, "When I was in your shoes, I never imagined this would be my answer, but collecting and analyzing data and effectively marketing your school counseling program are essential skills for school counselors today. I can work extremely hard, but if I don't demonstrate and share the impact of my work, neither teachers, administrators, nor families will understand the benefit of a comprehensive school counseling program. Learning about data and marketing allows you to both measure and share program results for future improvement and to ensure the sustainability of your role as a school counselor."

Elementary school counselors are vital members of the school team who help ensure the success of all students. Through developing and evaluating a data-driven school counseling program, counselors create and continually improve school counseling lessons and activities based on school and community needs, and they share these successes with stakeholders. Data analysis helps school counselors determine what has worked and what hasn't, and clarifies what needs to be changed or improved. Through showcasing process, perception, and outcome data (reviewed in Chapter 8), school counselors demonstrate how students have benefited from school counseling services. In addition, evaluation allows for analysis of effectiveness and helps inform decisions related to program improvement, while guiding future planning (Duarte & Hatch, 2014). Ultimately, evaluation of the impact of school counseling Tier 1 activities, as well as strengths and areas for improvement, drives updates to counseling program SMART goals and future program implementation to achieve the desired results.

There are many ways to showcase school counseling program results, whether through presentations using different technology tools or by highlighting successes more informally. Regardless of the style, sharing is important to increase understanding about the school counselor's role and to build program sustainability. This chapter walks school counselors through a variety of ways to share results.

ASCA RESULTS REPORTS

The American School Counselor Association (ASCA) provides Results Report templates—the School Counseling Core Curriculum Results Report (see is appropriate for Tier 1 lessons. Results Reports serve as documentation tools for ensuring that the counseling program was carried out as planned, that every student was served, and that developmentally appropriate standards were addressed. In addition, Results Reports share process, perception, and outcome data, reflections on curriculum activities' effectiveness and impact, and ideas for improving the activity

Figure 9.1   School Counseling Core Curriculum Results Report Template

Grade Level	Lesson Topic	ASCA Domain and Mindsets & Behaviors Standard(s)	Projected Start/End	Process Data (Projected number of students affected)	Perception Data (Achievement, attendance and/or behavior data)	Outcome Data (Achievement, attendance and/or behavior data to be collected)	Implications

Figure 9.2   How to Write a Results Report

[DISTRICT NAME] & [YEAR]
School Counselor Core Curriculum
Results Report – [LESSON TITLE]

Grade Level	Lesson Topic	ASCA Domain & Standards	Curriculum and Materials	Start/End Date	Process Data (Number of students affected)	Perception Data: Pre/post assessments (What students learned, believe, think, or can demonstrate)	Outcome Data How did students' behavior change because of the lesson? (Improved achievement, attendance and/or behavior)	Limitations, Implications & Next Steps (So, what does the data tell you?)
What grade level(s) did you service?	What was the content of your core curriculum lesson? Describe the topics covered	What domain(s) were addressed? (Academic, career, social/ emotional)	What materials did you use? Were they pre-packaged or counselor generated?	When did you begin and end the lesson?	How many students received the lesson(s)?	**Results of Pre-Test / Post-Test** (Pick a few relevant samples and attach the rest of the results to the report) **Attitude:** Prior to counseling lesson ___% believed _XYZ__ Afterwards ___% indicated they believe XYZ **Skills:** Prior to counseling lesson ___% demonstrated XYZ Afterwards ___% demonstrated XYZ **Knowledge:** Prior to counseling lesson ___% knew XYZ Afterwards ___% know XYZ	**Achievement-Related Data** Report any achievement-related data you collected or are monitoring for improvement (this will vary depending on activity) e.g. *Homework rates? Attendance? Discipline? etc.* **Achievement Data** Report any academic achievement data you collected or are monitoring for improvement (this will vary depending on activity) e.g. *Test scores At or above grade level on achievement test etc.*	What worked? What didn't? What will you do differently next time? Were there limitations to your results? What recommendations do you have for improvement?

or program. This tool is particularly useful for keeping track of core curriculum data throughout the year and for sharing information with administrators, teachers, and families. See Figure 9.2 for a results report template with prompts to support creating your own report.

Figure 9.3 is a results report from school counselor Felipe Zañartu sharing results from his third- and fourth-grade *Second Step* Emotion Management lessons.

FLASHLIGHT RESULTS PRESENTATIONS

A Flashlight Presentation shines a light on *one* thing that the school counseling program has measured well through a simple PowerPoint or another visual presentation software. School counselors are encouraged to present a brief Flashlight Presentation of 6 to 10 minutes to stakeholders, post the presentation to a school website, and/or share it at a district level meeting with other counselors as a way to communicate the school counseling program's activities and impact.

What is the Flashlight Presentation?

- A tool that shares the school counseling program's effectiveness and impact
- A tool to educate others about school counseling and the school counselor's role as a valuable educator

Figure 9.3   Example Results Report

RESULTS REPORT
Avaxat School Counseling Program
Core Curriculum (3ʳᵈ & 4ᵗʰ Grade Emotion Management)

Grade Level	Lesson Topic	ASCA Domain and Mindsets & Behaviors Standard(s)	Projected Start/ End	Process Data (Number of students affected)	Perception Data (Data from surveys/ assessments)	Outcome Data (Achievement, attendance and/or behavior data)	Implications
3ʳᵈ	Emotion Management Unit 4 Lessons from Second Step	Social/ Emotional M 6 SE B-LS 9 SE B-SMS 2 SE B-SMS 2 SE B-SMS 6 SE B-SMS 7 SE B-SSS 4 MVUSD LCAP GOAL #2 Prevention, Intervention & Acceleration	Jan. 24-27, 2017	120	**Attitude** 89% of students now believe that identifying their feelings can help them calm down (Previously 80%) **Knowledge** 66% of students now can identify the Calm Down Steps "Stop, Name, Your Feeling, Calm Down" (Previously 38%) 56% of students can identify listening body cues that signal a strong feeling/emotion (Previously 45%)	**Behavior Data (N's)** 15.7% drop from 51 to 43 **Reading Scores (SRI)** 12% increase from 554 to 624 **Math Scores (SMI)** 63.6% increase from 272 to 445 *(Data collected reflects Q1 and Q3)*	The inverse relationship between academic scores and negative behavior grades (N's) suggests that emotion management is contributing in a meaningful way to improved outcomes for students. More research is needed here to indicate a correlation. In the future, we would like to implement the Emotional Management lesson during the 2ⁿᵈ quarter of the year to be more preventative, rather than reactive.
4ᵗʰ	Emotion Management Unit 4 Lessons from Second Step	SE M 6 SE B-LS 9 SE B-SMS 2 SE B-SMS 2 SE B-SMS 6 SE B-SMS 7 SE B-SSS 4 MVUSD LCAP GOAL #2 Prevention, Intervention & Acceleration	Feb. 14-21, 2017	101	**Attitude** 70% of students strongly agree that it's important to control their emotions (Previously 50%) **Knowledge** 84% of students can identify the Calm Down Steps "Stop, Name, Your Feeling, Calm Down" (Previously 48%) **Skill** 50% of students selected the correct response to a scenario of what to do when they had a strong feeling and how to calm down (Previously 21%)	**Behavior Data (N's)** 35% drop from 31 to 20 **Reading Scores (SRI)** 20% increase from 582 to 699 **Math Scores (SMI)** 53% increase from 323 to 628 *(Data collected reflects Q1 and Q3)*	Both reading and math scores are showing improvement, while N's (needs improvement) are decreasing. This inverse relationship suggests that teaching emotional management may support student academic success. In the future, we would like to teach this series of lessons during the 2ⁿᵈ quarter of the year to be more preventative and compare the difference between 1ˢᵗ and 2ⁿᵈ quarter data.

- A tool that shares the positive outcomes of an activity (in this case, core curriculum classroom lessons)
- A tool for reflecting on the successes of the school counseling program and areas for growth
- A tool to advocate for the work of a school counselor in the school building
- A tool to gauge readiness for ASCA's Recognized ASCA Model Program (RAMP) recognition
- A possible artifact/evidence for the school counselor's performance evaluation

How Does One Create a Flashlight Presentation?

To complete a Flashlight Presentation, select a visual presentation software. For most people, information transmitted visually makes a greater impression than text alone, so the likelihood of stakeholders' remembering information presented is greater with the use of visuals.

The Flashlight PowerPoint Template

A time-saving Flashlight PowerPoint Presentation Template for core curriculum is provided in Figure 9.4, which includes the essential elements of an effective Flashlight; each slide in the template is juxtaposed to a completed sample slide to show how the template can be used. School counselors can modify and adapt the template to enter details about their school, activities, and data; they can also add or delete slides as needed. The full downloadable template, which includes slide notes that give helpful guidance on editing and creating presentations, is available in the online appendix.

Figure 9.4   Flashlight PowerPoint Template for Core Curriculum Compared With Example Flashlight Results Presentation

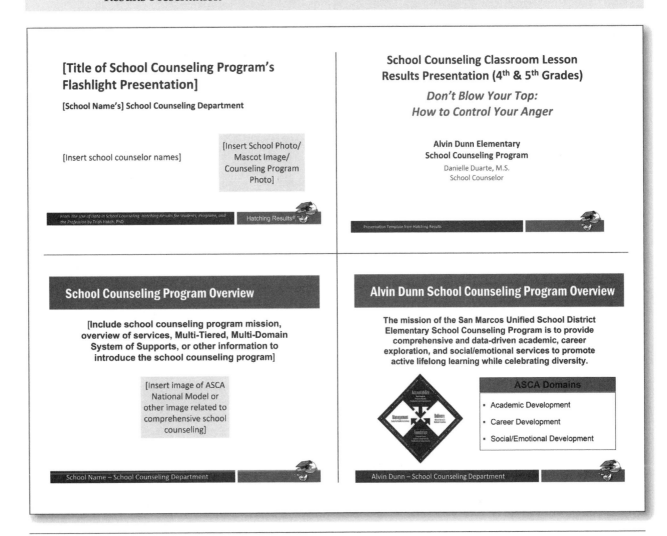

(Continued)

Figure 9.4 (Continued)

School Counseling Program Goal

[Write the relevant SMART goal statement here]

School Name – School Counseling Department

School Counseling Program SMART Goal

By the end of the school year there will be a 20% decrease in school-wide discipline referrals.
(From 287 referrals to 230 referrals or less)

School Counseling Activities to Support this Goal:

- All student in grades K-5 will receive a <u>minimum of 10 Second Step classroom lessons</u> teaching <u>emotional regulation</u> & <u>problem solving</u>, plus additional lessons supporting anger management

- School counselor is an active member of the <u>**PBIS Team**</u>
  - Co-presenting *school-wide expectations assembly* twice a year
  - Supporting the implementation of *school-wide positive incentives*
  - Developing presentations & *training staff* on <u>proactive classroom management</u>, <u>reasons for referrals</u>, & <u>restorative practices</u>

- *Intentional interventions* for students with 2+ significant referrals

- <u>Data monitoring</u> monthly/each trimester to determine areas of focus as well celebrate successes

Alvin Dunn – School Counseling Department

Rationale

[Insert information about why you are teaching this curriculum/lesson using school data]

[Insert relevant data graphic from previous school years or complete this chart below]

[INSERT TOPIC/DATA METRIC SUCH AS G.P.A. OR SCHOOL CLIMATE]		
PREVIOUS SCHOOL YEAR DATA 20XX – 20XX	**PREVIOUS SCHOOL YEAR DATA 20XX – 20XX**	**DATA GOAL 20XX – 20XX**
[Insert previous school year data]	[Insert previous school year data]	[Insert school data goal]

School Name – School Counseling Department

Rationale – Why Did We Teach This Lesson?

Of the 287 behavior referrals last year, 130 were given to 3rd and 4th graders (45%)

37% of referrals included yelling, bad words, aggressive behavior, and/or fighting (behaviors related to anger)

This year, 4th and 5th grade students reported anger management as one of their top areas they to learn (through school counselor survey)

Lesson expands upon anger management taught through Second Step and incorporates family participation

Alvin Dunn – School Counseling Department

Rationale

" "

[Insert quote from research or survey results]
--Name of Source
Year
" "

[Insert screenshots of article/research publications (OPTIONAL)]

School Name – School Counseling Department

Rationale – Supporting Research

" " Social-emotional competencies are key academic enablers that help form the bridge between instruction and learning. " "

--Flook, Repetti, & Ullman
2005

The Alvin Dunn School Counseling Program supports the school's academic mission,

School Name – School Counseling Department

Student Standards: ASCA Domain + Mindsets & Behavior

ASCA DOMAIN
[Insert ASCA Mindset Standard in format such as:
M 3. Sense of belonging in school environment]

ASCA MINDSET & BEHAVIOR STANDARDS
[Insert multiple ASCA Mindset and/or Behavior Standard(s) in format such as:
- Mindset 3. Sense of belonging in school environment
- B-SS 2: Create positive and supportive relationships with other students
- Behavior Self Management Skill 7: Demonstrate effective coping skills when faced with a problem]

School Name – School Counseling Department

Student Standards: ASCA Domain + Mindsets & Behavior

ASCA DOMAIN
SOCIAL/EMOTIONAL

ASCA BEHAVIOR STANDARDS
- Mindset 1: Believe in development of whole self, including a healthy balance of mental, social/emotional and physical well-being
- Behavior Self Management Skill 2: Demonstrate self-discipline and self-control
- Behavior Social Skill 1: Use effective oral and written communication skills and learning skills

Alvin Dunn – School Counseling Department

Other Standards, School Initiative, District Strategic Plan, or State Goals Aligned with Lesson (OPTIONAL)

[INSERT NAME OF STATE/LOCAL STANDARD]
[Insert identified standard(s)]

OR

[INSERT INITIATIVE/STRATEGIC PLAN/GOAL]
[Include information about how the lesson aligns to or supports these goal]

School Name – School Counseling Department

Supporting District Goals

Don't Blow Your Top & other school counseling classroom lessons align with Tier 1 services to support the following school district goal & data:

"Provide a clearly defined tier of academic and behavioral interventions for students not progressing toward the expectation of college and career as noted by data."

Measurement of goal includes reducing discipline referrals

Alvin Dunn – School Counseling Department

Process Data

[IDENTIFY STUDENT GRADE LEVEL OR GROUP]
Insert bulleted list with details about how
- [Insert text: When? Days/months]
- [Insert text: What frequency/how often?]
- [Insert text: Lesson topics?]
- [Insert text: Where? Which class?]
- [Insert text: How many students impacted?]

[Insert Graphic/ Image of Curriculum/ Photo, etc. (OPTIONAL)]

School Name – School Counseling Department

Process Data

4th & 5th Grade Students
- Lessons delivered in February
- All students receive lesson about identifying feelings of anger & ways to calm down
- Students wrote & shared letter about the lesson with their families
- 179 students received the lesson

Alvin Dunn – School Counseling Department

(Continued)

Figure 9.4 (Continued)

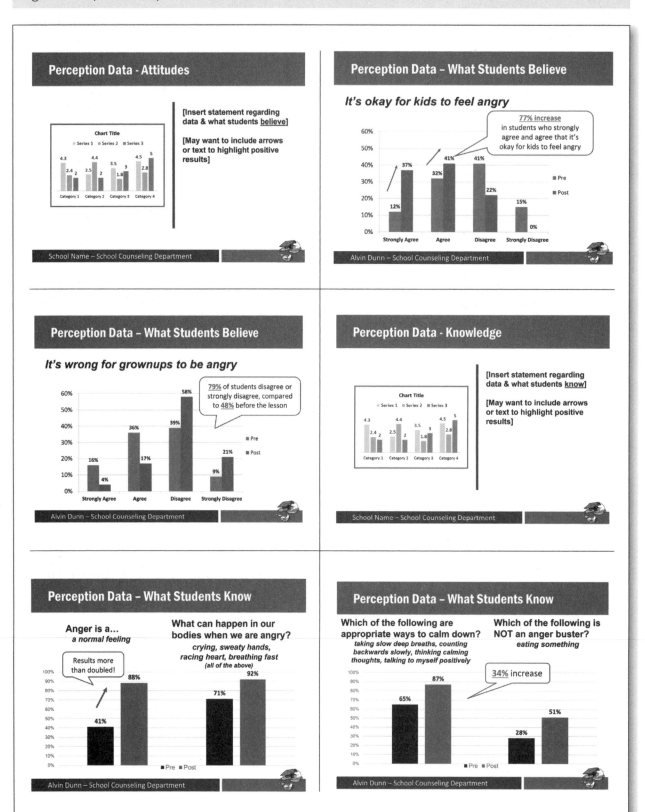

Perception Data - Skill

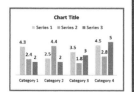

[Insert statement regarding data & what students <u>students can do/what skill they learned</u>]

[May want to include arrows or text to highlight positive results]

School Name – School Counseling Department

Perception Data – What Students Can Do (Skill)

All students wrote a letter about how anger affects their body and what helps them calm down
(supported by teachers – thanks!)

154 returned their signed letter by someone in their family (84%)

Alvin Dunn – School Counseling Department

Outcome Data

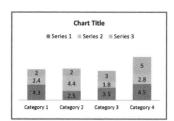

[Insert Statement Regarding Outcome Data]

School Name – School Counseling Department

Outcome Data - Discipline Referrals

SMART Goal: By the end of the school year there will be a 20% decrease in school-wide discipline referrals.
(From 287 referrals to 230 referrals or less)

Based on ALL the school's work to decrease discipline referrals, including the Don't Blow Your Top Lesson, *referrals have consistently decreased this year* and we are *projected to reach our goal!*

Only 95 discipline referrals at this point in the year, compared to 196 last year

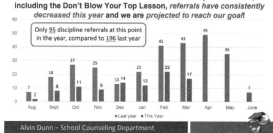

Alvin Dunn – School Counseling Department

Summary and Implications

- [Insert summary bulleted list of your results and the overall impact of your curriculum]
- Cont.
- Cont.
- Cont.

School Name – School Counseling Department

Summary and Implications

- All 4th & 5th grade students received valuable information about how to identify anger and calm down

- Students showed growth in attitudes and knowledge related to the lesson, & demonstrated a skill

- The Don't Blow Your Top Lesson supports the reduction in discipline referrals by teaching students how to calm down

- Second Step lessons are continuing to reinforce students identifying emotions & finding ways to calm down, along with teaching problem solving skills

Alvin Dunn – School Counseling Department

(Continued)

Figure 9.4   (Continued)

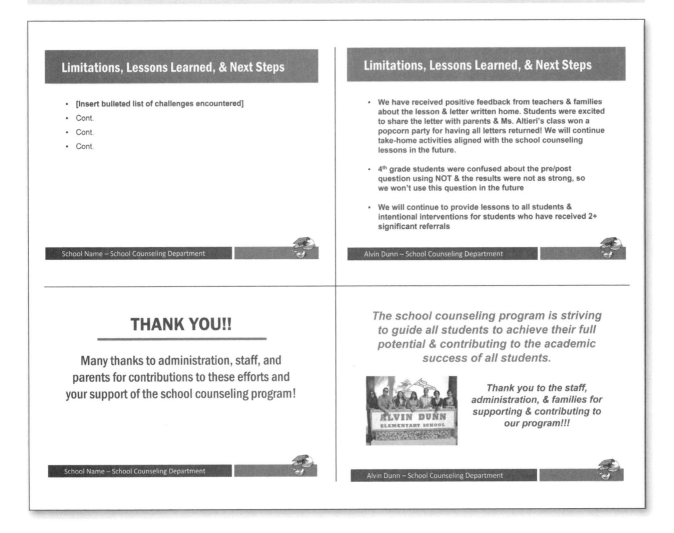

Creating Data Presentation Slides

There are a variety of ways to showcase data slides when creating Flashlight or other results presentations. Review the following data slides from schools we have worked with, which provide examples of ways to share data with school stakeholders. Full presentations were shared with school faculty, district-level leaders, families, and school board members and can also be found in the online appendix.

Figures 9.5 and 9.6 feature slides that serve as an overview to introduce school counseling programs and delivery of services.

Figures 9.7 and 9.8 show perception data based on school climate surveys. In Figure 9.7, the school counselor shared activities related to improving school climate. Figure 9.8 includes a quote from a teacher (qualitative data).

Figures 9.9, 9.10, and 9.11 are examples of achievement-related outcome data. The school counselors tracked citizenship marks from report cards to showcase

Figure 9.5 Introduction to School Counseling Program Slide

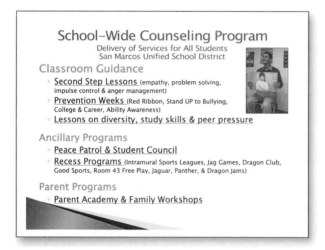

Figure 9.6 Delivery of School Counseling Services Slide

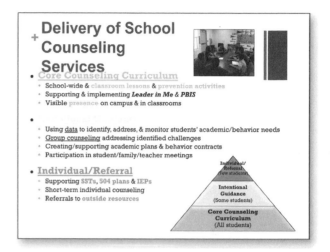

Figure 9.7 Perception Data Slide: School Climate

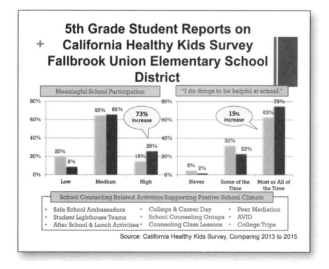

Figure 9.8 Perception Data Slide: Feelings of Safety

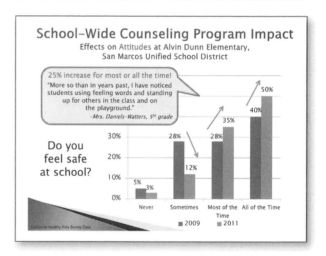

improvement in student behavior. Note that in Figure 9.9, the axis does not begin at zero. Typically, it's best to use a zero axis so that an increase doesn't appear larger than it actually is; however, when gains are smaller, they are harder to see. When a zero axis is not used, school counselors are encouraged to point out that the gains may appear larger, to avoid misleading the audience.

Figures 9.12, 9.13, and 9.14 present ways to showcase improvements in achievement-related behavior data showing declines in behavior referrals and suspensions.

Figure 9.15 displays achievement-related attendance data. Note how the school counselors aligned the decreased absences with the monetary value of attendance to show how funding was "earned" from improving attendance rates.

Figure 9.9 Achievement-Related Data: Citizenship Marks

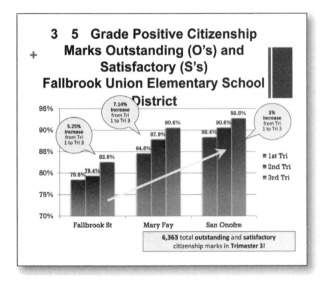

Figure 9.10 Achievement-Related Data: Behavior Grades

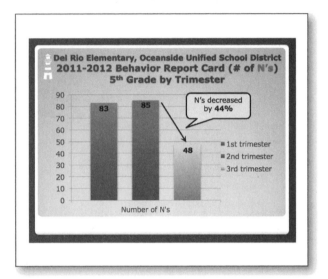

Figure 9.11 Achievement-Related Data: Improved Report Card

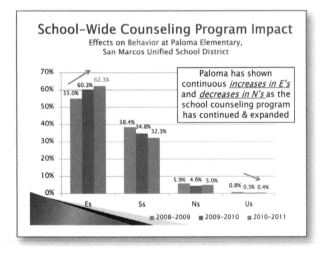

Figure 9.12 Improvements in Achievement-Related Data: Reduction in Discipline Referrals

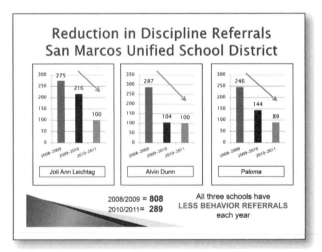

Different software programs with a variety of features are available to help school counselors present their results effectively. While PowerPoint may be the industry standard, there are other cloud-based and internet options to consider that offer varying levels of ease of use, cost, and so on. School counselors may choose programs readily available at their workplace or may want to look at the alternatives listed in Table 9.1.

Figure 9.13 Improvements in Achievement-Related Data: Decreased Discipline Referrals

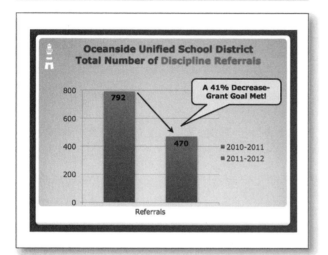

Figure 9.14 Improvements in Achievement-Related Data: Fewer Suspensions

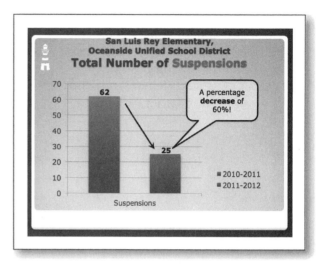

Figure 9.15 Improvements in Achievement-Related Data: Attendance

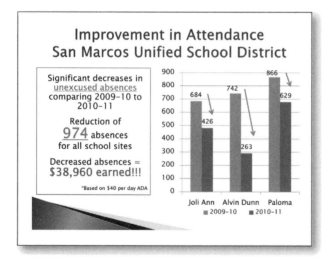

FLASHLIGHT PRESENTATION "ONE-PAGER"

The Flashlight Presentation One-Pager is a one-page, double-sided tool that provides stakeholders with a lasting visual reference of the delivered Flashlight Presentation in a simple, summative format. The Flashlight One-Pager allows audience members to take notes directly as they are listening to the school counselor present and/or refer to the information at a later time.

The Flashlight Presentation One-Pager can be shared with stakeholders as a standalone document as well. Stakeholders who do not hear a live presentation from the school counselor can still reference the Flashlight Presentation One-Pager and understand the presented information. Additionally, this document can easily be distributed in staff mailboxes, e-mailed as an attachment, included in a newsletter, shared with the school board or parent teacher organization, posted on the school counseling program website, or displayed at conferences when exhibiting your school counseling program.

Table 9.1 Program Results Presentation Software

Software	Description	Cost
Prezi https://prezi.com	This visual storytelling software features a map-like, schematic overview that lets users pan between topics at will, zoom in on desired details, and pull back to reveal context. This freedom of movement enables a "conversational presenting" style, in which presentations follow the flow of dialogue, instead of vice-versa.	Free public account (limited); 14-day free trial; three monthly subscription plans with various additional features at a cost.
Google Slides https://www.google.com/slides/about	Praised for its simplicity and frequent product updates, this presentation program offered by Google within its Google Drive service allows users to create and edit files online while collaborating with other users in real-time.	Free.
Piktochart https://piktochart.com	The Piktochart web-based infographic application allows users to easily create professional designer-grade infographics using themed templates. It features HTML publishing capability, which generates infographics that are viewable online with multiple clickable elements, such as videos, hyperlinks, and charts for users. See Figure 9.20 for an example.	Free lifetime account, with options to upgrade anytime to access additional features.
(Apple) Keynote https://www.apple.com/keynote	This presentation software application includes beta release so that your team can work together collaboratively in real time on a Mac, iPad, iPhone, or even on a PC using iWork for iCloud. With Keynote Live, many people in different places can be invited to watch your presentation.	Included in the iWork productivity suite by Apple Inc. Cost varies for Mac OS or iOS.
Visme https://www.visme.co	Visme is a one-stop shop for all visual design needs to develop engaging content in the form of presentations (online and offline), infographics, reports, web products, etc.	Basic plan (limited) is free; monthly subscription plans with premium features are available at a cost. Student and teacher discounts are available.
Presbee https://presbee.com/index	This tool is simple to use, with full multimedia functionality, including live websites, streamed video, timing controls, full analytics, nonlinear presentations, prestyled tables and data charts, and remote meetings.	Free (limited) for beginners, with two subscription plan options for professionals or teams needing additional features.

Flashlight Presentation One-Pager Template and Example

A user-friendly reproducible template that sums up a Flashlight Presentation in a one-page, double-sided document is available here and in the online appendix (https://www.hatchingresults.com/books/elementary-t1/), simply type over it and insert your text, graphs, and/or photos. Developing a Flashlight Presentation One-Pager to showcase your results has never been easier! See Figures 9.16 and 9.17 for the template and example.

Figure 9.16   Flashlight One-Pager Template

[INSERT FLASHLIGHT PRESENTATION TITLE]
[INSERT SCHOOL NAME] SCHOOL COUNSELING PROGRAM

20XX-20XX

Abstract/Summary

Lorem ipsum dolor sit amet, consectetur adipiscing elit. Nam faucibus urna vitae pellentesque porta. Etiam tristique dapibus viverra. Maecenas rutrum nec eros eu varius. Suspendisse sit amet est justo. Vivamus sed facilisis purus. Donec laoreet nulla dui, ac sagittis mauris hendrerit vel.

Lorem ipsum dolor sit amet, consectetur adipiscing elit. Nam faucibus urna vitae pellentesque porta. Etiam tristique dapibus viverra. Maecenas rutrum nec eros eu varius. Suspendisse sit amet est justo. Vivamus sed facilisis purus. Donec laoreet nulla dui, ac sagittis mauris hendrerit vel. Lorem ipsum dolor sit amet, consectetur adipiscing elit. Nam faucibus urna vitae pellentesque porta.

School Counseling Program Activities

- [Insert text]
- [Insert text]
- [Insert text]

[Insert photo of counseling program at work or other image]

Rationale and Need

- [Insert text]
- [Insert text]
- [Insert text]
- [Insert text]
- [Insert text]

Mindsets & Behaviors/Standards

- **[Standard bullet point]**
  [Description/details]
- **[Standard bullet point]**
  [Description/details]
- **[Standard bullet point]**
  [Description/details]
- **[Standard bullet point]**
  [Description/details]

Competencies

- **[Competency bullet point]**
  [Description/details]
- **[Competency bullet point]**
  [Description/details]
- **[Competency bullet point]**
  [Description/details]
- **[Competency bullet point]**
  [Description/details]

Source: From *Hatching Results for Elementary School Counselling: Implementing Core Curriculum and Other Tier One Activities* (Hatch, T., Duarte, D., & De Gregorio, L. k., 2018).

(Continued)

Figure 9.16 (Continued)

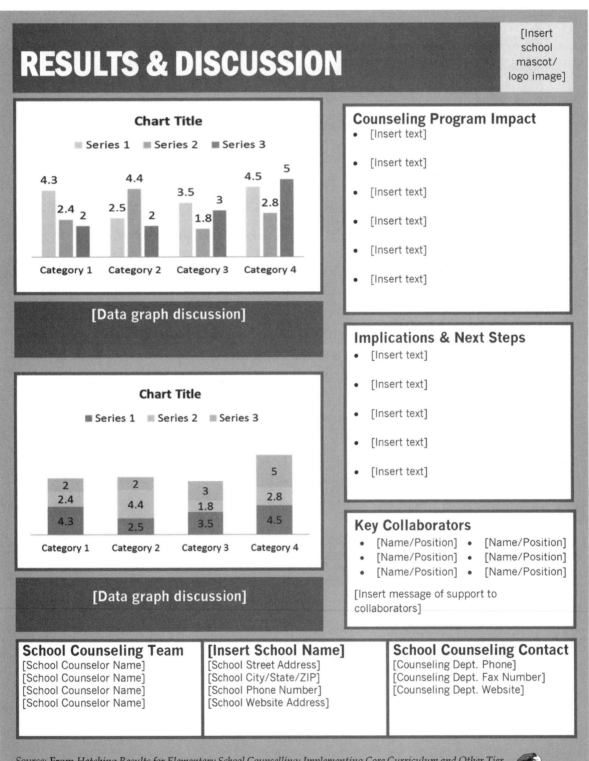

Source: **From** *Hatching Results for Elementary School Counselling: Implementing Core Curriculum and Other Tier One Activities* (Hatch, T., Duarte, D., & De Gregorio, L. k., 2018).

Figure 9.17 Flashlight One-Pager Example: "Don't Blow Your Top!" Lesson

School Counseling Class Lesson Overview

Don't Blow Your Top: How to Control Your Anger

Alvin Dunn Elementary School Counseling Program

Summary

Alvin Dunn Elementary is working to decrease the number of behavior referrals through <u>teaching students to manage strong emotions & to use problem solving steps</u>. Based on a high number of behavior referrals in upper grades last year, and students requesting additional support with anger management (through school counselor survey) *Don't Blow Your Top: How to Control Your Anger* was taught in 4th and 5th grade classes by the school counselor.

In February 179 students (all 4th & 5th graders) received the lesson about identifying feelings of anger

Counseling Program SMART Goal

By the end of the school year there will be a 20% decrease in school-wide discipline referrals.

Program Activities Aligned to Goal

- Second Step lessons teaching emotional regulation/problem solving, & additional lessons supporting anger management
- Intentional interventions for students with 2+ significant referrals

Rationale and Research

Social-emotional competencies are key academic enablers that help form the bridge between instruction and learning.

--Flook, Repetti, &

America School Counselor Association Domain & Standards

<u>Domain</u>: Social/Emotional

<u>Mindset & Behavior Standards:</u>
- M 3: Believe in development of whole self, including a healthy balance of mental, social/emotional & physical well-being
- B-SMS 2: Demonstrate self-discipline & self-control
- B-SS 1: Use effective oral & written communication skills & learning skills

Alvin Dunn Elementary School Counseling Program Information

School Counselor – Danielle Duarte, MS

Supported by school counseling trainees from San Diego State University (Thursdays)

3697 La Mirada Drive, San Marcos, CA 92078
www.smusd.org/ad | (760) 290-2000

Created using a Hatching Results Template

(Continued)

Figure 9.17   (Continued)

School Counseling Class Lesson Results
Don't Blow Your Top: How to Control Your Anger
Alvin Dunn Elementary School Counseling Program

It's okay for kids to feel angry

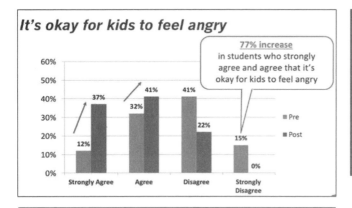

77% increase in students who strongly agree and agree that it's okay for kids to feel angry

Counseling Program Impact

- All 4th & 5th grade students received valuable information about how to identify anger & calm down.

- The Don't Blow Your Top! Lesson supports the reduction in discipline referrals by teaching students how to calm down.

Results from Students' Improved Attitudes & Knowledge After the Lesson

Students can identify...

What can happen to their body when feeling angry   **Appropriate ways to calm down**

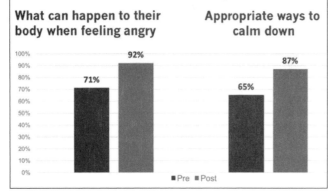

Implications & Next Steps

- Positive feedback was received from teachers & families about the lesson & letter written home. We will continue take-home activities aligned to school counseling lessons.

- Students with 2+ significant referrals are receiving intentional interventions for additional support.

Perception & Outcome Data Review

- Students showed growth in attitudes and knowledge related to the lesson, & applied their knowledge to writing a letter about what they learned to their family

- Behavior referrals have decreased significantly due to the variety of prevention and intervention activities, including the Don't Blow Your Top! Counseling Lesson.

Comparing This Year to Last Year:
Discipline referrals August through March

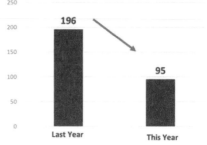

Created using a Hatching Results Template

OTHER "ONE-PAGERS"

Another use for a one-pager is to highlight the work and results of one or more lessons or schoolwide activities. School counselors can include program descriptions, ASCA standards, testimonials, photographs, and data charts to share results. One-pagers allow school counselors to describe these schoolwide activities within their program in a simple yet powerful way. The four examples shared in Figures 9.18 through 9.21 are different ways to explain the school counseling lessons or programs while showcasing process, perception, and outcome data. School counselors can include student and teacher testimonials aligned with standards, results data, and photos to bring the school counseling activities to life. One-pagers can be shared with teachers, families, and community partners to share the activities and successes within the school counseling program.

Activity 9.1

Consider the one-pagers presented in the following pages—what does each one teach the reader? What components are most powerful? What might you change? For what schoolwide school counseling program or activity could you create a similar one-pager?

Figure 9.18 shows a one-pager developed from Tier 1 college readiness lessons and a field trip to a local university within the Alvin Dunn Elementary School Counseling Program. The action plan featured in Chapter 2 includes this lesson, and the one-pager highlights the accompanying college trip. How could you use a "one-pager" like this to highlight your Tier 1 classroom lessons and/or schoolwide activity?

Figure 9.19 is an example of one way to showcase your program. It features the new student welcome program and provides an overview of the activities, action steps, and impact on students, along with outcome data related to attendance, truancy, and students on track academically. Teachers and other school staff were highlighted in the one-pager for their support of the program. How could you create something similar to highlight a program within your school counseling department?

The one-pager shown in Figure 9.20 was created by elementary school counselor Alexandra Todd using Piktochart (piktochart.com) to share the progress of her Tier 1 lessons and schoolwide activities and to market her school counseling program. While this report is especially strong on process data, it is recommended that counselors also include perception and outcome data. What types of Tier 1 activities do you notice Alexandra is implementing? What kind of perception (attitudes, knowledge, and skills) and outcome (achievement-related and achievement) data might she include in her next edition?

Figure 9.21 presents a one-pager called a Support Personnel Accountability Report Card (SPARC) created by school counselor Zorayda Delgado. This is a document on continuous improvement that focuses on key college and career readiness outcomes for students, and it can be voluntarily submitted to the California Department of Education. Creating a SPARC at the elementary level can be used to

- Demonstrate the school counselor's commitment to students' career and college readiness

Figure 9.18   College Readiness One-Pager Example

COLLEGE STUDENTS FOR THE DAY AT CSUSM!!

On Friday, May 4th, Alvin Dunn Elementary School's 4th grade students were "college students for the day" at **California State University, San Marcos (CSUSM)!** To prepare for their trip, 4th graders received classroom lessons from their school counselor about the importance of college and the **P.A.C.E. Promise** admission agreement and practiced filling out a "college application." Some highlights from their applications included:

- *"I want to be a vet when I grow up. College could help me with my career because I learn more about animals and how to take care of them when they are sick."*—Gisel
- *"I'm excited because when I graduate my parents will be proud of me."*—Omero
- *"I want to go to college because I want to study hard to get a good job and make a good example for my children."*—Stephanie

While at CSUSM, students and their families participated in various activities through generous funding from the **Current Wisdom Foundation** and support from **CSUSM's Early Outreach Program** and **Athletics Department**, including:

- Budget Game where students learned the value of a college education and money
- Question and answer session with CSUSM students
- *College: Making it Happen* Bilingual Parent Workshop
- Campus tour of classrooms, library, cafeteria, and science lab
- Inspirational speech from Olympic Gold Medalist and CSUSM Track and Field Coach—Steve Scott—with a tour of the athletic facilities

Students Are Gaining Knowledge, Attitudes, & Skills to Help Them Succeed!

American School Counselor Association Mindsets & Behaviors for Student Success
Students will employ strategies to achieve future career goals with success and satisfaction

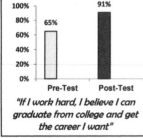

"If I work hard, I believe I can graduate from college and get the career I want"
Pre-Test: 65%   Post-Test: 91%

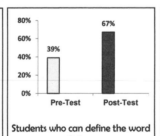

Students who can define the word *diploma*
Pre-Test: 39%   Post-Test: 67%

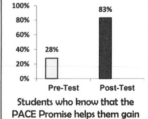

Students who know that the PACE Promise helps them gain admission to Cal State San Marcos
Pre-Test: 28%   Post-Test: 83%

The classroom lesson and field trip promote increased college-going rates for students, most of whom will be first generation college students.

Figure 9.19 New Student Welcome Program One-Pager Example

NEW STUDENT ORIENTATION PROGRAM
THOMAS KELLY ELEMENTARY SCHOOL COUNSELING

EVELYN GATSBY, School Counselor
(555) 555-5555 ext.55
egatsby@kellyedu.com

Abstract/Summary
With restructured school boundaries, many students have begun to transfer into Kelly Elementary School. Historical data reveals that these students tend to exhibit greater misconduct and poorer academics—a large percentage of students 'off track' in 3rd grade are new students. To better support them and greet with a warm welcome, the New Student Orientation Program was developed this school year.

Key Collaborators
- Mr. Reynolds—5th
- Mrs. Huffman—3rd
- Ms. Jenkins—4th
- Mr. McGuire—Music
- Mrs. Marshall—Psych
- Mr. Simpson—SW
- Mrs. Carter—Principal
- Miss Libby—AP

Thank you to the whole MTSS Team as well! A big thanks for your great effort, ideas, and diligence—I appreciate your energy and time spent at weekly meetings!

Action Steps
- Created a 'Passport to Success' for students—meet staff and explore the school and get a 'stamp' in your passport
- Conduct Orientation/Family Night with key staff, teachers, pupil services personnel, etc. to review policies and procedures and key graduation requirements
- Partner each incoming 3rd grader with a current 4th or 5th grader to be peer mentor
- School counselor met 2x/month in small group setting to support and teach life skills

Results & Discussion
- Greater 'On Track' rate after participating in the PASSPORT program!!
  Semester 1: 12 students 'Off Track'; **Semester 2:** 4 students 'Off Track' (n=18)
- Reduced 'Truancy' after participating in the PASSPORT program!
  Semester 1: 7 students had truancy rate exceeding yellow level; Semester 2: 3 students
- Improved Attendance rate after participating in the PASSPORT program!
  Average attendance rate **increased 1%** from Semester 1 to Semester 2

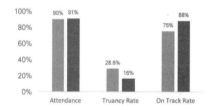

Comparison of Data of 3rd Graders
Semester 1 vs. Semester 2

Recommendations & Next Steps
- Inconsistency of 'buddies' in the program; needs to become part of the culture here. Seek t-shirt donations to help identify participating students and be source of pride!
- Greater time investment than anticipated! WANTED: A Co-Coordinator of the Program next year who can focus solely on non-peer mentoring tasks!
- Start sooner! Involve the feeder primary school's counselor and/or attend a transition event at the primary school. Possibly coordinate a summer transition event.

Pre/post-test survey results **AND** teacher observations show that students in the New Student Orientation Program gained 21st century skills and are able to get acclimated to our school more quickly!

- Describe alignment with local, state, and national career and college readiness initiatives
- Proactively promote the school counseling program to administrators, teachers, school boards, parents/guardians, community partners, businesses, and legislators

All SPARC submission requirements are recognized by receiving a SPARC Seal and Certificate of Participation from the California Department of Education. Other states have adopted similar documents under a different name; non-California schools can use the same components to create a document comparable to the SPARC. See http://www.sparconline.net and Figure 9.21 for more information. What are the ways in which Zorayda could share this document with staff, administrators, families, and community members?

Figure 9.20   Tier 1 Lesson Progress One-Pager Example

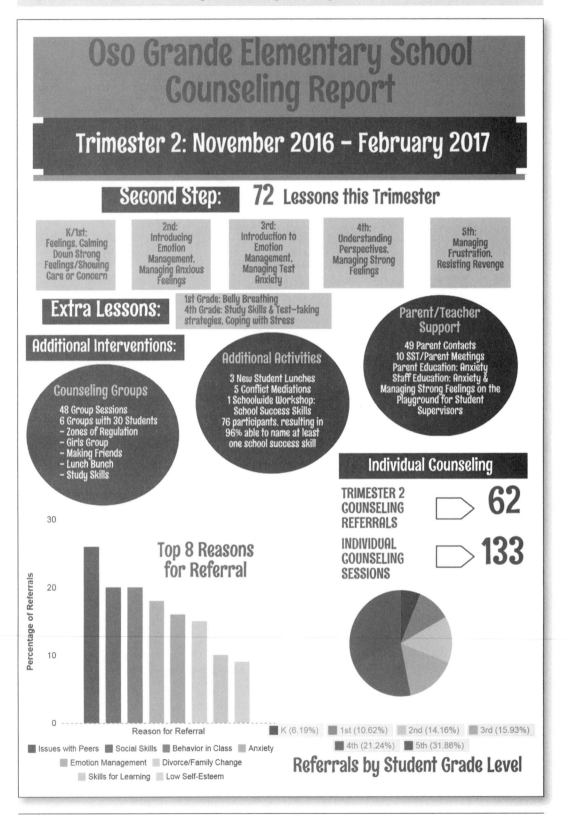

Created by elementary school counselor Alexandra Todd.

Figure 9.21 Support Personnel Accountability Report Card (SPARC) One-Pager Example

Fallbrook Street Elementary School
2016 SPARC
Support Personnel Accountability Report Card
A continuous improvement document sponsored by the
California Department of Education

Address: 405 West Fallbrook Street, Fallbrook, CA 92028
Phone: 760-731-4000 **Website:** http://www.fuesd.k12.ca.us/fss
Principal: Stephenie Martinez **District:** Fallbrook Union Elementary School District
Grade Levels: TK-6 **Enrollment:** 550

Principal's Message

Fallbrook Street Elementary School (FSS) has a dedicated and knowledgeable staff that is committed to supporting students in their academic journey and to ensure career and college readiness for all. We recognize, honor and celebrate the leaders within us by: "Loving Learning, Excelling in all we do, Achieving goals together, Doing what is right, Inspiring STEM, Navigating College and Career readiness through a Growth Mindset."

The collaboration between our staff, students, families and community, along with the programs mentioned below foster a safe school climate. We do this through implementing the Leader in Me program that encourages our students to develop leadership and 21st century skills including critical thinking and

creativity. Our Positive Behavior Intervention Supports Program and Restorative Justice practices promote character development. Lastly, our school counselor delivers activities that support students in academic, college/career, and personal/social domains as outlined in the American School Counselor Association National Model framework. In 2016-2017 our focus-for-improvement goals are to expand college and career activities school wide and to increase leadership opportunities for students during unstructured times like recess and lunch time.

Career and College Readiness Student Outcomes

The Student Support Team (SST) and School Counseling Department at FSS collects and analyzes student outcomes data to determine the effectiveness of school-wide interventions and programs. We are committed to improve our support programs that prepare students to successfully transition to junior high school and beyond. The two outcomes presented below highlight results from our career exploration activity and classroom lessons focused on skills for college readiness.

Career Readiness: The SST members collaborate with school staff to create a college and career mindset. Some of the activities include a college corner in each classroom, career exploration activities and all students having "classroom leadership jobs." This year the school counselor presented college and career lessons in 6th grade. Students were introduced to post-secondary options (vocational schooling, community colleges and four-year universities). The students also participated in a career assessment survey and discovered possible career opportunities based on their interest results. After the activity, 35% of 6th grade students identified one career of interest, 40% identified 2 careers of interests and 25% were undecided.

College Readiness: To support our students with their academic and positive social skills development, the school counselor delivers weekly classroom lessons. The chart illustrates the percentage of our student population who have received Second Step lessons. In 2014-2015 Second Step curriculum was taught in two grade levels (30% of our school population). This year it's implemented in grades second through fifth (55% of our student population). Second Step curriculum provides students the opportunity to learn skills that are essential for rigorous academic learning and college readiness. The content in the lessons include: Skills for Learning, Problem Solving, Empathy and Emotion Management. The goal is to provide students with study tools and work habits early in their education through engaging activities, role-plays and videos.

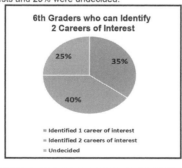

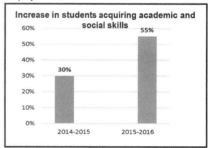

Figure 9.21 (Continued)

21st Century Skills

At FSS 21st Century Skills are developed both in the classroom and through extracurricular activities. The implementation of using a school-wide leadership initiative, the Leader in Me, has been crucial in empowering students to be leaders in our school and the community. In 2014- 2015 SST members collaborated with our Student Lighthouse Team to establish after school clubs. Since our first year, 150 students participate each trimester in after school clubs and many are taking on leadership roles. For example, some are dance instructors in the Fitness club, tutors in homework and reading club and manage fundraisers for our local animal sanctuary. Students are not only exploring their interests and talents but also developing their interpersonal skills while working with their peers.

Additional Achievements:
- Chromebooks for each 4th-6th grade student to integrate technology into everyday classroom activities
- Junior Achievement BizTown provides our 5th grade students with professional work experience
- Leadership assemblies are student-led to celebrate student achievements and events

College and Career Readiness School Site Programs and Community Partnerships

The SST members work closely with school site and community programs to provide students and families with resources that will lead students to academic success. Our current partnerships support the needs of our diverse student population and are fundamental for their college and career readiness. Through our partnerships we promote parent engagement, empower families in their child's education and address social and emotional needs.

School Site Programs
21st Century Skills Readiness Curriculum
- *The Leader in Me* by Stephen Covey
- *7 Habits of Highly Effective Teens* by Sean Covey
- Safe School Ambassadors
College and Career Readiness Curriculum
- College and Career Lessons
- J.A. BizTown Curriculum
Parent Outreach
- Parent Workshops
- English Language Advisory Committee (ELAC)
- English as a Second Language (ESL) Classes
Student Outreach
- Student Forums

- Student Lighthouse
Community Partnerships
Student Outreach
- Palomar Family Counseling
- Fallbrook Rotary Club
- Department of Migrant Education Services
Parent Support Services
- Parent Institute for Quality Education (PIQE)
- Sharing the Table
- Computers 2 SD Kids
After School Programs
- Boys and Girls Club
- After School Clubs

Student Support Team

The FSS Student Support Team (SST) is committed to providing an equitable support system for academic, personal/social and 21st century skills development. By implementing and monitoring school-wide programs, the SST members collaborate often to evaluate the effectiveness of programs. We want all students to be academically successful while attaining career and college readiness.

Our SST members have the appropriate credentials and training to contribute in supporting the diverse needs of our students. SST members participate in the following professional organizations: Association of California School Administrators, American School Counselor Association, California Association of School Counselors, National Association of School Psychologists, California Association of School Psychologists and National Student Nurses' Association.

Certificated Team Members		
Position	Academic Degree/Education	Years in Education
Principal	M.A. Administration	19
Assistant Principal	M.A. Administration	11
School Counselor	M.S. Counseling	2
School Psychologist (3/5 FTE)	M.A. School Psychology, Ed. S.	3
Speech Therapist	M.A. Speech Language Hearing Sciences	8
Teacher on Special Assignment	B.S. Early Childhood Education	20

Classified Team Members		
Position	Academic Degree/Education	Years in Education
Administrative Secretary	Some College	14
Bilingual Attendance Clerk	Some College	18
Health Care Specialist	BSN, RN, PHN	4
Reading Intervention Specialist (2/5)	B.A. Cred. CLAD	13
Reading Intervention Specialist (2/5)	Some College	5

Source: Created by school counselor Zorayda Delgado.

Percent Change Calculator

When sharing results with faculty, administrators, families, and other school stakeholders, it is important to accurately present the impact of the Tier 1 lessons and activities. Therefore, school counselors are encouraged to calculate improvements in pre- and post-assessment scores, attendance, behavior, or achievement using percentage change. In *The Use of Data in School Counseling* (Hatch, 2013), the following notes are included to describe percentage change:

> One important point to remember is the distinction between the terms increase and improvement. For example, if someone had a quarter and was given an additional quarter, the increase would be 25 cents, but the improvement to the total amount of funds would be 100%, because the total amount of money doubled. In the same way, if the percentage of correct responses on a test shifted from 25% to 50%, this represents an increase of 25%, and an improvement of 100%. (p. 230)

> The book goes on to describe the mathematical formula used to calculate percentage change, but now school counselors can easily find percentage change online! Just by Googling "percentage change," multiple sites can be found. Figure 9.22 shows one located at http://www.percent-change.com. School counselors input the pre-assessment data in the "1st Value" box and the post-assessment data in the "2nd Value" box, click "Calculate," and the percentage change will be calculated!

Figure 9.22 Percent Change Calculator

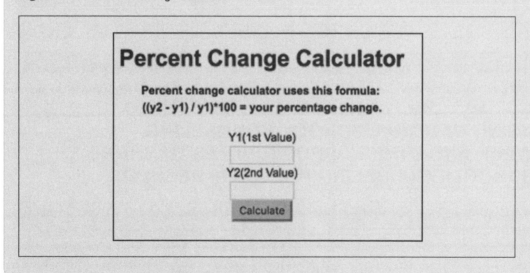

Elementary school counselor Kathie Ketcham used the percent change calculator to assess the percent reduction in negative "Skills and Behaviors That Support Learning" (i.e., citizenship) from student report cards. She calculated the number of Areas of Concern (AC) and Unacceptable (U) marks given in the year prior to the district's hiring of elementary school counselors (the baseline), and compared the

Figure 9.23   Percent Change Calculation Example: 56% Decrease in Negative Citizenship Marks

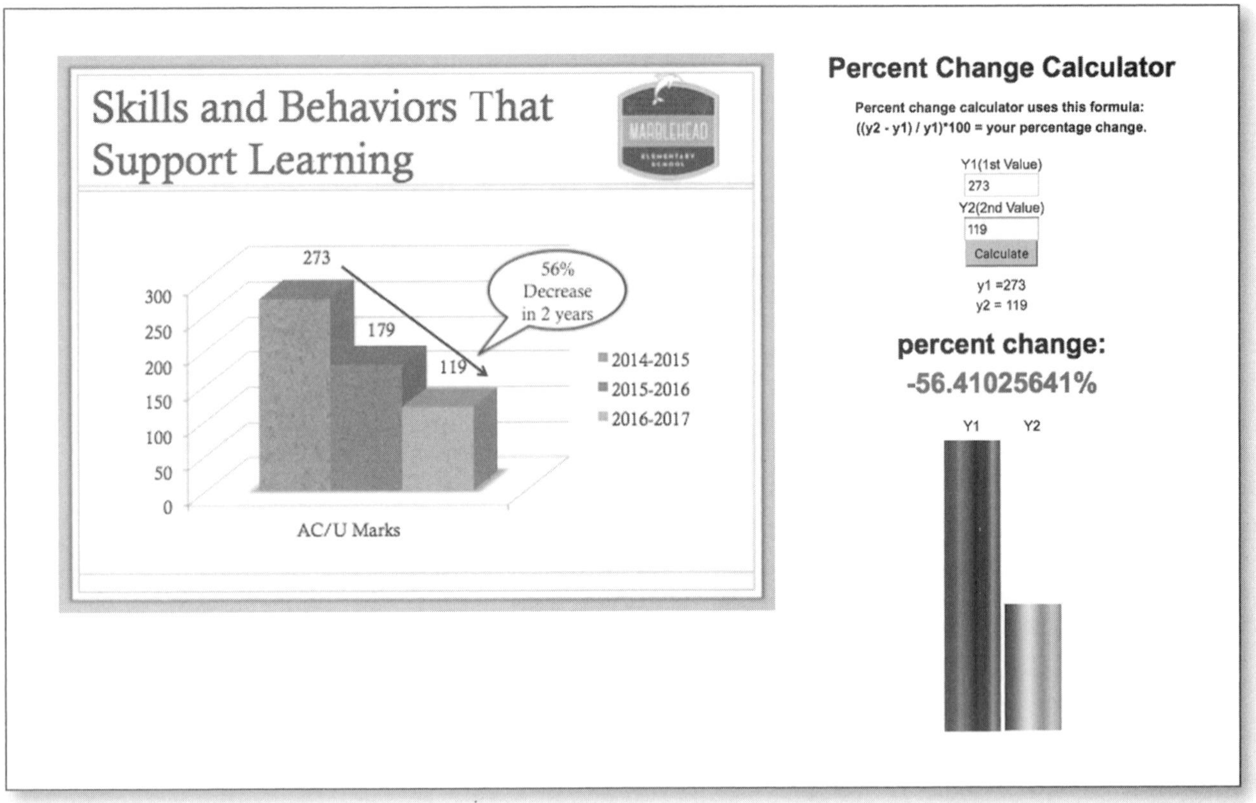

Source: Created by elementary school counselor Kathie Ketcham.

number to two years later, correlating the reduction in negative marks with her classroom lessons and intentional interventions. Over two years, Kathie saw a 56% reduction in negative "Skills and Behaviors That Support Learning" marks!

USING NATIONAL SCHOOL COUNSELING WEEK AND OTHER OPPORTUNITIES TO SHARE SCHOOL COUNSELING PROGRAM RESULTS

National School Counseling Week (NSCW), celebrated annually during the first week of February, focuses public attention on the unique contribution of school counselors within the school system and how students improve as a result of school counselors' work. This week is a wonderful opportunity for school counselors to promote the services and outcomes of their school counseling program, while also thanking the school staff for their support. Presented here are different ways in which elementary school counselors have shared results during NSCW.

Classroom Lessons Guessing Contest

During NSCW, elementary school counseling trainee Courtney Lloyd wanted to increase awareness of the comprehensive school counseling program at her internship site. She created a contest asking staff members to guess how many

Figure 9.24 School Counseling Program Awareness Staff E-mail

Did you know...
- Teaching classroom lessons is an integral part of the school counselor role.
- The Los Pen counseling team teaches lessons about social emotional skills, bullying prevention, and college and career readiness.

CONTEST

How many classroom lessons have the Los Pen counseling team (Mrs. H, interns, Mrs. McCombs) taught so far in the 2016-2017 school year?

Submit your guess with your name into the mason jar by end of day Wednesday 2/7. The two closest guesses will win a jar of candy!

HAPPY NATIONAL SCHOOL COUNSELING WEEK!

classroom lessons the school counseling team had presented so far that year. Courtney set up a guessing station with jars filled with candy, to mirror how folks might guess the number of pieces inside, just as they would guess the number of counseling lessons taught. The staff received an e-mail about the activity, and the guessing station included a flyer with information about the importance of school counseling core curriculum class lessons and the topics taught at the school (see Figure 9.24). Submitted guesses ranged from 5 to 1,900, which demonstrated that many teachers and other staff were uninformed about the work of the school counseling program.

At the end of NSCW, Courtney sent an e-mail revealing the winners, which also included more information about the number of classroom lessons taught to date, process data related to other school counseling services, and perception data about the *Second Step* classroom lessons (See Figure 9.25). Through her advocacy, Courtney helped educate the school staff and build collaborative relationships by thanking them for their support of the comprehensive school counseling program.

Results and Treats

Co-author Danielle Duarte used NSCW to celebrate her counseling program through sharing treats and data. Each year, Danielle created a PowerPoint highlighting program information and results, including those from Tier 1, in an easy-to-read format. On the first day of NSCW, Danielle set up a table in the staff lounge decorated with printed-out school counseling program slides and also set out cookies and candy. Danielle sent an e-mail to the staff thanking them for their support of school counseling and inviting them to enjoy treats in celebration of NSCW during lunch. At the end of the day, she sent another thank-you e-mail to the staff with the PowerPoint presentation attached so that all staff had access to the information. Figure 9.26 shows the table from Danielle's NSCW celebration, and Figure 9.27 shows her PowerPoint presentation.

Figure 9.25   Sample National School Counseling Week Counseling Data

Los Pen School Counseling Data
August 2016 - February 2017

As a part of National School Counseling Week, we would like to present some data about the services that the Los Pen school counseling program provides.

School Counseling Program Process Data

Classroom lessons	271 lessons taught
Parent/family consultations	More than 160 consultations
Individual student meetings	More than 90 meetings
Responsive (behavior support) services	More than 50 students
Small groups	14 sessions
Family forums and workshops	10 forums and workshops held
CPS reports	4 reports filed

Classroom Lessons: Attitude, Knowledge, and Skills Data

91% of 5th grade students believe that the Second Step lessons have made Los Pen a better place.
91% of 5th grade students have *learned* at least one new skill during their Second Step lessons this year.
72% of 5th grade students have *used* at least one skill that they learned from their Second Step lessons. <ul><li>"I have used empathy when my friend was sad and I cheered her up."</li><li>"I used different perspectives because when my friend was having trouble in life, I tried to see that maybe she was also having personal problems. That skill helped me because it helped me to not judge people."</li><li>"When I disagreed with my mom I didn't yell at her instead i disagreed respectfully."</li><li>"I have used the way that Ms.Lloyd told us to us a nice firm voice and make eye contact especially when we had our biztown interviews."</li><li>"I used attentive listening skills during class when Mrs. D'Acquisto was talking."</li></ul>

Thank you for helping us take care of our students. We are honored to continue serving Los Pen!

Source: Created by Courtney Lloyd.

Activity 9.2

Reflect on the variety of ways to share program results. What do you like about them? How can you modify one of these examples or create your own to showcase the work you are doing in your elementary school counseling program?

Figure 9.26 Danielle's NSCW Celebration

Figure 9.27 NSCW Program Highlight Slides

Happy National School Counseling Week!

The school counseling program is striving to guide all students to achieve their full potential and contributing to the academic success of all students.

More Students Feel Safe at School

Do you feel safe at school?

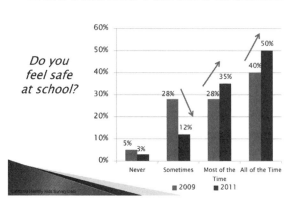

More Students Are Coming to School!!!

Significant decreases in <u>unexcused absences</u> comparing 2009–10 to 2010–11

Reduction of

2<u>58</u> absences!!!

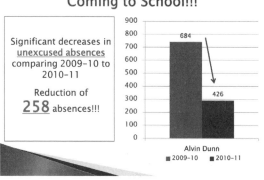

Figure 9.27 (Continued)

Positive Effects on Behavior

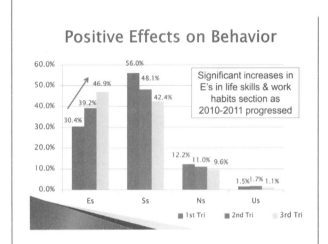

Significant increases in E's in life skills & work habits section as 2010-2011 progressed

Reduction in Discipline Referrals

Compared to prior to the program, discipline referrals have decreased school-wide.

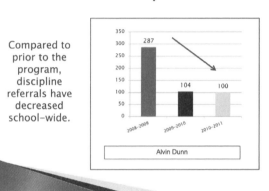

Students Are Learning about College & Careers

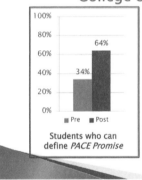

Students who can define *PACE Promise*

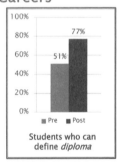

Students who can define *diploma*

Intentional Guidance (group counseling) Finds Improvements in Behavior

- 25 4th & 5th grade students with 5 or more N's or U's
- Eight week group (40 min)
  - Goals & weekly progress checks
  - Self control
  - Solving problems
- N's and U's *DECREASED* from 129 to 75
- S's and E's *INCREASED* from 196 to 250

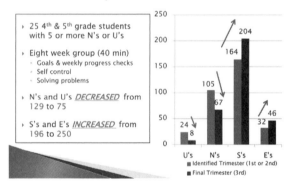

Thank you to the teachers, administration, and other school staff for your support of the school counseling program!

We ♥ your support!!!

Please enjoy some treats in celebration of the week! ☺

~Danielle & Judy

For additional ideas of ways to celebrate National School Counseling Week, listen to Episode 4 of the Hatching Results Podcast, available at http://www.stitcher.com/podcast/hatching-results-podcast.

ADDITIONAL IDEAS FOR SHARING RESULTS

There are many ways to share school counseling program results throughout the year. Below are some suggested activities and strategies. Which opportunities fit your skills, level of comfort in public speaking, use of technology, and available resources best? Making a commitment to sharing program results benefits both the school counseling program and the entire profession.

- Contact the local newspaper before a schoolwide activity, such as Character Counts Week or College and Career Day, and ask the paper to cover the event. If a reporter is unable to attend, the newspaper often allows for stories and photos to be submitted. For example, San Onofre K–8 school counselor Joy Beidel reached out to the local newspaper about her school's College and Career Day. The *Fallbrook Village News* was unable to attend the event, so Joy submitted the article with photos shown in Figure 9.28, which was featured on the newspaper's website ("San Onofre School Holds College and Career Day," 2015).
- Publicize a few highlights of your school counseling program's process, perception, and/or outcome data in a regular school or counseling program newsletter for families and staff. Figure 9.29 presents a newsletter from school counselor Ashley Kruger that includes information about her school counseling classroom lessons and ways for families to reinforce the concepts at home. The newsletter also shares attendance and citizenship data (achievement-related) aligned with the work of teaching students social skills and supporting schoolwide activities to create a positive school climate.
- Display a summary of counseling activities and outcomes on the school counseling program's or the school's website.
- Present a report to the local school council or school site council or the parent-teacher association.
- Share about the school counseling program during open sessions of district school board meetings. Anyone from the public is welcome to attend and share at these meetings with a written request before the meeting begins. Generally, the time allotted to speak is three to five minutes. Prepare a brief statement and bring a results report or other program information and outcomes to share with those in attendance. (Note: Be sure to discuss this presentation with site administrators beforehand for approval.)
- Share with other school counselors by presenting a workshop session at state and national conferences.

Figure 9.28 San Onofre College and Career Day News Article

San Onofre School holds College and Career Day

By Newsroom on March 19, 2015 · No Comment

San Onofre students line up for an up-close look at a military police vehicle during College and Career Day on Feb. 27.

Commander Lt. David Mauerman spoke about commanding a nuclear submarine to San Onofre students during College and Career Day.

The keynote speaker, Lorenzo Romero, spoke about his experience as a student at San Onofre School and his journey through high school and college that lead to his career at Wells Fargo Bank.

Students were able to try on military gear and climb through a military vehicle, just like many of their parents.

CAMP PENDELTON – On Feb. 27, San Onofre School celebrated its first school-wide College and Career Day. The school's counseling department organized the speakers and events to motivate students to be college-bound and career-ready.

There were a variety of presentations and speakers to appeal to different interest levels of a K-8 school population. The kindergarten through second graders attended an assembly on the importance of reading by Mrs. Crandall, a Scholastic representative. She shared why reading is essential in each career as she read the book LMNOPeas.

The third graders requested hearing from an engineer, as a follow up to a recent field trip about the math and science of hockey. The fourth through eighth graders had the opportunity to hear from many career presenters, such as a veterinarian, a florist, a physician's assistant, a photographer, engineers, a real estate agent, a district attorney, an electrician, a submarine lieutenant, an insurance agent, a band director, an associate creative director in advertising, a writer, etc.

In addition to hearing the speakers, students also had the opportunity to check out a police car, fire truck, ambulance, and a military truck! They loved crawling through each of the cars, testing out the siren, and talking to the service men and women.

By the end of the day, students were beginning with the end in mind: creating goals for future careers and the steps needed to get there. Students were proactive in thanking many of their presenters as they left the classrooms.

Source: Fallbrook & Bonsall Village News, March 19th, 2015. Retrieved from http://villagenews.com/education/san-onofre-school-holds-college-and-career-day.

Figure 9.29 Counselor's Corner Newsletter

Ashley Kruger
E Hale Curran RAIN Counselor
951-696-1405 ext 2271

Counselor's Corner

June 2017

Classroom Lessons

During the month of May, students in Tk-2nd grade received four weekly lessons in their classrooms. These lessons focused on teaching students problem solving skills. Students learned the acronym STEP. S: Say the problem without blame; T: Think of solutions (safe and respectful), E: Explore Consequences (what could happen if I choose this solution?); P: Pick the best solution. Students had the opportunity to engage in role play activities to practice using these four steps to solve problems.

HOW TO REINFORCE AT HOME: If a problem occurs at home, please encourage your students to go through each of these steps to solve the problem. Students learned that using words like "always" and "never" can be considered "blaming words." Therefore, students must practice saying the problem WITHOUT blame!

E Hale Curran's School Counseling Program Results:

Each year, the E Hale Curran School Counseling Program uses data to determine the effectiveness of the program. The outcome data below compares last year's data with this years data in the areas of chronic absenteeism and social skills/work habits on the report card.

The E Hale Curran school counseling program worked hard to reduce the percent of students who were chronically absent (students missing 10% or more of the school year). The goal was to reduce the percent of students who were chronically absent by 10%. Here are the results!

In addition to academic grades, students are measured on their social skills/word habits. Students are given an "O" for outstanding, an "M" for meets expectations and an "N" for needs improvement. The goal set forth this year was to decrease the number of students receiving N's in social skills/work habits by 10%! Here are the results

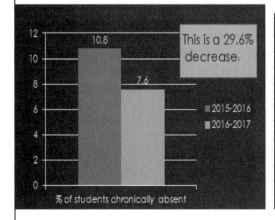

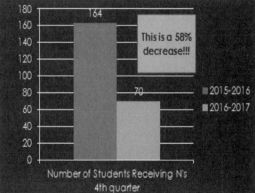

A Powerpoint with more outcome data can be found on the school counseling website. Thank you to teachers, staff, parents,, PTA, students and community members for supporting the E Hale Curran school counseling program! We could not do it without you! Have a wonderful summer!!

Source: Created by school counselor Ashley Kruger.

- Invite school board members to visit your site and use the opportunity to share program activities and results (remember to always discuss this idea with your administrators first).
- Submit photos and achieved results to state/national/district offices seeking "good news" stories and articles for publication.
- Participate in a district or conference poster exposition featuring school counseling program services and outcomes.
- Network with other counselors using social media exchanges and blogs—share program results and activities with them virtually.
- Create an end-of-the-year bulletin board or other visual display stating "Thanks for a great year!" with highlights of the program's impact that school year.

Sharing school counseling program results is an essential component of the elementary school counselor's role. Whether presented through a Flashlight Results Presentation, a one-pager, or a newsletter article, there are a variety of ways to showcase the work of elementary school counselors. Sharing results increases the understanding among faculty and families of the importance of the role and contributes to garnering buy-in for the program. Through highlighting the successes supported by their work, school counselors build program credibility, sustainability, and, hopefully, growth (Duarte & Hatch, 2014). As you reflect on your program and the desired effect of sharing counseling program outcomes, consider the following:

How will your experience documenting your work using the School Counseling Core Curriculum Results Template help your practice?

How will you commit to sharing and celebrating your program successes with others?

What audience most needs to hear about your school counseling activities and outcomes?

Based on your results, what are the future implications and next steps for counseling program goals for your next school year?

10

Management Systems and Putting It All Together

TRISH'S STORY

As an elementary school counselor, each year I was provided with a teacher's yearly lesson plan book to use (see Figure 10.1). I scheduled the curriculum lessons first in my calendar before scheduling interventions such as groups. It was a primitive approach compared to today's Apple, Google, and Outlook calendars, but it worked for me. This chapter will cover recommendations for efficient and effective management systems that will support elementary school counselors in "putting it all together."

School counselors often report that they spend far too much time responding to unexpected crises and "putting out fires." While it is true that school counselors are often first responders to crisis situations, best practice is to "happen to your day" as opposed to having "your day happen to you" (Hatch, 2013). Calendaring a daily, weekly, monthly, and annual schedule is key to ensuring that proactive management systems are in place for students.

The average school counselor–to-student ratio is 491:1, which can make it difficult to meet the needs of every student (ASCA, n.d.) In addition to serving *all* students, school counselors are also expected to provide support for staff, parents, and other stakeholders. Therefore, creating systems that allows school counselors to use their time efficiently is crucial.

Figure 10.1 Excerpt From Trish Hatch's Calendar as a School Counselor

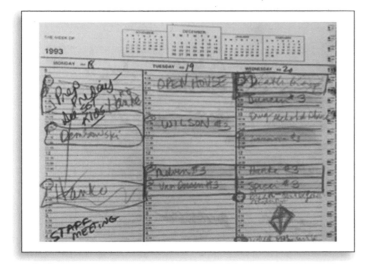

Proactive school counselors do not sit in their offices and wait for students or staff to come to them. Rather, they create an annual and weekly calendar that outlines all school counseling program activities; this also sends a message to stakeholders that counselors are not "always available" and that those in need of school counseling support may have to schedule an appointment, as is the case with other professionals. Developing effective management systems ensures that students receive prescheduled and consistent preventative school counseling services, such as core curriculum classroom lessons. By maintaining a strong time-management system, counselors will be less likely to be asked to engage in "non–school counseling activities" that are not "fair-share responsibilities," such as proctoring state testing, supervising the playground, substitute teaching, disciplining students, or providing long-term therapy in the school setting.

SCHEDULING CORE CURRICULUM

To make the process of collaborating with teachers to schedule core curriculum counseling lessons most efficient, consider these suggestions:

- Attend grade-level team meetings to share a schedule and ask teachers to sign up for a convenient time.
- Post a signup sheet in the staff lounge asking teachers to mark their preferred time slot (see the example in Figure 10.2).
- Create an online signup system and e-mail directions on how to use it to teachers (refer to Figures 10.3 and 10.4 for examples created using SignUpGenius.com).
- Work with administrators to identify times to push into teachers' classrooms or how to become part of the master schedule.

Using a signup sheet for school counseling lessons, whether paper or electronic, could allow teachers the option of not signing up at all. However, if the school counselor is clear that all teachers will have school counseling lessons and then follows up with individuals who did not sign up, there is a system of accountability. One way to promote signup is to implement a "freedom within limits" approach, such as "Would you prefer your lessons in October or November?" Note that in this case, the lesson delivery itself is not an option; rather, the month of delivery is negotiated. If possible, schedule all class lessons for a specific grade level on the same day, so that you teach the same lesson plan repeatedly throughout a single day and avoid having to "rewire" your brain for different lessons. Additionally, when scheduling, keep in mind the time needed in between lessons to set up and put away materials, travel between classrooms, and prepare yourself for the next class.

Figure 10.2 School Counseling Classroom Lesson Signup Sheet

SCHOOL COUNSELING CLASSROOM CURRICULUM LESSONS SIGN-UP

Please provide two options that are best for monthly core classroom curriculum lessons of 30-45 minutes as part of the school counseling program. Sign up by <u>September 6, 2018</u>. Thank you!

	TEACHER	DAY AND TIME PREFERENCE
	Example	1. Thursdays from 9-9:30 AM 2. Wednesdays from 12:45-1:15 PM
GRADE K	Teacher Name	1. 2.
GRADE K	Teacher Name	1. 2.
GRADE K	Teacher Name	1. 2.
1ST GRADE	Teacher Name	1. 2.
1ST GRADE	Teacher Name	1. 2.
1ST GRADE	Teacher Name	1. 2.
2ND GRADE	Teacher Name	1. 2.
2ND GRADE	Teacher Name	1. 2.
2ND GRADE	Teacher Name	1. 2.
3RD GRADE	Teacher Name	1. 2.
3RD GRADE	Teacher Name	1. 2.
3RD GRADE	Teacher Name	1. 2.
4TH GRADE	Teacher Name	1. 2.
4TH GRADE	Teacher Name	1. 2.
4TH GRADE	Teacher Name	1. 2.
5TH GRADE	Teacher Name	1. 2.
5TH GRADE	Teacher Name	1. 2.
5TH GRADE	Teacher Name	1. 2.

Source: Adapted from Kate Bailin, EduKate & Inspire Blog: http://edukateandinspire.blogspot.com/2016/07/google-docs-for-school-counselors.html.

Trish shares her story: One of my favorite trainings I went to as a school counselor was "Love and Logic" by Jim Fay. It was helpful not only in my role as a school counselor but also as a parent. In one particular training, Fay talked about the "freedom within limits" approach (Cline & Fay, 2014). I used that technique more often than I can say, not only professionally but also in my parenting. For instance, I used it with my sons when it was time to go out to dinner or to go visit relatives. I would say, "You can pick any shirt in the closet you want to wear; it's your choice, your decision—the only requirement is that it has to have a collar." With this approach, my sons were able to feel completely in control, and I was able to have what I needed, which was a shirt with a collar. In the same way, I would suggest that school counselors say to teachers when they are scheduling their core curriculum lessons, "You can have your lesson any day of the week or anytime you like, as long as it's during the month of October."

Ashley was a new school counselor at E. Hale Curran Elementary School. Prior to her arrival, the school did not have a counselor, and Ashley was given a caseload of 650 students. As Ashley began implementing the school counseling program, she recognized the need to do the following:

1. Educate the staff on the school counseling program

2. Explain the purpose and goals of core curriculum classroom lessons

3. Provide an example of a core curriculum lesson and explain that topics are developed/selected based on data-driven needs

4. Gather data and review the schedule of existing school activities (such as set times for library, art, or reading intervention)

5. Analyze available times in the teacher's schedule and compare each grade level for possible core curriculum times

6. Collaborate with staff and send out a signup sheet to solidify a schedule for core curriculum (Ashley chose to use SignUpGenius.com; see Figures 10.3 and 10.4)

7. Align the core curriculum class lesson schedule with school calendars to ensure that reminders would be sent to teachers prior to their lesson

By offering open time slots and asking teachers to sign up for one of those available times, Ashley sent the message that core curriculum is a necessary and integral part of a student's learning environment. Providing teachers this "freedom within limits" allowed them to be involved in the process, and also ensured that the times selected fit within Ashley's schedule.

CALENDARS

As school counselors schedule core curriculum and other program activities, calendars are a vital component in planning and ensuring appropriate allocation of time and services. School counselors utilize their calendar as a marketing tool to keep stakeholders and administrators informed of their school counseling program and encourage active participation in activities throughout the year. Additionally, a well-planned calendar puts school counselors in the driver's seat by allowing them to control the direction and implementation of their program, protecting counselors' time for their work, and providing programmatic legitimacy. Within the Tier 1 system, calendars allow scheduling of core curriculum lessons and school-wide activities in a systematic manner that guarantees consistent instruction for all students.

Figure 10.3 Example of Using Technology to Schedule Core Curriculum Lessons: A Message to Teachers

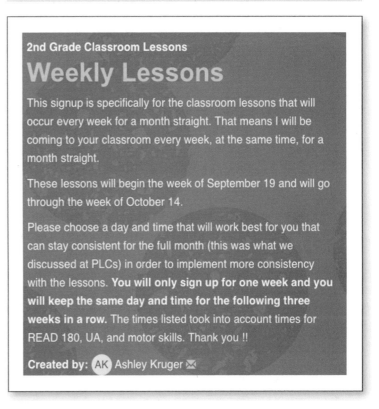

Figure 10.4 Using Technology to Schedule Core Curriculum Lessons With SignUpGenius.Com

Date (mm/dd/yyyy)	Time (PST)	Available Slot	Calendar View
09/19/2016 (Mon.)	1:00pm - 1:45pm	Select One	Sign Up ☐
09/20/2016 (Tue.)	1:00pm - 1:45pm	Select One	AS Alexandra Shores
	1:45pm - 2:30pm	Select One	KO Kim Ordinario
09/21/2016 (Wed.)	1:00pm - 1:45pm	Select One	HG Heather Goka
	1:45pm - 2:30pm	Select One	AS Alexandra Shores
09/22/2016 (Thu.)	1:00pm - 1:45pm	Select One	Sign Up ☐

Source: Created by Ashley Kruger.

Sharing the school counseling calendars with teachers, parents, administrators, and students is a critical aspect of ensuring buy-in and support for the school counseling program. Calendars also invite family and community involvement beyond the school staff and foster partnerships with additional resources. Some common ways in which school counselors share their calendars are through

- School counseling websites
- Weekly/monthly/quarterly newsletters
- Bulletin boards
- E-mail
- Shared Google Calendars
- Printouts posted outside the counseling office

Tips for creating school counseling program calendars:

- Create complete, timely, visually appealing and organized calendars
- Format calendars for ease of understanding, attractive design, color, and detail
- Identify grade level, dates, and activities
- Distribute calendars to appropriate stakeholders
- Use a template that resonates best with you

Annual Calendars

Annual calendars are comprehensive and identify all Tier 1 activities, including schoolwide programs and the full scope and sequence of lessons and activities scheduled for delivery. Although not the focus of this text, Tier 2 and 3 activities (such as small counseling groups and individual sessions) would also be calendared.

When creating an annual calendar, school counselors collaborate with all stakeholders to ensure that core curriculum lessons and schoolwide activities are developed and delivered in a purposeful way. For example, when determining which core

Figure 10.5   Annual Calendars

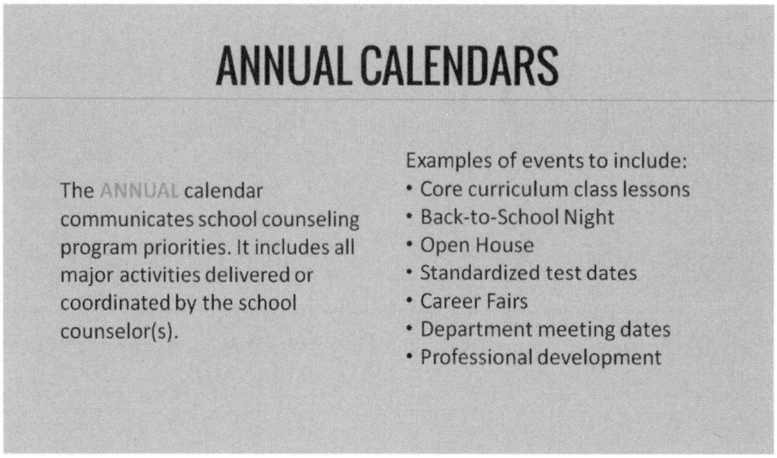

ANNUAL CALENDARS

The ANNUAL calendar communicates school counseling program priorities. It includes all major activities delivered or coordinated by the school counselor(s).

Examples of events to include:
- Core curriculum class lessons
- Back-to-School Night
- Open House
- Standardized test dates
- Career Fairs
- Department meeting dates
- Professional development

curriculum lessons to teach fifth-grade students in October, transitioning to middle school would not be included, because the timing would not be appropriate. Rather, providing such lessons in the spring is more logical. In addition, school counselors will want to consider national awareness campaigns (see Chapter 7) when planning the annual calendar.

School counseling calendars convey professionalism through visual appeal and ease of reading. While there is no specified format to use, school counselors should create a calendar that fits their needs and keeps them on track. While some go so far as to color-code activities per type of direct/indirect counseling service to assist in giving a visual picture of the amount of time spent in different activities, or color-code according to the school counseling program SMART goals, the calendar should help and not hinder you.

See Figures 10.6 through 10.8 for examples from annual calendars, noting the differences. Figure 10.6, provided by K–8 school counselor Martha Williams of Crown Community Academy, is an example of an annual calendar in a linear monthly list view, with the added feature of identifying recurring weekly and monthly activities. Figure 10.7 is an example of a month excerpted from an annual calendar with a traditional calendar view. Figure 10.8, provided by Angela Shanahan in Chicago, is another example with a traditional calendar view; it has the added feature of using color-coding to connect activities to school counseling program SMART goals.

It can also be beneficial to create a calendar of monthly activities for your parent education program (see Figure 10.9 for an example). Figure 10.10 is an excerpt from an annual school counseling calendar template that can be modified for your use in the online appendix.

Weekly Calendars

The weekly calendar keeps the elementary school counselor organized and communicates general whereabouts and availability daily. While the weekly calendar provides a detailed plan of the school counselor's activities, it is important that stakeholders understand that the calendar is somewhat flexible, based on the possibility of needing to deal with crises or other situations that may require immediate attention.

See Figures 10.12 and 10.13 for sample weekly calendars. Figure 10.14 presents a weekly school counseling calendar template that can be modified for your use. Notice that you have the option to color-code by the type of service if you choose to do so, which can easily be modified to coordinate with SMART goals. The complete template is available in the online appendix. Figure 10.13 displays a weekly calendar from Rebecca Lallier in Vermont, with the added features of color-coding by type of direct/indirect counseling service and the corresponding use of time calculation.

MONTHLY PLANNING GUIDES

A monthly planning guide of suggested school counseling activities, when reviewed and updated each year, is helpful to ensure that school counselors keep in mind the rhythm of regular events and action items throughout the academic school year when creating their calendars. The sample that follows has been updated since Trish's use of a hardcopy planner with her district in the 1990s (see Figure 10.15). Note that the guide presented here doesn't include state or local activities, which counselors can add themselves.

Figure 10.6 Annual Calendar Example: Linear Monthly List View

CROWN COMMUNITY ACADEMY
2016–2017 ... SCHOOL COUNSELING ANNUAL CALENDAR

AUGUST 2016

8/24 Consulting Educator Training
8/30 Meeting – new SEL program; UIC
8/30 Team Meeting – preparation for staff PD on Thriving Communities SEL program
8/31-9/2 Scheduled Staff PD's and preparation for the start of the new school year
- **8/31** Intro. to Thriving Communities; facilitate staff Character Strengths survey, and reading assignment
- **9/1** Facilitate Staff (MS) Thriving Communities PD
- **9/1** Moderate Staff Refresher on CHAMPS and Second Step by Network SEL Specialist; distribute kits and overview of roll out
- **9/2** BoY Counselor/Coach Meeting 9/2 School Staff PD's Community Walk; Committees / Calendar; SEL Calendar; Thriving Communities Evaluation; Distribution of remaining SEL kits (Thriving Communities and Second Step), Selection of 8th grade Mentees (Kick-off 9/19), etc.

"TEAMWORK MAKES THE DREAM WORK
ONE TEAM, ONE DREAM"

SEPTEMBER 2016

National Hispanic Month (9/15-10/15)... daily PSA's

9/6 First Day School for Students
Assist w/student entry and transition to classes
Meet & greet students and new families
9/6-10/7 BoY MAP / NWEA (K-8)
9/7-9/9 Know Your School Counselor Week
- **9/7** ASAS meeting
- **9/7** Select students for Illinois Prevention Bowl
- **9/7** CISC BoY meeting
9/8-9/9 Prevention Bowl Practice w/students
- **9/8** UIC meeting for SEL/Nutrition program
- **9/9** Kick Off school-wide PBIS
9/12-9/16 Prevention Bowl Practice w/students
9/12-9/16 PBIS/CHAMPS ... classroom assistance
- **9/12** Counselor/Social Worker Planning
- **9/12** Recruit Student Ambassadors
- **9/13** Crown Teacher after-school PD
9/19-9/21 Prevention Bowl Practice w/students
- **9/19** Kick Off Thriving Classrooms (5-8) & Second Step school-wide (PK-8), Mentoring
- **9/20** Back to School Open House & 8th grade Parent/Student Night
9/22 Illinois Prevention Bowl (U.S. Cellular Field)
9/23 Student Ambassador meeting/training
9/26 New Student Social
9/26 Prep for Groups (small & large)
9/28 MS Naviance training
9/29 One Fund Emerald City Field Trip
9/29 Crown Teacher after-school PD
9/30 Back-to-School w/the HistoryMakers Assembly

(RECURRING)
Weekly
MS High School Readiness classes
MS Thriving Communities assistance
Teacher Team meetings
Team Day, MTSS & Records Management
ILT Meeting
Monthly Meetings
Community Mental Health/Mentoring Service Providers
Art Teacher/CCCAS Resource Coordinator/Counselor
BHT: PBIS, 2nd Step, CHAMPS, Thriving Classrooms
Network 5 Professional School Counselors

MARTHA WILLIAMS, PROFESSIONAL SCHOOL COUNSELOR ... ROOM 115

CROWN COMMUNITY ACADEMY
2016–2017 … SCHOOL COUNSELING ANNUAL CALENDAR

OCTOBER 2016

National Hispanic Month (9/15-10/15)… projects/PSA's

Bully Prevention … class projects/PSA's

10/1 CPS HS Application Process Kick-Off
10/3 BOY MAP / NWEA (K-8) *cont'd*
10/5 Crown High School Fair & CTE workshops (6-8) … Ambassadors help w/event
10/6 Master Counselor/Coach Orientation
10/11-6/17 ASAS – We Are Ready HS, College, Career begins (Class of 2017 lessons/units, 1-on-1 sessions)
10/12 Teacher after-school PD
10/13 New Counselor Orientation
10/14 Ronald McDonald Assembly (K-4)
10/19 Stop Bullying Day of Action – School-wide Activity
10/24-10/31 Red Ribbon Week … class Drug Awareness/Prevention projects

(RECURRING)
Weekly
MS High School Readiness classes
MS Thriving Communities assistance
Teacher Team meetings
Team Day, MTSS & Records Management
ILT Meeting

Monthly Meetings
Community Mental Health/Mentoring Service Providers
Art Teacher/CCCAS Resource Coordinator/Counselor
BHT: PBIS, 2nd Step, CHAMPS, Thriving Classrooms
Network 5 Professional School Counselors

NOVEMBER 2016

11/1 HS Application Process *cont'd*
11/2 Teacher after-school PD
11/3 End 1st Qtr.
11/4 School Improvement Day
11/7 Ageless Eye Center – Eye Exams … Ambassadors assist
11/9 1st Qtr. Report Card Conferences
11/9 HS Application Parent/Student Workshops
11/14 Parent Involvement Week … Volunteers (IS; OS)
11/10 Story Bus – primary
11/15 MC Meeting
11/16 PBIS "102"
11/21-12-9 Service Learning … Canned Food Drive (led by Ambassadors)

(RECURRING)
Weekly
MS High School Readiness classes
MS Thriving Communities assistance
Teacher Team meetings
Team Day, MTSS & Records Management
ILT Meeting

Monthly Meetings
Community Mental Health/Mentoring Service Providers
Art Teacher/CCCAS Resource Coordinator/Counselor
BHT: PBIS, 2nd Step, CHAMPS, Thriving Classrooms
Network 5 Professional School Counselors

DECEMBER 2016

12/1 HS Application Process *cont'd*
12/2 Disabilities Awareness Day
12/5 Teacher after-school PD
12/9 HS Application DEADLINE
11/21-12-9 Service Learning … Canned Food Drive (led by Ambassadors)
12/12 Community Service Week … various projects
12/19-1/27 MoY MAP / NWEA (K-8)
12/26-1/6 Winter Vacation

(RECURRING)
Weekly
MS High School Readiness classes

JANUARY 2017

1/9 Return from Winter Vacation
1/9-1/27 MoY MAP / NWEA (K-8)
1/13 Donuts for Dad Event … embracing male supports
1/16 "No Name Calling Week"
1/26 Teacher after-school PD

(RECURRING)
Weekly
MS High School Readiness classes
MS Thriving Communities assistance
Teacher Team meetings
Team Day, MTSS & Records Management
ILT Meeting

MARTHA WILLIAMS, PROFESSIONAL SCHOOL COUNSELOR … ROOM 115

(Continued)

Figure 10.6 (Continued)

CROWN COMMUNITY ACADEMY
2016-2017 ... SCHOOL COUNSELING ANNUAL CALENDAR

MS Thriving Communities assistance
Teacher Team meetings
Team Day, MTSS & Records Management
ILT Meeting

Monthly Meetings
Community Mental Health/Mentoring Service Providers
Art Teacher/CCCAS Resource Coordinator/Counselor
BHT: PBIS, 2nd Step, CHAMPS, Thriving Classrooms
Network 5 Professional School Counselors

Monthly Meetings
Community Mental Health/Mentoring Service Providers
Art Teacher/CCCAS Resource Coordinator/Counselor
BHT: PBIS, 2nd Step, CHAMPS, Thriving Classrooms
Network 5 Professional School Counselor

FEBRUARY 2017

Black History Month (2/1-2/28)... projects/PSA's

2/6-2/10 *NATIONAL SCHOOL COUNSELING WEEK*
2/7 Teacher after-school PD
2/14 Valentine's Day
2/20 President's Day

(RECURRING)
Weekly
MS High School Readiness classes
MS Thriving Communities assistance
Teacher Team meetings
Team Day, MTSS & Records Management
ILT Meeting

Monthly Meetings
Community Mental Health/Mentoring Service Providers
Art Teacher/CCCAS Resource Coordinator/Counselor
BHT: PBIS, 2nd Step, CHAMPS, Thriving Classrooms
Network 5 Professional School Counselors

MARCH 2017

Women's History Month (3/1-2/31)... projects/PSA's

3/1 Teacher after-school PD
3/2 Celebrate Reading Day
3/6-4/6 PARCC 3-8
6/8 Muffins for Moms ... Celebrating "Mothers" support
3/22 MC Meeting
3/27-3/31 Youth Violence Prevention Week
3/27 Teacher after-school PD

(RECURRING)
Weekly
MS High School Readiness classes
MS Thriving Communities assistance
Teacher Team meetings
Team Day, MTSS & Records Management
ILT Meeting

Monthly Meetings
Community Mental Health/Mentoring Service Providers
Art Teacher/CCCAS Resource Coordinator/Counselor
BHT: PBIS, 2nd Step, CHAMPS, Thriving Classrooms
Network 5 Professional School Counselors

APRIL 2017

4/3-4/6 PARCC Ends
4/7 School Improvement Day
4/10-4/14 National Library Week ... D.E.A.R.
4/10-4/14 Spring Vacation
4/19 3rd Qtr. Report Card Conferences
4/21 Annual School-wide Career Day
4/17-4/28 ISBE Science 5-8
4/24 Teacher after-school PD

MAY 2017

5/1-5/5 Health Awareness Week
5/4 MC Meeting
5/9 Teacher after-school PD
5/15-6/16 EoY MAP / NWEA (K-8)
5/31 Teacher after-school PD
(RECURRING)
Weekly
MS High School Readiness classes

MARTHA WILLIAMS, PROFESSIONAL SCHOOL COUNSELOR ... ROOM 115

CROWN COMMUNITY ACADEMY
2016-2017 ... SCHOOL COUNSELING ANNUAL CALENDAR

(RECURRING)

Weekly
MS High School Readiness classes
MS Thriving Communities assistance
Teacher Team meetings
Team Day, MTSS & Records Management
ILT Meeting

Monthly Meetings
Community Mental Health/Mentoring Service Providers
Art Teacher/CCCAS Resource Coordinator/Counselor
BHT: PBIS, 2nd Step, CHAMPS, Thriving Classrooms
Network 5 Professional School Counselors

MS Thriving Communities assistance
Teacher Team meetings
Team Day, MTSS & Records Management
ILT Meeting

Monthly Meetings
Community Mental Health/Mentoring Service Providers
Art Teacher/CCCAS Resource Coordinator/Counselor
BHT: PBIS, 2nd Step, CHAMPS, Thriving Classrooms
Network 5 Professional School Counselors

JUNE 2017

6/1 Celebrate Children's Day
5/15-6/16 EoY MAP / NWEA (K-8)
6/16 EoY Counselor/Coach Meeting
6/16 Celebrate the Young Child (EoY PK celebration)
6/19 8th grade Graduation
6/20 Last Day Classes
6/21 Teacher Institute

(RECURRING)

Weekly
MS High School Readiness classes
MS Thriving Communities assistance
Teacher Team meetings
Team Day, MTSS & Records Management
ILT Meeting

Monthly Meetings
Community Mental Health/Mentoring Service Providers
Art Teacher/CCCAS Resource Coordinator/Counselor
BHT: PBIS, 2nd Step, CHAMPS, Thriving Classrooms
Network 5 Professional School Counselors

Additional activities, events, programs, etc. to be Scheduled once dates are arranged

- North Lawndale Coalition on Underage Drinking
- Prevention Partnership Leadership workshops
- Junior Achievement
- MS grade mentoring project
- Youth Wellness Team
- Per Referrals (teacher, parent, other)
    1. SS Grin
    2. Zoo U
    3. Emote trial SEL program w/primary
    4. Girls / Boys groups
    5. Classroom units

Schedule, Facilitate, and Manage other health initiatives
    1. Oral Health Education
    2. Asthma Education
    3. Dental Exams & Cleanings
    4. CPS Vision/Hearing Screenings

As of 8/31/16 ... to be revised as Appropriate

MARTHA WILLIAMS, PROFESSIONAL SCHOOL COUNSELOR ... ROOM 115

Source: Crown Community Academy Calendar created by Martha Williams, Elementary School Counselor. Reproduced with permission.

Figure 10.7 Annual Calendar Example: Traditional Calendar View

K-8 School Counseling Calendar

October

Monday	Tuesday	Wednesday	Thursday	Friday
			1 *AVID Binder/ Planner Check* **Club Bond** **Grade Check Family Night @ 6pm (5-8)**	**2** *AVID Binder/ Planner Check Workshop*
5	**6** Monthly District Counseling Mtg @ DO	**7**	**8** *Citizenship Lunch Intervention (3-4)*	**9** *School Counselors @ CASC Conference*
	←Respect & Cyber Awareness Lessons→			
12 Grades Check Workshop (5-8)	**13** *Citizenship Lunch Intervention (1-2)*	**14** **AVID @ Lunch**	**15** **Club Bond** RAMP Application Due	**16**
19 Progress Report Grades Due	**20**	**21**	**22** *Citizenship Lunch Intervention (3-4)*	**23**
26 Grades Check Workshop (5-8)	**27** *Citizenship Lunch Intervention (1-2)*	**28**	**29** **Club Bond** **Gang/Drug Awareness Family Night @ 6pm**	**30** **Red Ribbon Weekly Assembly** **Staff Social**
	← Red Ribbon Week/Positive Decision Making Lessons →			

Updated September 10, 2015

Figure 10.8 Annual Calendar Example: Traditional Calendar View With Color-Coding

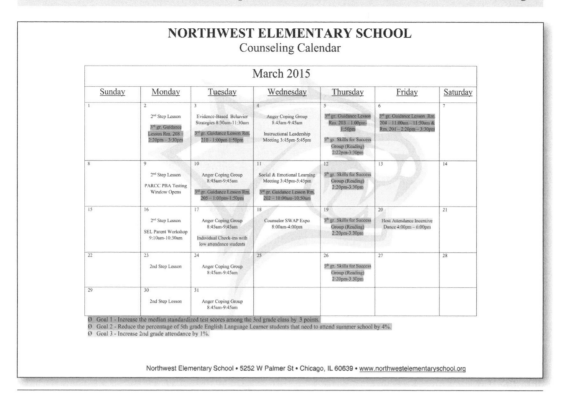

Source: Adapted from calendar created by Angela Shanahan, Northwest Elementary School, Chicago, IL.

Figure 10.9 Annual Calendar of Monthly Parent Activities

Figure 10.10 Annual School Counseling Calendar Template

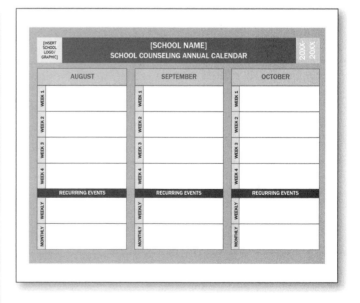

Figure 10.11 Weekly Calendars

WEEKLY CALENDARS

A WEEKLY calendar provides a detailed plan of the school counselor's activities for the week. It is somewhat flexible due to crisis response or immediate need situations.

Examples of events to include:
• Core curriculum lessons
• Small-group and individual counseling
• Committee meetings
• Fair-share responsibilities
• Collaboration or data analysis time
• Meetings with students or parents

Figure 10.12 Sample Weekly Calendar

BURNHAM/ANTHONY MATHEMATICS & SCIENCE ACADEMY

Dr. Linda J. Moore, Principal ● *Ms. Sheryl Freeman, Assistant Principal* ● *Ms. Krotiak, School Counselor*

SCHOOL COUNSELING WEEKLY SCHEDULE

	MONDAY	TUESDAY	WEDNESDAY	THURSDAY	FRIDAY
8:30 to 9:00 am	Data/Administrative	Data/Administrative	Data/Administrative	Meetings—Graduation & SEL Committees	Data/Administrative
9:00 to 11:00 am	Student Observations Burnham Bldg. (or Grade Level Mtg)	Administrative Tasks	Student Observations Burnham Bldg.	Classroom Walk Throughs/ Administrative Tasks	ILT TEAM
11:00 to 12:10 pm	Individual/Group/Class Guidance Preparation	Individual & Small Group Counseling—Burnham Bldg.	Individual & Small Group Counseling—Burnham Bldg.	High School Transition Tasks or Test Coordination	ILT TEAM and LUNCH BREAK
12:10 to 12:40 pm	LUNCH BREAK/ Lunch Social Club (Grades K and 2)	LUNCH BREAK	LUNCH BREAK	Individual/Group/Class Guidance Planning and Documentation	Pupil Support Services Meeting
12:40 to 1:10pm	Student Observations at Anthony Bldg. (or Grade Level Mtg.)	'Education to Careers' and 'Live Every Day with Character' Planning	Individual/Group/Class Guidance Preparation and/or Parent Correspondence	LUNCH BREAK/ Lunch Social Club (Grades 1 and 3)	Character Guidance— Ms. Porthan (#101) 3rd full week of Month (12:45 to 1:10)
1:10 to 1:50pm	Individual or Small Group Counseling—Anthony Bldg.	Character Guidance— Mr. Benson (#105) 3rd full week of Month (1:15 to 1:50)	Administrative Team Meetings Bi-Monthly (1:30 to 2:45)	Character Guidance— Ms. Langdon (#107) 3rd full week of Month (1:15 to 1:50)	Character Guidance— Mr. Lee (#102) 3rd full week of Month (1:15 to 1:50)
1:55 to 2:30 pm	Individual or Small Group Counseling—Anthony Bldg.	Character Guidance— Ms. Agyeman (#103) 3rd full week of Month (1:55 to 2:30)	Or Coordination of Outside Programs	Character Guidance—Ms. Pfieil (#104) 3rd full week of Month (1:55 to 2:30)	Individual Student Advisement
2:30 to 2:45 pm	◄——————— TRAVEL TO ANTHONY BLDG.——————►				Planning for Next Week
2:45 to 4:15 pm	◄——— ACADEMIC COMMUNITY SCHOOL PROGRAM, ROOM 113 ———►				

NOTE: Character Guidance occurs during 3rd week of month at Burnham Bldg. only. Class guidance at Anthony will be scheduled at this time. To be determined as needed. Family Connection Workshops are Wednesdays from 5:00 to 6:00 PM

Figure 10.13 Weekly Calendar With Additional Features

Lallier Weekly Counseling Schedule — September 29-October 3

Monday

7:30 – 8:00	IP: Targeted Check-In
8:00 – 8:20	Parent Consult
8:20 – 9:00	CC: Kindergarten KR1 *TIFY* Lesson 4: Body in the Group
9:00 – 9:10	Prep: Morning groups
9:10 – 9:55	3rd Grade Group: Self-Regulation-Empathy: Planning to Learn
9:55 – 10:00	Transition
10:00 – 10:45	2nd Grade Group: Self-Regulation - Skills for Learning: Being Assertive
10:45 – 11:05	Prep: Advisory Council, *Second Step* Lesson
11:05 – 11:20	RS: Kindergartner
11:20 – 11:35	Parent Consult
11:35 – 11:50	Lunch
12:10 – 12:50	CC: Kindergarten KR2 *TIFY* Lesson 4: Body in the Group
12:50 – 12:55	Transition
12:55 – 1:40	IP: 1st grader
1:40 – 1:45	Transition
1:45 – 2:25	CC: Kindergarten KR3 *TIFY* Lesson 4: Body in the Group
2:25 – 2:45	IP: Targeted Check Out
2:45 – 3:45	Advisory Council

Tuesday

7:30 – 8:00	IP: Targeted Check-In
8:00 – 8:15	RS: Kindergartner
8:15 – 8:35	CC: KS *Second Step:* Self Talk for Staying on Task
8:35 – 9:15 / 8:35 – 9:15 concurrent	CC: Kindergarten KR4 (Lallier) & KS1 (Nichols) *TIFY* Lesson 4: Body in the Group
9:15 – 10:00	DBS Counselor/SLP meeting
10:00 – 10:30	Behavior plan update; parent call
10:30 – 10:45	IP: 4th Grader
10:50 – 11:35	4th Grade Team Consult/Behavior Planning
11:35 – 11:50	Parent Consult
11:50 – 12:10	Lunch
12:10 – 12:50	CC: Kindergarten KS2 *TIFY* Lesson 4: Body in the Group
12:50 – 12:55	Transition
12:55 – 1:40	Kindergarten Team Consult/Behavior Planning
1:40 – 1:45	Transition
1:45 – 2:30	2nd Grade Teacher Consult/Behavior Planning: A-2S
2:30 – 2:45	IP: Targeted Check Out
2:45 – 3:00	OC Para Consult
3:00 – 4:00	Staff Meeting

Wednesday — Not scheduled to work on Wednesdays

CALENDAR CODING

Direct & Indirect Services
Direct
- Core Curriculum
- Group Counseling
- Individual Planning/ Responsive Services

Indirect
- Consultation
- Individual Student Team Meetings
- Targeted, Intensive, CPT & EST Meetings

Program Management/ School Support
- Prep
- Meetings
- School-Wide Events
- Duties
- Other
- Transition
- Lunch

Thursday

7:30 – 8:00	IP: Targeted Check-In
8:00 – 8:20	RS: Kindergartner
8:20 – 9:05	CC: 4th Grade 4W Bullying Lesson 2: Goodbye Bully Machine
9:05 – 9:15	Prep: Intensive Meeting
9:15 – 10:00	Intensive Team Meeting
10:00 – 10:30	RS: Kindergartner
10:30 – 11:00	Intern Consult/IP & Behavior Planning
11:00 – 11:45	CC: 4th Grade 4T Bullying Lesson 2: Goodbye Bully Machine
11:45 – 11:50	Transition
11:50 – 12:10	Recess Duty
12:15 – 12:40	4th-5th Lunch Group: SS: Conversation
12:40 – 1:00	Lunch
1:00 – 1:40	CC: Kindergarten KS3 *TIFY* Lesson 4: Body in the Group
1:40 – 1:45	Transition
1:45 – 2:30	Student Team Meeting 5th grader
2:30 – 2:45	IP: Targeted Check Out
2:45 – 3:15	Parent calls
3:45 – 4:45	SIBS Matching

Friday

7:20 – 8:00	Targeted Team Meeting
8:00 – 8:30	RS: Kindergartner
8:30 – 10:00	District Elementary/Middle School Counselor Meeting
10:00 – 10:15	RS: Kindergartner
10:15 – 10:30	OC Para Consult
10:30 – 10:50	Targeted behavior plan updates
10:50 – 11:35	5th Grade Teacher Consult/Behavior planning A-5T
11:35 – 11:55	Consult: Mental Health Clinician
11:55 – 12:10	Lunch
12:10 – 12:50	CC: Kindergarten KS4 *TIFY* Lesson 4: Body in the Group
12:50 – 12:55	Transition
12:55 – 1:15	RS: 4th Grader
1:15 – 1:35	IP: Kindergartner
1:35 – 2:00	RS: Kindergartner
1:45 – 2:00	K Teacher Consult
2:00 – 3:00	Student 504 Meeting 5th Grader
3:00 – 3:30	Prep: CC Lessons

Source: Created by Rebecca Lallier at Dothan Brook School.

Figure 10.14 School Counseling Weekly Calendar Template

[INSERT SCHOOL LOGO/ GRAPHIC]

[SCHOOL NAME]
[SCHOOL ADDRESS] • [SCHOOL CITY/STATE/ZIP] • [SCHOOL PHONE NUMBER]
[Name of principal] • [Name of assistant principal] • [Name of school counselor]

20XX-20XX

SCHOOL COUNSELING WEEKLY CALENDAR

	MONDAY	TUESDAY	WEDNESDAY	THURSDAY	FRIDAY
8:00 to 8:30 am					
8:30 to 9:00 am					
9:00 to 9:30 am					
9:30 to 10:00 am					
10:00 to 10:30 am					
10:30 to 11:00 am					
11:00 to 11:30 am					
11:30 to 12:00 pm					
12:00 to 12:30 pm					
12:30 to 1:00 pm					
1:00 to 1:30 pm					
1:30 to 2:00 pm					
2:00 to 2:30 pm					
2:30 to 3:00 pm					
3:00 to 3:30 pm					

LEGEND: DIRECT • INDIRECT • STUDENT SUPPORT

online resources

Sample Year-at-a-Glance Planning Guide of Elementary School Counselor Activities

AUGUST (BEFORE THE START OF THE SCHOOL YEAR)

- Revise and update the school counseling calendar
- Review data (attendance, behavior, etc.) and create SMART goals with tiered prevention and intervention lessons/activities to support the goals
- Create core curriculum (Tier 1) and Intentional Guidance Action Plans (Tiers 2 and 3)
- Determine which core curriculum lessons and interventions will be measured/reported
- Create an Annual Agreement and review it with your administrator (see page 254)
- Identify possible retained students for monitoring, if applicable
- Review students with IEPs and consult with support staff to determine appropriate counseling services
- Check supplies and order materials for core curriculum and small groups
- Design or update a school counseling page on the school's website, including an overview of the school counseling program, a school counselor bio and photo, and contact information
- Ensure that the student referral form is available to teachers and students
- Create or update the school counseling program brochure
- Schedule and begin planning topics for family workshops for the year
- Update membership in state and national school counseling associations and register for annual conference(s)
- Identify professional development opportunities/dates for the year
- Meet with administrators to review action plans, calendars, etc. and discuss next academic year planning

AUGUST/SEPTEMBER (FIRST MONTH OF SCHOOL)

- Support kindergarten transition (for students and parents)
- Provide orientation for students new to the school
- Meet with students experiencing adjustment challenges (consider a peer buddy or group)
- Visit all classes and introduce yourself and the school counseling program. See the online appendix for examples and templates.
- Present information about the school counseling program at a staff meeting, including program goals, core curriculum lessons, and activities for the year
- Participate in Back to School Night
- Finalize dates and times for classroom lessons with teachers
- Meet with the school site council, parent-teacher association, etc. to acquaint them with the school counseling program and yearly goals
- Send a letter (or newsletter) to families describing your program and goals for this year and post it on your website
- Start core curriculum lessons
- Calendar the district school counselor meetings for the year
- Attend SSTs, IEPs, 504s, etc. as appropriate

Figure 10.15 Don't forget to talk to your administrator about flexing your schedule if you need to attend your own child's awards ceremony! And remember to attend your "School Counselor in the '90s Conference"! LOL!

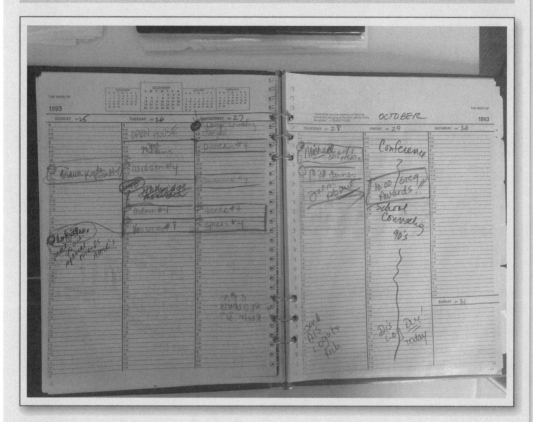

OCTOBER

- Make the staff aware of school counseling program activities for the month
- Continue teaching core curriculum lessons
- Develop student leaders/conflict manager training and select students to participate
- Participate in Red Ribbon Week activities (and calendar other national/local campaign events)
- Begin data analysis to determine students for interventions (groups, etc.)
- Be available for parent conferences at report card pickup
- Plan for groups (curriculum, schedules) after getting data from the first report card
- Facilitate family workshops
- Attend SSTs, IEPs, 504s, etc. as appropriate
- Attend the state school counseling conference (if applicable)

NOVEMBER

- Continue delivering core curriculum lessons
- Use the report card (end-of-quarter data) to determine which students will receive Tier 2 interventions (i.e., students with *x* or more absences for attendance group, students

(Continued)

(Continued)

with *x* or more referrals for behavior group, students with Us in behavior on their report cards, etc.)
- Consult with teachers regarding student attendance or behavior challenges
- Plan core curriculum and train selected student leaders/conflict managers
- Consult with school staff and community organizations to help coordinate donations for Thanksgiving and other winter holidays for low-income families served by your school
- Facilitate family workshops
- Attend SSTs, IEPs, 504s, etc., as appropriate

DECEMBER

- Deliver December core curriculum lessons
- Develop and/or revise lessons for the remainder of the year
- Attend district school counselors' holiday luncheon and gift exchange (if applicable)
- Be on the lookout for students with holiday crisis issues
- Continue facilitating groups
- Attend SSTs, IEPs, 504s, etc., as appropriate

JANUARY

- Begin planning for the spring College and Career Day Event (and ask for parent volunteers)
- Continue facilitating family workshops
- Plan activities for National School Counseling Week (the first week in February)
- Teach core curriculum lessons
- Finish/evaluate groups from the first quarter
- Coordinate and lead a refresher training for student leaders/conflict managers
- Review data from the second quarter (or semester) to determine groups for the third quarter
- Attend SSTs, IEPs, 504s, etc., as appropriate

FEBRUARY

- Develop a "wish list" to spend all your program money by March 1
- Continue delivering core curriculum lessons
- Begin facilitating a new round of groups for students who meet semester criteria for intentional (Tier 2) intervention
- Continue to plan for the College and Career Day Event and reach out to community partners, such as the local chamber of commerce, fire and police departments, etc.
- Celebrate National School Counseling week—inform, advertise, and promote staff awareness
- Deliver family workshops
- Present Flashlight Results presentation to faculty on core curriculum from the fall
- Attend SSTs, IEPs, 504s, etc., as appropriate

MARCH

- Work with teachers to plan lessons on how to take/prepare for standardized tests and deliver lessons

- Start groups for students who meet semester criteria for intentional (Tier 2) intervention
- Schedule spring break massage ☺
- Finalize volunteers for College and Career Day and send information to volunteers with details
- Contact the local middle school to arrange a date, time, and schedule for an orientation presentation and/or school visit in May
- Conduct additional training for student leaders/conflict managers
- Attend SSTs, IEPs, 504s, etc., as appropriate

APRIL

- Teach core curriculum lessons
- Continue intervention groups
- Communicate with middle school counselors about the transition process and plan an orientation, a school visit, and a family workshop to support the fifth-grade transition
- Lead College and Career Day, including a core curriculum lesson before and/or after the event
- Begin to prepare for the closure of groups
- Meet with teachers/parents of students who are in danger of retention (Tier 3)
- Be aware of standardized test dates—support student attendance during these times
- Attend SSTs, IEPs, 504s, etc., as appropriate

MAY/JUNE (LAST MONTH OF THE SCHOOL YEAR)

- Participate in middle school orientation activities
- Teach core curriculum lessons on preparing for middle school
- Participate in formal teacher discussions of student classroom placements for next year
- Facilitate final core curriculum classroom lessons
- Attend SSTs, IEPs, 504s, etc., as appropriate, including transition meetings for students going to middle school
- Notify students and families of summer school opportunities and summer educational activities (such as summer reading programs at the local library)
- End and evaluate small counseling groups
- Evaluate the effectiveness of the school counseling program—survey teachers, administrators, students, and families
- Take notes on ways to improve the school counseling calendar next year
- Reflect on successes and areas for growth from the past year
- Review and report to administration results of the comprehensive school counseling program (core curriculum and intentional interventions)
- Conduct a Flashlight Results presentation for staff and administration
- Update your records
- Schedule end-of-year massage ☺

JULY

- Attend the American School Counselor Association (ASCA) national conference

SYSTEMATIC REFERRAL PROCESS

As shown in Figure 10.16, it is recommended that school counselors at the elementary level spend approximately 35% to 45% of their time providing core curriculum lessons (formerly called "guidance curriculum" in the second edition of the ASCA model; ASCA 2005). While the focus of this book is Tier 1, counselors may have a high number of individual student referrals, which may not allow them to effectively implement Tier 1 core curriculum services. One way to address this challenge is to ensure that a systematic referral process is in place.

Similar to creating a structured calendar, school counselors are encouraged to develop and implement a systematic referral process to ensure that students are

Figure 10.16   ASCA National Model Suggested Use of Time

ASCA National Model (third edition) Delivery	K-12	ASCA National Model (second edition) Delivery	Elementary	Middle	Secondary
Direct Services School ■ Counseling Core Curriculum ■ Individual Student Planning ■ Responsive Services **Indirect Services** ■ Referrals ■ Consultation ■ Collaboration	80% or more	Guidance Curriculum	35%-45%	25%-35%	15%-25%
		Individual Student Planning	5%-10%	15%-25%	25%-35%
		Responsive Services	30%-40%	30%-40%	25%-35%
		System Support	10%-15%	10%-15%	15%-20%

Adapted from Gysbers, N.C. & Henderson, P. (2012) *Developing and managing your school counseling program* (5th ed.), Alexandria, VA: American Counseling Association.

Included in Other Components

Program Planning and School Support ■ Program management and operations (management) ■ Professional development (foundation and management) ■ Data analysis (accountability) ■ Fair-share responsibilities (management)	20% or less

Source: American School Counselor Association (ASCA). (2012). *ASCA national model: A framework for school counseling programs* (3rd ed.). Alexandria, VA: Author.

being identified for Tier 2 and 3 supports using data (Chapter 1) rather than teacher referrals. One important exception to consider is students who have had an extreme change in behavior, attendance, affect, or academic achievement. These students may need immediate support and may not be identified via the data. For example: Martin's father recently committed suicide, and Martin's teacher has noticed that he has been extremely angry and withdrawn; Luisa is exhibiting isolating behaviors that would not be recognized through discipline referrals; Tyson is normally happy and energetic, but has been extremely sullen and lethargic during the last two weeks. In addition, unless a student's mood is causing his or her grades to drop dramatically, data would not be a useful tool to identify that this student needs support. Therefore, creating a referral form for teachers to complete in extraordinary situations, such as those listed previously, ensures that students in need of immediate support are serviced. Refer to the sample on page 131 of *The Use of Data in School Counseling: Hatching Results for Students, Programs, and the Profession* (Hatch, 2013). Utilizing a systematic referral process is vital for effective time management within a tiered school counseling program.

MARKETING THE SCHOOL COUNSELING PROGRAM AND TIER 1 SERVICES

With access to technology at school counselors' fingertips, it is easier than ever to inform families, students, staff, and the school community about core curriculum lessons and schoolwide activities. Marketing yourself and the program is essential in providing professional legitimacy and inciting participation from others. Introductory letters, counseling program brochures, and websites provide a clearer understanding of how school counselors support students, families, and the entire school community. School counselors should conduct classroom lessons with students that introduce themselves and their role in the school. Various counselor blogs and Pinterest boards have a wealth of creative ideas—whether you dress up like a fictional character to relay a message of leadership, create a trivia game, or utilize a bag of props to discuss each role of the counselor, try to make it fun and different each year! School counselors can seek opportunities to discuss the counseling program during staff, local school council, or board meetings and family events. Be sure to get on the agenda of the initial staff meeting for each new school year. School counselors who work in diverse schools are encouraged to translate family information into their community's native language(s).

Activity 10.1

Figures 10.17 through 10.19 show examples of a school counselor's welcome letter, brochure, and website. What do you like about each one? What might you change? How can you use and adapt the different examples to market your own school counseling program and role in the school?

One of the ways school counselor Ashley introduced herself to the families at E. Hale Curran Elementary was through an introduction letter. Because the school previously did not have a school counselor, explaining Ashely's role and services was especially important to bring clarity to her position.

Figure 10.17   Ashley's School Counselor Introduction Letter

Dear Parents/Guardians,

Welcome to the 2015–2016 school year! My name is Ashley Kruger and I am the new, full-time school counselor at E. Hale Curran! I wanted to take this opportunity to introduce myself and discuss some of the counseling services that will be available to your child and the E. Hale Curran community. I am very excited to be a part of the team and look forward to meeting you!

I am extremely passionate about school counseling and believe that every child has the ability to flourish when given the proper resources and support. Children come to school with unique experiences and perspectives. I believe that every child deserves a secure, caring, and stimulating atmosphere that allows them to grow emotionally, intellectually, physically, and socially.

Our school's vision to **"inspire every student to think, to learn, to achieve, and to care"** is closely aligned with the goals of the school counseling program. Elementary school is the time in which students begin to explore the world independently and create an identity. As a counselor, I will encourage students to identify their skills and interests and develop future goals and aspirations. I believe that in order for a student to be a successful learner at school, their social and emotional needs must be met. Although excelling academically is extremely important, learning how to be a strong, independent and respectful individual is equally valuable.

My counseling practices are based off of the American School Counseling Association (ASCA) National Model and I focus on developing a program that removes barriers to learning. In order to implement effective interventions for your children, I believe it is essential to view the child as a whole. Understanding the community in which the child lives, the culture the child comes from, and the beliefs and values of the families I am working with are all crucial aspects of creating a program that benefits all students. Some of the services I will provide include:

- **Core Curriculum Classroom Lessons:** These services will be provided to all students. All students will receive lessons utilizing a curriculum called Boystown and Second Step. This curriculum focuses on providing students with tools to improve social skills, solve conflicts, and identify and express emotions in an appropriate manner.
- **Small Groups:** Small groups provide extra support for students who may be having difficulty in a specific area. For example, group topics may include controlling emotions, coping with change, self-control, or social skills.
- **Individual Support:** In some circumstances, it may be beneficial to provide short-term individual services for students.
- **Parent Support:** In addition to student services, I am also here to provide you with support! I will be holding monthly "Coffee with the Counselor" sessions which will provide you with the opportunity to come to my office and discuss your child and their progress. I also will be developing parent workshops and will be sending home a survey to understand which topics would be most helpful/relevant to you. I encourage you to attend the workshops and learn how you can be the best advocate for your child!

I know this is going to be a great year. Please feel free to contact me at anytime with any questions or concerns at akruger@murrieta.k12.ca.us. Thank you.

Ashley Kruger
E. Hale Curran School Counselor

Figure 10.18 School Counseling Program Brochure

Meet your School Counselor

As a former bulldog Mrs. Melissa Lafayette is honored to return and work with the students, families, military community, and the Mary Fay Pendleton community to provide students the opportunity to be leaders in school and in the community.

A little bit about me…I received my bachelor's degree in Psychology from Chapman University and my master's degree in educational & clinical counseling from Azusa Pacific University.

∽ ∾

110 Marine Drive
Oceanside, CA 92058

760-847-9329

mlafayette@fuesd.org

School Counseling Program Development

School counseling services are provided as a result of the U.S. Department of Education's Elementary and Secondary School Counseling Program Grant. FUESD was one of only 41 districts nationwide to receive the grant funding.

The Fallbrook Unified School District Comprehensive School Counseling Program aligns with the American School Counselor Association (ASCA) National Model. The ASCA Model provides a framework for developing, implementing, and evaluating data-driven services within the school counseling program to support the grant goals for improving student success.

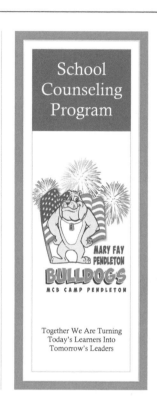

School Counseling Program

Together We Are Turning Today's Learners Into Tomorrow's Leaders

Leader in Me

Developing a culture of leadership in our schools is about inspiring children to be leaders of their own lives; it helps them identify their own unique talents and abilities and encourages them to make a positive difference in the world.

Getting Help for my Child

Please contact the school counselor directly by setting up a phone or in person meeting to discuss your child's situation; an appointment will ensure the availability of the counselor. You can also encourage your child to stop by the school counseling office to fill out a Request to See Ms. Lafayette.

School Counseling Services

- Being Proactive through providing Core Curriculum Counseling lessons in the classrooms on themes including conflict resolution, mistreatment/bully prevention, and study skills for all students

- Beginning with the End in Mind through College and Career Readiness activities and learning to set goals

- Providing individual and small group counseling for students needing extra support for topics such as social skills, managing feelings, deployment, peer pressure, divorce, grief, etc.

- Creating win-win experiences by referring to outside services and providing resources to additional community support services for the student and family

- Synergizing with parents, teachers, administration and support staff

Benefits

- Help students balance their academic, personal, and social skills

- Foster a positive school environment of cultural diversity and safety

- Value each students' individuality and help them make meaningful connections at school

- Empower students to be leaders at school and in the community

Mission

The mission of the Fallbrook Union Elementary School District (FUESD) School Counseling Program, in partnership with the Department of Student Services, is to provide comprehensive and data-driven academic, college and career exploration, and social/emotional services to promote active lifelong learning while celebrating diversity.

Source: Created by Melissa Lafayette and Chad McGough, Fallbrook Union Elementary School District.

Figure 10.19 School Counseling Program Website Created by Heidi Mejia From Monte Vista Elementary in California

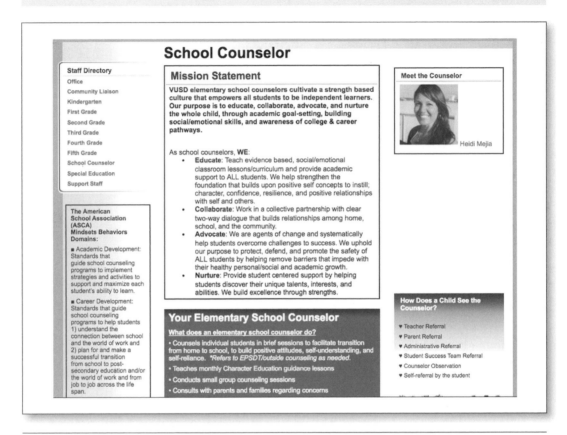

Source: https://mv-vistausd-ca.schoolloop.com/cms/page_view?d=x&piid=&vpid=1420326785098.

Note: Additional elementary school counseling website examples include the following:

Matoka Elementary School, Williamsburg, Virginia: https://wjccschools.org/mes/school-counseling/#tab-id-7

Avaxat Elementary School, Murrieta, California: http://www.murrieta.k12.ca.us/Domain/3415

Orchard View Elementary School, Winchester, Virginia: http://ove.frederick.k12.va.us/parents___students/school_counseling

COLLABORATION WITH STAFF

Elementary school counselors are leaders, advocates, and change agents, which often involves being a coach or consultant. Consistent communication, accessibility, and visibility are vital to enhancing relationships with staff and faculty. Teachers must have explicit means and methods to approach, communicate with, and share feedback and concerns with the counselor, whether via "drop-in" office hours, an online appointment calendar for conferences that displays available time slots, an advisory council for your school counseling program, or feedback forms for the school counseling core curriculum lessons. Be mindful of providing clear instructions when issuing forms or signup sheets, include deadlines, and give plenty of advanced notice whenever possible.

COLLABORATION WITH ADMINISTRATORS

The influence and expectations of administrators, their knowledge of the role of the school counselor, and their understanding of program development and implementation have been identified as significant factors affecting the development of exemplary school guidance and counseling programs (Ponec & Brock, 2000) and as aspects of school counselor efficacy (Sutton & Fall, 1995). Often, administrators have not been trained in the role of school counselor. Therefore, supporting the improvement of the principal–school counselor relationship is important in developing the school counseling program.

In *A Closer Look at the Principal-Counselor Relationship: A Survey of Principals and Counselors* (Finkelstein, 2009), the College Board holds that the principal-counselor

Figure 10.20   10 Characteristics of an Effective Principal-Counselor Relationship

10

Characteristics of an Effective Principal-Counselor Relationship*

1. Open communication that provides multiple opportunities for input to decision making

2. Opportunities to share ideas on teaching, learning and schoolwide educational initiatives

3. Sharing information about needs within the school and the community

4. School counselor participation on school leadership teams

5. Joint responsibility in the development of goals and metrics that indicate success

6. Mutual trust between the principal and school counselors

7. A shared vision of what is meant by student success

8. Mutual respect between the principal and school counselors

9. Shared decision making on initiatives that impact student success

10. A collective commitment to equity and opportunity

* The questions on the national survey of principals and counselors, including the characteristics of effective principal-counselor relationships, were suggested by experts at the College Board, ASCA and NASSP. While this is not an exhaustive list and there may be additional important characteristics of these relationships, all 10 presented here were endorsed by both principals and counselors as important characteristics of an effective principal-counselor relationship.

8   **Finding a Way:** Practical Examples of How an Effective Principal-Counselor Relationship Can Lead to Success for All Students

relationship is dynamic and evolves over time in response to the ever-changing needs of a school. Effective principal-counselor relationships are used to collaboratively lead school reform efforts to increase achievement for all students. Review Figure 10.20 and assess which of the characteristics of an effective counselor-principal relationship are currently in place in your school.

Annual Agreement

To create an effective management system for your school counseling program, administrator support is essential. One useful tool to develop a coordinated plan between school counselors and administrators, as well as to clarify expectations related to formal performance evaluations, is the Annual Agreement. Developed prior to or at the beginning of the school year in collaboration with and approved by administrators, the Annual Agreement is an organizational tool provided by the American School Counselor Association (ASCA) that outlines the roles and responsibilities of the school counselor. This tool promotes discourse between counselors and administrators, as the components prompt questions about effective use of the school counselor's time, ways in which the school counseling program is organized, alignment of goals to the school's mission, professional growth needs, and opportunities for collaboration with other stakeholders. Current needs data and previous results can be shared by the elementary counselor, along with relevant materials (results reports, ASCA Executive Summary, lesson plans, etc.) to increase administrator awareness. ASCA's Annual Agreement template can be modified to include the site- and counselor-specific details most relevant to each school counseling program. Find the Annual Agreement Template at https://www.schoolcounselor.org/asca/media/asca/ASCA%20National%20Model%20Templates/AnnualAgreementTemplate.pdf.

The Annual Agreement Meeting

The tone and body language of collegial conversation matters as much as the content, so begin your meeting with a tenor of mutual respect. Below is a list of possible talking points to enlist support for Tier 1 activities and interventions when discussing the Annual Agreement with administrators:

- Ways in which the school counseling program's mission statement supports the school's mission, vision, and goals supporting all students
- Development of an annual calendar, including schoolwide activities, core curriculum lessons, and small-group services
- Agreement on the school counselor referral system
- Collaboration efforts with other school staff, community partners, and parents to implement MTMDSS
- Curriculum and materials needed to provide all students with a standards-based school counseling core curriculum to address universal academic, college/career, and social/emotional development
- The difference between direct and indirect services and the amount of time recommended for classroom lessons (35%–45% at the elementary level [ASCA, 2005])
- The list of inappropriate and appropriate duties in the ASCA National Model, to explore the reassignment of duties that are not in line with best practices; find this in the Executive Summary at https://schoolcounselor.org/Ascanationalmodel/media/ANM-templates/ANMExecSumm.pdf (ASCA, 2012)

As a new school counselor, Ashley set out to meet with her principal to share her program ideas and goals to support positive student outcomes. During their first meeting, the administrator requested that Ashley be available for supervision time during recess and lunch on a daily basis. Ashley decided to show her administrator ASCA's list of appropriate versus inappropriate school counselor duties (see Figure 10.21) and ASCA's Annual Agreement. The school administrator indicated that she wasn't aware that the majority of a school counselor's time should be spent on direct and indirect student support services. Ashley and her administrator worked together to complete the Annual Agreement, which focused on providing service to all students through a tiered model of prevention and intervention activities.

Figure 10.21 ASCA List of Appropriate and Inappropriate School Counselor Duties

Executive Summary

School counselors design and deliver comprehensive school counseling programs that promote student achievement. These programs are comprehensive in scope, preventive in design and developmental in nature. "The ASCA National Model: A Framework for School Counseling Programs" outlines the components of a comprehensive school counseling program. The ASCA National Model brings school counselors together with one vision and one voice, which creates unity and focus toward improving student achievement.

A comprehensive school counseling program is an integral component of the school's academic mission. Comprehensive school counseling programs, driven by student data and based on standards in academic, career and personal/social development, promote and enhance the learning process for all students. The ASCA National Model:

- ensures equitable access to a rigorous education for all students
- identifies the knowledge and skills all students will acquire as a result of the K-12 comprehensive school counseling program
- is delivered to all students in a systematic fashion

- is based on data-driven decision making
- is provided by a state-credentialed school counselor

Effective school counseling programs are a collaborative effort between the school counselor, parents and other educators to create an environment that promotes student achievement. Staff and school counselors value and respond to the diversity and individual differences in our societies and communities. Comprehensive school counseling programs ensure equitable access to opportunities and rigorous curriculum for all students to participate fully in the educational process.

School counselors focus their skills, time and energy on direct and indirect services to students. To achieve maximum program effectiveness, the American School Counselor Association recommends a school counselor to student ratio of 1:250 and that school counselors spend 80 percent or more of their time in direct and indirect services to students. School counselors participate as members of the educational team and use the skills of leadership, advocacy and collaboration to promote systemic change as appropriate. The framework of a comprehensive school counseling program consists of four components: foundation, management, delivery and accountability.

(Continued)

Figure 10.21 (Continued)

FOUNDATION

School counselors create comprehensive school counseling programs that focus on student outcomes, teach student competencies and are delivered with identified professional competencies.

Program Focus: To establish program focus, school counselors identify personal beliefs that address how all students benefit from the school counseling program. Building on these beliefs, school counselors create a vision statement defining what the future will look like in terms of student outcomes. In addition, school counselors create a mission statement aligned with their school's mission and develop program goals defining how the vision and mission will be measured.

Student Competencies: Enhancing the learning process for all students, the ASCA Mindsets & Behaviors for Student Success: K-12 College- and Career-Readiness for Every Student guide the development of effective school counseling programs around three domains: academic, career and social/emotional development. School counselors also consider how other student standards important to state and district initiatives complement and inform their school counseling program.

Professional Competencies: The ASCA School Counselor Competencies outline the knowledge, attitudes and skills that ensure school counselors are equipped to meet the rigorous demands of the profession. The ASCA Ethical Standards for School Counselors specify the principles of ethical behavior necessary to maintain the highest standard of integrity, leadership and professionalism. They guide school counselors' decision-making and help to standardize professional practice to protect both students and school counselors.

MANAGEMENT

School counselors incorporate organizational assessments and tools that are concrete, clearly delineated and reflective of the school's needs. Assessments and tools include:

- **School counselor competency and school counseling program assessments** to self-evaluate areas of strength and improvement for individual skills and program activities
- **Use-of-time assessment** to determine the amount of time spent toward the recommended 80 percent

or more of the school counselor's time to direct and indirect services with students

- **Annual agreements** developed with and approved by administrators at the beginning of the school year addressing how the school counseling program is organized and what goals will be accomplished
- **Advisory councils** made up of students, parents, teachers, school counselors, administrators and community members to review and make recommendations about school counseling program activities and results
- **Use of data** to measure the results of the program as well as to promote systemic change within the school system so every student graduates college- and career-ready
- **Curriculum, small-group and closing-the-gap action plans** including developmental, prevention and intervention activities and services that measure the desired student competencies and the impact on achievement, behavior and attendance

APPROPRIATE ACTIVITIES FOR SCHOOL COUNSELORS	INAPPROPRIATE ACTIVITIES FOR SCHOOL COUNSELORS
individual student academic program planning	coordinating paperwork and data entry of all new students
interpreting cognitive, aptitude and achievement tests	coordinating cognitive, aptitude and achievement testing programs
providing counseling to students who are tardy or absent	signing excuses for students who are tardy or absent
providing counseling to students who have disciplinary problems	performing disciplinary actions or assigning discipline consequences
providing counseling to students as to appropriate school dress	sending students home who are not appropriately dressed
collaborating with teachers to present school counseling core curriculum lessons	teaching classes when teachers are absent
analyzing grade-point averages in relationship to achievement	computing grade-point averages
interpreting student records	maintaining student records
providing teachers with suggestions for effective classroom management	supervising classrooms or common areas
ensuring student records are maintained as per state and federal regulations	keeping clerical records
helping the school principal identify and resolve student issues, needs and problems	assisting with duties in the principal's office
providing individual and small-group counseling services to students	providing therapy or long-term counseling in schools to address psychological disorders
advocating for students at individual education plan meetings, student study teams and school attendance review boards	coordinating schoolwide individual education plans, student study teams and school attendance review boards
analyzing disaggregated data	serving as a data entry clerk

- **Annual and weekly calendars** to keep students, parents, teachers and administrators informed and to encourage active participation in the school counseling program

DELIVERY

School counselors provide services to students, parents, school staff and the community in the following areas:

Direct Student Services

Direct services are in-person interactions between school counselors and students and include the following:

- **School counseling core curriculum:** This curriculum consists of structured lessons designed to help students attain the desired competencies and to provide all students with the knowledge, attitudes and skills appropriate for their developmental level. The school counseling core curriculum is delivered

(Continued)

Figure 10.21 (Continued)

throughout the school's overall curriculum and is systematically presented by school counselors in collaboration with other professional educators in K-12 classroom and group activities.

- **Individual student planning:** School counselors coordinate ongoing systemic activities designed to assist students in establishing personal goals and developing future plans.

- **Responsive services:** Responsive services are activities designed to meet students' immediate needs and concerns. Responsive services may include counseling in individual or small-group settings or crisis response.

Indirect Student Services

Indirect services are provided on behalf of students as a result of the school counselors' interactions with others including referrals for additional assistance, consulta-

tion and collaboration with parents, teachers, other educators and community organizations.

ACCOUNTABILITY

To demonstrate the effectiveness of the school counseling program in measurable terms, school counselors analyze school and school counseling program data to determine how students are different as a result of the school counseling program. School counselors use data to show the impact of the school counseling program on student achievement, attendance and behavior and analyze school counseling program assessments to guide future action and improve future results for all students. The performance of the school counselor is evaluated on basic standards of practice expected of school counselors implementing a comprehensive school counseling program.

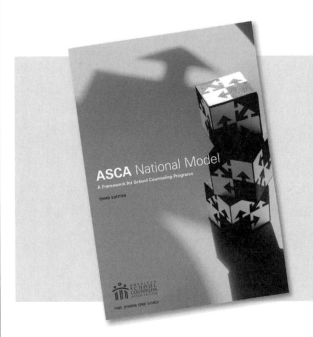

ORDERING INFORMATION

"The ASCA National Model: A Framework for School Counseling Programs (third edition)" is $34.95 for ASCA members or $44.95 for nonmembers. Bulk pricing of $29.95 is available for 10 copies or more. Order no. 289325.

Four easy ways to order:
Online: *www.schoolcounselor.org*
Phone: (800) 401-2404
Fax: (703) 661-1501
Mail: ASCA Publications,
P.O. Box 960, Herndon, VA 20172

AMERICAN
SCHOOL
COUNSELOR
ASSOCIATION

1101 King St., Suite 310, Alexandria, VA 22314 ▪ Phone: 703 683 ASCA ▪ *www.schoolcounselor.org*

Source: American School Counselor Association. Executive Summary. Retrieved from https://schoolcounselor.org/Ascanationalmodel/media/ANM-templates/ANMExecSumm.pdf.

School Counselor–Administrator Supervision Meetings

Scheduling a consistent and regular meeting time with administrators promotes the success of elementary school counselors, as the time to communicate and collaborate ensures that everyone is on the same page and support is provided as necessary. Keeping in mind that the administrator's priority is academic instruction, make connections between what is being taught and how it impacts academics with collected data so that the value of the school counseling lesson is seen to be worth the resource of time. During these meetings, school counselors can also present their weekly calendar, discuss current Tier 1 activities, and strategize solutions regarding classroom management, scheduling, or other issues impacting the effective delivery of core curriculum. School counselors may want to use this time to discuss logistics and planning for schoolwide activities and/or parent events.

RECOMMENDATIONS FOR NEW SCHOOL COUNSELORS RELATED TO DELIVERY OF TIER 1 SERVICES

As new school counselors begin their work, the success of implementing core curriculum and other Tier 1 activities can be enhanced through learning about the school culture, building relationships, and creating effective systems. Below are some tips for new school counselors:

- Schedule a meeting with administrators to develop a collaborative relationship, learn about the school's goals, and discuss school counseling program services such as core curriculum. New school counselors may want to share educational literature such as ASCA's "The Role of the School Counselor" document. (https://www.schoolcounselor.org/asca/media/asca/home/RoleStatement.pdf).
- Build relationships with teachers and visit their classrooms to learn about expectations, observe their student engagement and classroom management styles, and get to know students. School counselors can learn from great teachers and incorporate this knowledge into their style as they teach core curriculum.
- Begin by teaching lessons on specific topics to a few grade levels and then incorporate additional lessons as confidence and skills build.
- Consider the number of lessons to be provided and scheduling—try not to schedule more than three to four lessons per day and allow for at least 15 minutes in between sessions to account for unexpected occurrences and time to set up and clean up.
- Know your boundaries. From time to time, a teacher may ask you to teach a lesson that is specific to a classroom issue (e.g., stealing, cyberbullying), but it is important for school counselors to balance scheduled and developmentally appropriate core curriculum with supporting specific teacher needs. Use professional wisdom to set appropriate boundaries to prioritize core curriculum while supporting needs and building relationships.
- Remember to dress for success and demonstrate confidence when entering classrooms, building your credibility by showing your professionalism outwardly. Arrive early to set up and support the teacher in transitioning instruction to the counselor.

CLOSING

The goal of this book is to provide a practical hands-on guide to creating and implementing high-quality Tier 1 school counseling systems of supports with a focus on *effective teaching strategies* and the *use of measurement tools*. As authors, we set out to include best practices, examples, and resources from elementary school counselors across the country that have been proven to be effective.

Throughout this text, we have shared with you the knowledge, attitudes, skills, and behaviors recommended for school counselors in implementing Tier 1 core curriculum and schoolwide activities within an elementary school counseling program.

This text is written by three authors who have served as elementary school counselors in different parts of the country at different times, and even within different generations. Though each of us may have operationally approached the work in different ways, we are in fundamental agreement about how to structure a school counseling program aligned with the ASCA National Model and a Multi-Tiered, Multi-Domain System of Supports.

We have combined our "art" with "science," thereby developing our "wisdom" within the work. *And now it is your turn!* We hope this text will help you blend your art and science, develop your wisdom, and grow as a professional school counselor. It is our hope that you will identify new or innovative ways to improve outcomes for students as you collect and share results to improve your program. We look forward to your stories regarding the outcomes you achieve, both professionally and personally. We hope you will share your data, your courageous moments, and your wisdom with other elementary school counselors at local state and national conferences. The profession truly needs this.

Finally, we hope that you will share your feedback with us. If you have any suggestions for ways in which we might improve this text or recommendations for the online appendix, please contact us at office@hatchingresults.com.

Trish

Lisa

Danielle

References

Action Learning Systems. (2012). *Direct interactive instruction.* Pasadena, CA: Author.

AIM Education (Producer). (2010). *Essential elementary issues series: Super study skills (#394645)* [Motion picture on DVD]. United States: Cerebellum Corporation. http://www.library videocompany.com/Essential-Elementary-Issues-Super-Study-Skills-p/394645.htm

American School Counselor Association (ASCA). (2004). *ASCA national standards for students* (Rev. ed.). Alexandria, VA: Author.

American School Counselor Association (ASCA). (2005). *ASCA national model: A framework for school counseling programs* (2nd ed.). Alexandria, VA: Author.

American School Counselor Association (ASCA). (2008). The school counselor and multitiered system of supports [Press release]. Retrieved June 9, 2017, from https://www.schoolcounselor .org/asca/media/asca/PositionStatements/PS_MultitieredSupportSystem.pdf

American School Counselor Association (ASCA). (2012). *ASCA national model: A framework for school counseling programs* (3rd ed.). Alexandria, VA: Author.

American School Counselor Association (ASCA). (2014). *Mindsets and behaviors for student success: K–12 college- and career-readiness standards for every student.* Alexandria, VA: Author.

American School Counselor Association (ASCA). (2016). *ASCA ethical standards for school counselors.* Alexandria, VA: Author. Retrieved June 9, 2017, from https://www.schoolcounselor .org/asca/media/asca/Ethics/EthicalStandards2016.pdf

American School Counselor Association (ASCA). (n.d.). *Student-to-school-counselor ratio 2013–2014* [PDF document]. Retrieved June 9, 2017, from https://www.schoolcounselor .org/asca/media/asca/home/Ratios13-14.pdf

Anderson, C. M., & Borgmeier, C. (2010). Tier II interventions within the framework of school-wide positive behavior support: Essential features for design, implementation, and maintenance. *Behavior Analysis in Practice, 3*(1), 33–45. doi:10.1007/bf03391756

Armstrong, P. (n.d.). *Bloom's taxonomy.* Retrieved from https://cft.vanderbilt.edu/guides-sub-pages/blooms-taxonomy

Baker, K. (2010). *LMNO peas.* New York, NY: Beach Lane Books.

Bloom, B. S., Englehart, M. B., Furst, E. J., Hill, W. H., & Krathwohl, O. R. (1956). *Taxonomy of educational objectives: The classification of educational goals. Handbook 1: The cognitive domain.* New York, NY: Longman.

Campbell, C. A., & Dahir, C. A. (1997). *Sharing the vision: The ASCA national standards for school counseling programs.* Alexandria, VA: American School Counselor Association.

Canter, L. (2010). *Assertive discipline: Positive behavior management for today's classroom.* Bloomington, IN: Solution Tree Press.

Classroom management skills: From chaos to calm, from inattentive to inspired. (2016). *ASCA School Counselor, 53*(6) [Special issue].

Cline, F., & Fay, J. (2014). *Parenting with love and logic.* Colorado Springs, CO: NavPress.

Collaborative for Academic, Social, and Emotional Learning (CASEL). (2013). *CASEL guide to effective social and emotional learning programs.* Chicago, IL: Author. Retrieved October 8, 2017, from http://casel.org/guide

College Board. (2012). *Elementary school counselor's guide: NOSCA's eight components of college and career readiness counseling*. New York, NY: Author. Retrieved from https://secure-media .collegeboard.org/digitalServices/pdf/advocacy/nosca/11b-4383_ES_Counselor_Guide_ WEB_120213.pdf

Committee for Children. (2014). *Second step: A violence-prevention curriculum*. Seattle, WA: Author.

Cowan, K. C., Vaillancourt, K., Rossen, E., & Pollitt, K. (2013). A framework for safe and successful schools [Brief]. Bethesda, MD: National Association of School Psychologists.

Dimmitt, C., Carey, J. C., & Hatch, T. (2007). *Evidence-based school counseling: Making a difference with data-driven practices*. Thousand Oaks, CA: Corwin.

Duarte, D., & Hatch, T. (2014). Successful implementation of a federally funded elementary school counseling program: Results bring sustainability. *Professional School Counseling, 14*(1).

Easton, J. Q., & Engelhard, G. (1982). A longitudinal record of elementary school absence and its relationship to Reading Achievement. *The Journal of Educational Research, 75*(5).

Evertson, C. M., & Weinstein, C. S. (Eds.). (2013). *Handbook of classroom management: Research, practice, and contemporary issues*. New York, NY: Routledge.

Farrington, C. A., Roderick, M., Allensworth, E., Nagaoka, J., Keyes, T. S., Johnson, D. W., & Beechum, N. O. (2012). *Teaching adolescents to become learners: The role of noncognitive factors in shaping school performance: A critical literature review*. Chicago, IL: University of Chicago Consortium on Chicago School Research.

Finkelstein, D. (2009). *A closer look at the principal-counselor relationship: A survey of principals and counselors*. New York, NY: College Board Advocacy & Policy Center.

Frey, K. S., Nolen, S. B., Edstrom, L. V. S., & Hirschstein, M. K. (2005). Effects of a school-based social–emotional competence program: Linking children's goals, attributions, and behavior. *Journal of Applied Developmental Psychology, 26*(2), 171–200.

Gay, G. (2010). *Culturally responsive teaching: Theory, research, and practice*. New York, NY: Teachers College Press.

Gesek, T. (n.d.). Fight or flight: Anxiety in the classroom. *Special Education Advisor*. Retrieved May 15, 2017, from http://www.specialeducationadvisor.com/fight-or-flight-anxiety-in -the-classroom

Gettinger, M., & Kohler, K. M. (2006). Process-outcome approaches to classroom management and effective teaching. In C. M. Evertson & C. S. Weinstein (Eds.), *Handbook of classroom management: Research, practice, and contemporary issues* (pp. 73–95). New York, NY: Routledge.

Greenberg, M. T., Weissberg, R. P., O'Brien, M. U., Zins, J. E., Fredericks, L., Resnik, H., & Elias, M. J. (2003). Enhancing school-based prevention and youth development through coordinated social, emotional, and academic learning. *American Psychologist, 58*(6–7), 466.

Harris, A. (2016, December 1). ClassDojo is teaching kids empathy in 90% of K–8 schools nationwide. *Fast Company*. Retrieved May 12, 2017, from https://www.fastcompany .com/3065654/classdojo-is-teaching-kids-empathy-in-90-of-schools-nationwide

Hatch, T. (2005, June). *Data made easy: Using data to effect change*. Paper presented at the American School Counselor Association, Orlando, FL.

Hatch, T. (2017, March 8). Multi Tiered, Multi-Domain System of Supports by Trish Hatch, PhD. Retrieved from https://www.hatchingresults.com/blog/2017/3/multi-tiered-multi-domain-system-of-supports-by-trish-hatch-phd.

Hatch, T. (2013). *The use of data in school counseling: Hatching results for students, programs, and the profession*. Thousand Oaks, CA: Corwin.

Hawken, L., Vincent, C., & Schumann, J. (2008). Response to intervention for social behavior: Challenges and opportunities. *Journal of Emotional and Behavioral Disorders, 16*, 213–225.

Illinois State Board of Education. (2010). *Understanding RtI/MTSS: Multi-tiered system*. Retrieved June 9, 2017, from http://www.illinoisrti.org/i-rti-network/for-educators/ understanding-rti-mtss/multi-tiered-system

Jones, S., Brush, K., Bailey, R., Brion-Meisels, G., McIntyre, J., Kahn, J., Nelson, B., & Stickle, L. (2017, March). *Navigating SEL from the inside out: Looking inside and across 25 leading SEL programs: A practical resource for schools and OST providers (elementary school focus).* Cambridge, MA: Harvard Graduate School of Education, with funding from the Wallace Foundation.

Kennelly, L., & Monrad, M. (2007). *Approaches to dropout prevention: Heeding early warning signs with appropriate interventions.* Washington, DC: National High School Center. Retrieved June 9, 2017, from http://files.eric.ed.gov/fulltext/ED499009.pdf

Killian, S. (2015, August 28). *The I do WE do YOU do model explained.* Retrieved from the Australian Society for Evidence Based Teaching Web site: http://www.evidencebased teaching.org.au/the-i-do-we-do-you-do-model-explained

Lemov, D. (2015). *Teach like a champion 2.0: 62 techniques that put students on the path to college.* San Francisco, CA: Wiley.

Lopez, C. J., & Mason, E. C. M. (n.d.). School counselors as curricular leaders: A content analysis of ASCA lesson plans. Manuscript submitted for publication, *Professional School Counseling.*

Lorette, K. (n.d.). Definition of a franchise business. *Houston Chronicle.* Retrieved June 9, 2017, from http://smallbusiness.chron.com/definition-franchise-business-4467.html

Low, S., Cook, C. R., Smolkowski, K., & Buntain-Ricklefs, J. (2015). Promoting social–emotional competence: An evaluation of the elementary version of *Second Step®. Journal of School Psychology, 53*(6), 463–477.

Mason, E. C. M. (2010). Leveraging classroom time. *ASCA School Counselor, July/August,* 27–29.

Mason, E. C. M., Gupta, K., Sowers, M., & Sabens, F. (2014). Flip your lessons. *ASCA School Counselor, Mar/Apr,* 28–32.

Mitchell, M. M., & Bradshaw, C. P. (2013). Examining classroom influences on student perceptions of school climate: The role of classroom management and exclusionary discipline strategies. *Journal of School Psychology, 51*(5), 599–610.

National Office for School Counselor Advocacy (NOSCA). (2011). *Elementary counselor's guide: NOSCA's eight components of college and career readiness counseling.* New York, NY: The College Board.

O'Brennan, L., & Bradshaw, C. (2013, November). Importance of school climate. *National Education Association Research Brief no. 15584.* Retrieved from https://www.nea.org/assets/docs/15584_Bully_Free_Research_Brief-4pg.pdf

Ockerman, M. S., Mason, E., & Hollenbeck, A. F. (2012). Integrating RTI with school counseling programs: Being a proactive professional school counselor. *Journal of School Counseling, 10*(15), 15.

Ponec, D. L., & Brock, B. L. (2000). Relationships among elementary school counselors and principals: A unique bond. *Professional School Counseling, 3*(3), 208.

Sackett, D. L., Straus, S. E., Richardson, W. S., Rosenberg, W., & Haynes, R. B. (2000). *How to practice and teach EBM.* Edinburgh, Scotland: Churchill Livingstone.

San Onofre School holds college and career day. (2015, March 19). *Fallbrook & Bonsall Village News.* Retrieved May 15, 2017, from http://villagenews.com/education/san-onofre -school-holds-college-and-career-day

Schunk, D. H. (1989). Social cognitive theory and self-regulated learning. In B. J. Zimmerman & D. H. Schunk (Eds.), *Self-regulated learning and academic achievement: Theory, research, and practice* (pp. 83–110). New York, NY: Springer-Verlag.

Shapiro, E. S. (n.d.) Tiered instruction and intervention in a response-to-intervention model. *RTI Action Network.* Retrieved October 8, 2017, from http://www.rtinetwork .org/essential/tieredinstruction/tiered-instruction-and-intervention-rti-model

Siegle, D. (2010). *Likert scales.* Retrieved from University of Connecticut Web site: http://researchbasics.education.uconn.edu/likert_scales

Simonsen, B., Fairbanks, S., Briesch, A., Myers, D., & Sugai, G. (2008). Evidence-based practices in classroom management: Considerations for research to practice. *Education and Treatment of Children, 31*(3), 351–380.

Sparks, E., & American School Counselor Association. (n.d.). *ASCA mindsets and behaviors for student success: K–12 college- and career-readiness standards for every student* [PowerPoint slides]. Retrieved April 10, 2017, from https://www.schoolcounselor.org/asca/media/webinars/Mindsets-Beh-Presentation.pdf

Sugai, G., & Horner, R. H. (2009). Responsiveness-to-intervention and school-wide positive behavior supports: Integration of multi-tiered system approaches. *Exceptionality, 17*(4), 223–237.

Sutton, J. M., & Fall, M. (1995). The relationship of school climate factors to counselor self-efficacy. *Journal of Counseling & Development, 73*(3), 331–336.

U.S. Department of Education Office for Civil Rights. (2014, March 21). *Civil rights data collection data snapshot: School discipline*. Washington, DC: Author. Retrieved from http://blogs.edweek.org/edweek/rulesforengagement/CRDC%20School%20Discipline%20Snapshot.pdf

Vavrus, M. (2008). Culturally responsive teaching. In T. L. Good (Ed.), *21st century education: A reference handbook, vol. 2* (pp. 49–57). Thousand Oaks, CA: SAGE.

Walker, T. (n.d.). *Legal controversy over lesson plans*. Retrieved from the National Education Association Web site: http://www.nea.org/home/37583.htm

Weinstein, C., Curran, M., & Tomlinson-Clarke, S. (2003). Culturally responsive classroom management: Awareness into action. *Theory into Practice, 42*(4), 269– 276.

Index

A SAGE Publishing Company

Helping educators make the greatest impact

CORWIN HAS ONE MISSION: to enhance education through intentional professional learning.

We build long-term relationships with our authors, educators, clients, and associations who partner with us to develop and continuously improve the best evidence-based practices that establish and support lifelong learning.